THEORY AND INTERPRETATION OF NARRATIVE
James Phelan and Peter J. Rabinowitz, Series Editors

October 2007

# — Experiencing Fiction —

### Judgments, Progressions, and the
### Rhetorical Theory of Narrative

## James Phelan

For Jim,

Once again with deep
gratitude for your generosity, help,
and friendship

Jim

The Ohio State University Press
Columbus

Library of Congress Cataloging-in-Publication Data
Phelan, James, 1951–
  Experiencing fiction : judgments, progressions, and the rhetorical theory of narrative / James Phelan.
      p. cm. — (Theory and interpretation of narrative)
  Includes bibliographical references and indexes.
  ISBN-13: 978-0-8142-1065-9 (alk. paper)
  ISBN-10: 0-8142-1065-1 (alk. paper)
  ISBN-13: 978-0-8142-5162-1 (pbk. : alk. paper)
  ISBN-10: 0-8142-5162-5 (pbk. : alk. paper)
  [etc.]
  1. Narration (Rhetoric) 2. American fiction—20th century—History and criticism—Theory, etc. 3. English fiction—History and criticism—Theory, etc. 4. Reader-response criticism. 5. American literature—Explication. 6. English literature—Explication. I. Title.
  PS374.N285P47   2007
  809.3–dc22

                                        2007007830

This book is available in the following editions:
Cloth (ISBN 978-0-8142-1065-9)
Paperback (ISBN 978-0-8142-5162-1)
CD-ROM (ISBN 978-0-8142-9145-0)

Cover design by Dan O'Dair
Typeset in Rotis Serif
Type design by Juliet Williams
Printed by Sheridan Books, Inc.

9 8 7 6 5 4 3 2 1

In memoriam
Sheldon Sacks and Wayne C. Booth

# Contents

## PART TWO
## Judgments and Progressions in Lyric Narratives and Portrait Narratives

## APPENDICES

In the spring of 1973, when I was a very green M.A. student at the University of Chicago, I walked into the first session of Sheldon Sacks's course in the Eighteenth-Century Novel and heard him ask a question that has stayed with me ever since: "Do we read the same books?" Sacks wanted to point to a paradox: While most of us in that room, including him, would instinctively answer yes (critical orthodoxy in 1973 was much different than it is in 2007), once we set about discussing the meaning of any one novel—Sacks's example that day was *Pride and Prejudice*—our interpretations would suggest the opposite conclusion. We students started to express the meaning in thematic terms: *Pride and Prejudice* is a statement about marriage in an acquisitive society; it's a warning about the risks of putting too much stock in first impressions; it's an exploration of the vices named by the title. Sacks surprised me and, I believe, most of my classmates, not by explicitly disagreeing with these accounts but by saying that they all missed something crucial to the experience of reading Austen's novel: the pleasure and satisfaction it offered in the culminating marriage of Elizabeth Bennet and Fitzwilliam Darcy. In my case at least, the surprise was also a revelation: for the first time in my five years of formal study of literature someone was putting the experience of reading at the center of the interpretive enterprise. As the course went on, it opened up for me an entirely new way of doing criticism that made it both more appealing and more challenging: in this criticism my experiences as a reader matter a great deal and so do yours—but both mine and yours are responsible to the text as it has been constructed by an author who guides us to experience it in one way rather than another.

*Experiencing Fiction* is my attempt to lay out my principles and methods for connecting readerly experience to interpretation and theory, and to model the interpretive practice that follows from these principles and methods. My endeavor has its roots in Sacks's class (and its continuation in a three-quarter seminar the next year) and in my later engagement with the work of Wayne C. Booth—though neither Sacks nor Booth would agree with everything I argue here. To put this all another way, *Experiencing Fiction* is my effort to provide a persuasive affirmative answer to Sacks's initial question thirty-some years later when presumably I've learned a few more things.

Over time I've reformulated Sacks's question as I have encountered other takes on it. Both the empirical evidence provided by almost any poll of randomly selected readers and the theoretical evidence provided by post-structuralist thinking demonstrate that we have excellent reasons for concluding that, left to their own devices, readers do not respond in the same ways to the same books. Consequently, I began posing the question as "*can* we read the same books?" Then, as I became increasingly interested in accounting for the multi-leveled nature of our experience of narratives (we respond intellectually, emotionally, ethically, aesthetically), I came to articulate the question as "can we *experience* the same books in similar ways?" These changes in the overriding question, then, acknowledge the insights of post-structuralist theory without becoming committed to post-structuralist modes of interpretation, because I also have accumulated evidence throughout my many years of discussing narrative with others that often different readers do share (not totally but nontrivially) responses to the same narrative. I do not want to start, as Sacks did, with the underlying assumption that readers always have the same experience of a book, but I also do not want to start by assuming that language is inevitably indeterminate or that our reading experiences are wholly determined by our interpretive communities, or that they are only a function of the way ideology controls the production, dissemination, and consumption of discourse. Instead, I assume that, though shared experiences are far from inevitable, they are both possible and desirable, and from that assumption, as I note above in slightly different terms, I seek to identify and elaborate the theoretical principles underlying a viable and valuable reading practice that follows from that assumption and to exemplify the consequences of that practice in the analysis of individual narratives.

Although the theory behind the reading practice has multiple elements, I have chosen to focus here on the two concepts that I believe are most central to it: (1) judgments, which I break down into three main types, inter-

pretive, ethical, and aesthetic; and (2) progressions, which I break down
into twelve aspects that I describe in the Introduction. One consequence
of this focus is that I bring in other concepts of narrative theory such as
character, voice, focalization, and temporality not as part of a pre-existing
checklist for all analyses but as they are relevant to the examination of
judgments and progressions in my chosen texts. I believe that judgments
and progressions are central to accounting for the possibility of shared
experience because they are closely tied to the very concept of narrativity
(that which makes a given text a narrative), and because they both depend
on and influence every other element of narrative. I have also found that
the best way to demonstrate their centrality, and, thus, the powers of the
reading practice I want to advocate, is by formulating theoretical principles and then employing them in interpretations that demonstrate, test,
and refine those principles.

Indeed, as I shall explain at greater length in chapter 3, I believe that
the best test of the theoretical approach is its consequences for our understanding of individual narratives. For that reason, the Introduction focuses
on the key principles about progressions and judgments that will allow
me to get the detailed analysis of individual narratives underway. This
strategy, in turn, means that I defer two other theoretical discussions
until later chapters. The first, in chapter 3, characterizes my project as the
development of a "rhetorical poetics" of fiction, and it offers accounts of
how the reading practice that follows from it relates to the one I learned
during my training at Chicago many years ago and to the currently widespread practice of what I call cultural thematics. The second, in chapter
6, expands and refines an aspect of this rhetorical poetics whose complex
nature deserves special attention even after several exemplifications of the
reading practice: aesthetic judgments and their relation to interpretive and
ethical judgments.

Although focused on progressions and judgments, the interpretive
analyses are not designed to give a blow-by-blow account of the experience of reading or even to offer comprehensive accounts of every element
of each narrative. Instead, these analyses aim to give articulate expression to the multiple layers of what is sometimes explicit but just as often
tacit, intuitive, and even inchoate in our reading experience and to do so
through the focus on issues of judgment and progression that each narrative makes particularly salient. Given these analytical purposes, I have
selected a group of ten fictions that collectively constitute a very broad
range of interpretive challenges and an equally broad sample of the ways
in which narratives deploy judgments and progressions to affect (and,

indeed, to effect) our experience of them. Furthermore, I divide these ten fictions into two groups, one whose members have a high degree of *narrativity* and the other whose members synthesize narrativity with what I call *lyricality* (that which makes something lyric) or *portraiture* (that which makes something a character sketch).

Thus, after the Introduction, which makes extensive use of Ambrose Bierce's very short fable, "The Crimson Candle," to illustrate seven theses about narrative judgments, Part One looks at four different narratives with four very different progressions. Since a focus on progression means paying attention to the movement of a narrative from beginning to middle through ending, I pay some attention to all three parts in my discussion of each of these novels. Nevertheless, my own progression in Part One goes from primary attention to beginning and early middle in Jane Austen's *Persuasion,* to beginning and middle in Toni Morrison's *Beloved,* and to ending in Edith Wharton's "Roman Fever." My fourth narrative, Ian McEwan's *Atonement,* makes judgment itself a major thematic issue, while employing a tour de force progression the effect of which depends heavily on a disclosure that is delayed until almost the ending. Consequently, the analysis of *Atonement* calls upon most of the tools I develop in Part One.

Part Two then looks at how our experiences and our corresponding accounts of judgments and progression change when we leave the realm of texts dominated by narrativity and encounter hybrid forms that use principles of both narrativity and lyricality or narrativity and portraiture. My first two examples, Ernest Hemingway's "A Clean, Well-Lighted Place" and Sandra Cisneros's "Woman Hollering Creek," are lyric narratives, though I pair them because they demonstrate two significantly different ways to synthesize elements of narrativity and lyricality into an effective hybrid. My second examples, Alice Munro's "Prue" and Ann Beattie's "Janus," are what I call portrait narratives. These two stories by North American women written in the 1980s (reproduced in the Appendix) do not show any significant change in their women protagonists' situations, but effectively use narratives as part of the gradual unfolding of those protagonists' characters. In the final chapter of Part Two, I turn to Robert Frost's "Home Burial," because the powerful experience its offers provides a provocative demonstration of what a skillful poet can do with progression and judgment in a lyric narrative hybrid. In the Epilogue I reflect further on the relation between the rhetorical poetics of fiction and this corpus of narratives, and I offer brief accounts of how this poetics could be extended to both metafiction and to nonfictional narrative.

In shifting from a descriptive (do we read the same books?) to a normative question (can we experience the same books in similar ways?), I also take on the obligation of demonstrating what is to be gained by an affirmative answer. My brief answer here, which I elaborate in different ways throughout the book, is that attending to the various layers of our experience (especially the intellectual, the emotive, the ethical, and the aesthetic) and recognizing the sources of those experiences in authorial strategy and textual phenomena allow us to understand and value the power of fictional narrative. The reading practice and the associated critical approach ultimately want to give a plausible account of fictional narrative's ability to reinforce, extend, challenge, or sometimes change what we know, think, believe, and value—and to that extent, its ability to reinforce, challenge, or even change who we are.

*Experiencing Fiction* is also a fifth chapter in my ongoing effort to write a comprehensive account of the rhetorical theory of narrative. This book both draws on and seeks to go beyond the inquiries and conclusions in the previous four chapters: *Worlds from Words,* a study of style; *Reading People, Reading Plots,* a study of character and narrative progression; *Narrative as Rhetoric,* an articulation of the general theory and an illustration of how it would solve a number of interpretive problems; and *Living to Tell about It,* a study of character narration that also develops a more systematic approach to rhetorical ethics. This book seeks to expand the insights in *Reading People, Reading Plots* about narrative progression by elaborating the concept in several ways, and it seeks to develop much further that strand of the argument in *Living to Tell about It* concerned with the interrelations between (rhetorical) ethics and (rhetorical) aesthetics.

In the course of writing those four previous books, I have staged encounters with other theoretical positions from deconstruction to semiotics, from psychoanalysis to cognitive constructivism. I do not adopt a similar strategy here for two reasons. (1) Although I have no illusions that whoever reads this book will also have read the previous four, I have not found it productive to return to the same theoretical ground and till it once more. I invite those readers who would like more direct comparisons with other approaches to look at the earlier books. (2) As noted above, I believe that the best test of my rhetorical poetics as a way to account for the possibility of shared reading experiences lies in my engagements with individual narratives, and, I therefore want to keep the focus on those engagements.

Since I can locate the genesis of this book in an event that happened more than thirty years ago, it is not surprising that I have more people to thank than even the increasingly lenient rules of decorum for the genre of Acknowledgments will allow. Consequently, I focus primarily on those whose influence has been more direct and more recent. My research assistant, Elizabeth Marsch, has provided significant material assistance through her sharp-eyed copyediting and her thoughtful indexing. Lecture audiences at Peking University, the University of Tampere, Aarhus University, the University of Hamburg, the University of Bergen, the Centre for Advanced Study in Oslo as well as at Case Western University, the University of South Florida, and Auburn University have offered questions and comments that led me to rethink and revise important points of theory and interpretation. I am especially grateful for the invitations and responses from my hosts at those institutions, Dan Shen, Pekka Tammi and Markku Lehtimaki, Henrik Skov Nielsen and Stefan Iversen, Harry Muller, Randi Koppen, Willy Østreng and Jakob Lothe, Gary Lee Stonum, Susan Mooney, and Miriam Marty Clark. At the Centre for Advanced Study, I had the opportunity to try out my ideas with and learn from an excellent research team on Narrative Theory and Analysis assembled by Jakob Lothe: Jeremy Hawthorn, Daphna Erdinast-Vulcan, Beatrice Sandberg, J. Hillis Miller, Susan Suleiman, and Anniken Greve. I owe a debt to many friends and colleagues in the Society for the Study of Narrative Literature, especially the participants in the Contemporary Narratology Seminars, whose sessions continue to provide a wonderful environment in which to try out ideas. For careful readings of several parts of this manuscript and for almost thirty years of conversation, much of it conducted in the margins of my drafts, I am deeply grateful to my friend and colleague, James L. Battersby. My successor as chair of the English Department at Ohio State, Valerie Lee, has been so supportive that I would hope she would stay in the job until I retire—if my own experience in the chair's office didn't make me believe that I would be hoping for cruel and unusual punishment. My colleagues in Project Narrative at Ohio State, Frederick Aldama, David Herman, and Brian McHale, are so smart, generous, and funny that I can't imagine a better place to be doing narrative theory. I have been very fortunate in the Press's choices of readers for the manuscript, Harry Shaw and David H. Richter, who provided such healthy combinations of receptivity and skepticism that I couldn't help but feel motivated to write a better book. Above all, I am grateful to my friend and fellow rhetorical theorist, Peter J. Rabinowitz, whose ideas and ways of thinking about both narrative and theory have significantly influenced mine, and whose incisive reading of the manuscript—and many of its revisions—has improved it immeasurably. Once again, Peter has given me a vision of what ideal rhetorical reading looks like.

This book would not have been written at all, if I were not so fortunate as to live in the environment of generosity and thoughtfulness, kindness and understanding, laughter and love provided by my wife, Betty Menaghan. Being able to share experiences with her has been the greatest blessing of my life.

In living with this book over the last several years, I have spent many hours thinking about my intellectual and personal debts to my two extraordinary graduate school teachers at the University of Chicago, Sheldon Sacks and Wayne C. Booth. These debts go beyond anything I can register in this Preface or in my occasional direct discussions of their work in the later chapters. So I will just say that they taught me not just bodies of knowledge and ways of reading but what intellectual inquiry was all about: the pleasures and challenges of engaging with literature one cares about, the value of grappling with significant questions one does not have the answers to, the joys of arguing not to win (or not only to win) but to learn. For these lessons, and so much else, I dedicate this book to their memories.

Earlier versions of much of the material in this book have previously appeared in print, and though I have revised much of it, I am grateful for permissions from the publishers to draw on it here:

"The Beginning and Early Middle of *Persuasion;* Or, Form and Ideology in Austen's Experiment with Narrative Comedy." *Partial Answers* 1 (2003): 65–87.

"Judgment, Progression, and Ethics in Portrait Narratives: The Case of Alice Munro's 'Prue.'" *Partial Answers* 5 (2007): 115–29.

"Narrative as Rhetoric and Edith Wharton's "Roman Fever": Progression, Configuration, and the Ethics of Surprise." *A Companion to Rhetoric,* ed. Wendy Olmstead and Walter Jost. Oxford: Blackwell, 2004. 340–54.

"Narrative Judgments and the Rhetorical Theory of Narrative: The Case of McEwan's *Atonement.*" *A Companion to Narrative Theory.* Oxford: Blackwell, 2005). 322–36.

"Rhetorical Ethics and Lyric Narrative: Robert Frost's 'Home Burial.'" *Poetics Today* 25 (2004): 627–51.

"The Rhetoric and Ethics of Lyric Narrative: Hemingway's 'A Clean, Well-Lighted Place.'" *Frame* 17 (2004): 5–21.

"Sandra Cisneros's 'Woman Hollering Creek': Narrative as Rhetoric and as Social Practice." *Narrative* 6 (1998): 221–35.

"Sethe's Choice: The Ethics of Reading in *Beloved.*" *Style* 32, 2 (1998): 318–33.

"Prue," from *The Moons of Jupiter and Other Poems* by Alice Munro, copyright © 1982 by Alice Munro. Used by permission of Alfred A. Knopf, a division of Random House, Inc. and of the Virginia Barber Literary Agency.

"Janus," reprinted with permission of Simon & Schuster Adult Publishers Group and International Creative Management, Inc. from *Where You'll Find Me and Other Stories* by Ann Beattie. Copyright © 1986 by Irony & Piety, Inc. Originally appeared in *The New Yorker.*

"Home Burial" from *The Poetry of Robert Frost,* edited by Edward Connery Lathem. Henry Holt and Co., New York, 1966, 1969.

# Judgments, Progressions, and the Rhetorical Experience of Narrative

Critics love to reiterate the uninteresting idea that theatre depends on conflict. But actually it doesn't. It depends on engagement—engagement between the action on stage and the audience which attends.

David Hare, *The Guardian*, July 16, 2005

The word value is inseparable from the word judgment.

Gérard Genette, "What Aesthetic Values?"

## Judgments, Engagements, and Narrative as Rhetoric

When we first begin reading narratives (or have them read to us), we learn both that they typically have good guys (or gals), e.g., Cinderella and the Prince, and bad guys (or gals), e.g., Cinderella's stepmother and her stepsisters, and that the narrative itself signals which characters are which. In one version of "Cinderella," for example, the narrator tells us on the first page that Cinderella is a young woman "of unparalleled goodness and sweetness of temper, which she took from her mother, who was the best creature in the world" and that her stepmother is "the proudest and most haughty woman who ever lived." To put the effects of the narrator's comments in the terms that David Hare uses in the first epigraph, we become engaged on the side of Cinderella before the narrative introduces the nature of the conflict implicit in this contrasting description (and in our understanding that we are reading a fairy tale). We become engaged on Cinderella's side because, to borrow the terms that Gérard Genette uses in the second epigraph, we judge Cinderella positively and her stepmother negatively—we value her traits of character and do not value those of her stepmother. As "Cinderella" proceeds beyond its first paragraph, the narrative not only reinforces these initial judgments but also relies on them to influence significantly our hopes and desires for Cinderella

1

to escape from the tyranny of her stepmother. When we become more advanced readers and encounter more sophisticated narratives, we meet characters for whom the simple labels "good guys" and "bad guys" are no longer adequate, but we continue to make ethical judgments of them and, indeed, of the authors and narrators who tell us about them. One of the main arguments of this book will be that these judgments are as crucial for the kinds of engagements we make with these sophisticated narratives as our judgments in "Cinderella" are for our engagement with the fairy tale.

To take another example, consider this passage from Ring Lardner's "Haircut," in which Lardner's narrator, Whitey the barber, tells his new customer from out of town a little about Jim Kendall and his wife:

> As I say, she'd of divorced Jim, only she seen that she couldn't support herself and the kids and she was always hopin' that some day Jim would cut out his habits and give her more than two or three dollars a week.
>
> They was a time when she would go to whoever he was workin' for and ask them to give her his wages, but after she done this once or twice, he beat her to it by borrowin' most of his pay in advance. He told it all round town, how he had outfoxed his Missus. He certainly was a caution! (25)

What stands out here is not only that we judge Jim much more negatively than Whitey does (we recognize Jim's selfishness and meanness; Whitey regards him as an entertaining trickster), but also that we judge Whitey negatively too (though not mean and selfish himself, he is so morally imperceptive that he does not recognize Jim's meanness and selfishness). But as we judge this character and this narrator negatively, we are also approving the moral vision of the implied Ring Lardner because we feel he is guiding us to make those judgments. In addition, we are tacitly registering Lardner's skill in communicating these judgments to us while using only Whitey's discourse. Consequently, our engagement is similar to but more complicated than it is in "Cinderella." We regard Kendall as cruel and therefore dangerous, Whitey as obtuse and perhaps therefore dangerous, and Lardner as a skilled practitioner with whom we'd like to collaborate further.

We could of course continue up the ladder of sophisticated narratives to look at cases in which our moral discriminations among characters and our corresponding engagements are much more nuanced than they are in "Haircut"—and even to narratives that don't seem to give sufficient signals for us to make clear and firm discriminations. Later in this book I will climb that ladder, but now I want to pause at Lardner's rung because it is sufficiently high to allow me to lay out the threefold thesis of this book. (1) The judgments we readers of narrative make about characters and tellers (both narrators and authors) are crucial to our experience—and understanding—of narrative form. By form I mean the particular fashioning of the elements, techniques, and structure of a narrative in the service of a set of readerly engagements that lead to particular final effects on the implied audience.[1] (2) Narrative form, in turn, is experienced through the temporal process of reading and responding to narrative. Consequently, to account for that experience of form we need to focus on narrative progression, that is, the synthesis of both the textual dynamics that govern the movement of narrative from beginning through middle to end and the readerly dynamics—what I have so far been calling our engagement—that both follow from and influence those textual dynamics. (3) As key elements of narrative experience, narrative judgments and narrative progressions are responsible for the various components of that experience, especially the significant interrelation of form, ethics, and aesthetics—even as judgments and progressions do not totally explain everything we might want to know about ethics and aesthetics.

This threefold thesis itself is best understood within a broader rhetorical approach to narrative that can be sketched through a discussion of its five main principles.[2] The first principle is that narrative can be fruitfully understood as a rhetorical act: somebody telling somebody else on some occasion and for some purpose(s) that something happened. In fictional narrative, the rhetorical situation is doubled: the narrator tells her story

1. By "readerly" here I mean something different from Roland Barthes (1974) in his distinction between "readerly" (*lisible*) and "writerly" (*scriptible*) texts. Barthes uses "readerly" to refer to texts whose meanings appear fixed and conventional and "writerly" to refer to texts whose meanings are open-ended, I use "readerly" to refer simply to the activities of audiences. In the pages that follow, I often discuss "readerly dynamics" as a major element of narrative progressions.

2. The following discussion draws on material from the introduction to my previous book, *Living to Tell about It,* an introduction that also looks at what I call "redundant telling," the recounting of events and information that the audience already knows. Readers familiar with that introduction will find the next few paragraphs an instance of redundant telling.

In *Living to Tell* I also address the debate about the utility of the concept of the implied author (38–49). I argue that the concept is a good fit for the rhetorical approach, and redefine it as "a streamlined version of the real author, an actual or purported subset of the real author's capacities, traits, attitudes, beliefs, values, and other properties that play a role in the construction of the particular text" under consideration (45). In *Experiencing Fiction,* my references to "the author" and to the last names of the particular authors whose works I discuss are references to the implied author defined in this way. If I want to refer to the author as historical figure, I shall use the term "flesh-and-blood author."

to her narratee for her purposes, while the author communicates to her audience for her own purposes both that story and the narrator's telling of it. As I argue in *Living to Tell about It*, recognizing the consequences of this doubled communicative situation (one text, more than one teller, more than one audience, more than one purpose) is fundamental to a rhetorical understanding of character narration. (In nonfictional narrative, the extent to which the narrative situation is doubled will depend on the extent to which the author signals her difference from or similarity to the "I" who tells the story.) In the fictional "Haircut," Lardner uses Whitey's telling of his story about Jim's exploits and his "accidental" death to the new customer as a way to convey a quite different story to his (that is, Lardner's) implied audience. While Whitey's purpose is to entertain the customer with his tales of Jim's pranks and his unfortunate end, Lardner's is to convey the chilling consequences that follow from the inability of Whitey—and the group of men he represents—to recognize either the depth of Jim's cruelty or the very rough justice Doc Stair and Paul Dickson mete out separately and together.

Second, the approach assumes a recursive relationship (or feedback loop) among authorial agency, textual phenomena (including intertextual relations), and reader response. In other words, for the purposes of interpreting narratives, the approach assumes that texts are designed by authors in order to affect readers in particular ways; that those designs are conveyed through the words, techniques, structures, forms, and dialogic relations of texts as well as the genres and conventions readers use to understand them; and that reader responses are a function of and, thus, a guide to how designs are created through textual and intertextual phenomena. At the same time, reader responses are also a test of the efficacy of those designs.

Third, the model of audience behind the approach's conception of reader response is the one developed by Peter J. Rabinowitz that I have modified slightly (Rabinowitz 1977; Phelan 1996: 135–53). This model identifies four main audiences: the flesh-and-blood or actual reader, the authorial audience (the author's ideal reader or what I have called the implied reader above), the narrative audience (the observer position within the narrative world that the flesh-and-blood reader assumes), and the narratee (the audience addressed by the narrator). The model assumes that the flesh-and-blood (or actual) reader seeks to enter the authorial audience; hence, when I speak of what "we" readers do in response to a narrative text, I am referring to the activities of the authorial audience. In "Haircut," I as individual flesh-and-blood reader am distinct from the customer in

Whitey's barber chair, the narratee, but I enter both the narrative audience, which believes in the real existence of Whitey, the customer, Jim and the other characters (hence, the narrative audience is in the position of observing Whitey tell the story to the customer), and the authorial audience. The authorial audience recognizes Lardner's careful communication through Whitey's generally haphazard speech. The concept of the flesh-and-blood reader allows the rhetorical approach to recognize that differences among individual readers can lead to their different responses and interpretations, while the concept of the authorial audience allows the rhetorical approach to consider the ways in which readers can share the experience of reading narrative. Indeed, sometimes, the rhetorical theorist will use differences among flesh-and-blood readers as a way of identifying difficulties in the construction of a progression, a way, that is, of pointing to the sources of interpretive disagreement in the textual dynamics.

Methodologically, the feedback loop among author, text, and reader means that the rhetorical critic may begin the interpretive inquiry from any one of these points on the rhetorical triangle, but the inquiry will necessarily consider how each point both influences and can be influenced by the other two. With "Haircut," we might start with the way the text juxtaposes Jim's behavior and Whitey's judgments ("He told it all around town how he'd outfoxed his missus. He certainly was a caution!") in order to call attention to the incongruity between them. From there, it's a short step to Lardner as the designer of that incongruity and to the audience's judgments of Jim, Whitey, and Lardner himself. Alternatively, we might start with our overall sense that neither Jim nor Whitey is a character to be admired and then return to the text for the sources of that effect and then move from those sources to their designer. Or we might start with Lardner's agency, focusing on his clear judgments of his narrator and his protagonist, then moving to the textual phenomena by which he conveys those judgments despite his not having a spokesperson for his views in the narrative itself, and finally, considering the consequences of those judgments for readerly response to Jim's behavior and Whitey's reports of it.

4. Fourth, audiences will develop interests and responses of three kinds, each related to a particular component of the narrative: mimetic, thematic, and synthetic. Responses to the mimetic component involve an audience's interest in the characters as possible people and in the narrative world as like our own, that is, hypothetically or conceptually possible; responses to the mimetic component include our evolving judgments and emotions, our desires, hopes, expectations, satisfactions, and disappointments. Responses to the thematic component involve an interest in the ideational function

of the characters and in the cultural, ideological, philosophical, or ethical issues being addressed by the narrative. Responses to the synthetic component involve an audience's interest in and attention to the characters and to the larger narrative as artificial constructs. The relationship among an audience's relative interests in these different components will vary from narrative to narrative depending on the nature of its progression. Some narratives are dominated by mimetic interests, some by thematic, and others by synthetic, but developments in the progression can generate new relations among those interests. Furthermore, there is no necessary reason why a narrative cannot make two or even all three interests important. Still, a few generalizations are possible. In most realistic narratives, the audience has a tacit awareness of the synthetic while it focuses on the mimetic and the thematic components, but, as metafiction since *Don Quixote* has taught us, that tacit awareness can always be converted into something explicit. Furthermore, in metafiction that foregrounds the synthetic component from the beginning, the mimetic typically recedes into the background. In "Haircut," our main interest is in the mimetic and thematic components with the synthetic remaining in the background. The story is chilling both because we judge Jim, Whitey, and the others as if they were real people and because we recognize that Lardner also wants us to view them as representative inhabitants of the American small town in the 1920s. As noted above, the story's aesthetic effectiveness depends on Lardner's ability to foreground the mimetic—Whitey's story to the customer, told with artlessness and moral obtuseness—while tacitly using the details of that story in the synthetic construction of a very artful and thematically significant narrative.

Fifth, the approach assumes that the rhetorical act of telling a story entails a multileveled communication from author to audience, one involving the audience's intellect, emotions, and values (both moral and aesthetic), and that these levels interact with each other. In "Haircut," we interpret Lardner's meanings behind Whitey's communication, and then we judge the characters and become emotionally engaged with them; at the same time, we respond to the artfulness of Lardner's design. Again, one of the main points of my argument in this book is that judgments are crucial to the activation of our multileveled responses and to our understanding of the interrelations among form, ethics, and aesthetics. To develop these points further, I now offer the following seven theses about narrative judgments.

# Narrative Judgments: Seven Theses

*Thesis one* (a recapitulation and extension of the argument so far): *narrative judgments are the point of intersection for narrative form, narrative ethics, and narrative aesthetics.*

To substantiate this thesis further I turn to a rhetorical understanding of narrativity, one that is tied to both the rhetorical definition of narrative (somebody telling somebody else on some occasion and for some purpose that something happened) and the concept of narrative progression. From this perspective, narrativity is a double-layered phenomenon, involving both a dynamics of character, event, and telling and a dynamics of audience response. The phrase "somebody telling . . . that something happened" gets at the first layer: narrative involves the report of a sequence of related events during which the characters and/or their situations undergo some change. As I have discussed elsewhere (Phelan 1989), the report of that change typically proceeds through the introduction, complication, and resolution (in whole or in part) of unstable situations within, between, or among the characters. These dynamics of instability may be accompanied by a dynamics of tension in the telling—unstable relations among authors, narrators, and audiences—and the interaction of the two sets of dynamics, as in narratives that employ unreliable narration, may have significant consequences for our understanding of the "something that happened."

Turning to the second layer, the dynamics of audience response (or, in terms of the definition, the role of the "somebody else"), narrativity encourages two main activities: observing and judging. The authorial audience perceives the characters as external to themselves and as distinct from their implied authors, and the authorial audience passes interpretive and ethical judgments on them, their situations, and their choices. The audience's observer role is what makes the judgment role possible, and the particular judgments are integral to our emotional responses as well as to our desires about future events. In short, just as there is a progression of events there is a progression of audience response to those events, a progression rooted in the twin activities of observing and judging. Thus, from the rhetorical perspective, narrativity involves the interaction of two kinds of change: that experienced by the characters and that experienced by the audience in its developing responses to the characters' changes.

To turn from this abstract theorizing to its practical consequences, consider the relative narrativity of the following two short narratives.

### The Crimson Candle, by James Phelan

A man lying at the point of death said these words to his wife who had been constantly by his side throughout his long illness.

"I am about to say good-bye forever. I hope you know that I love you very much. In my desk you will find a crimson candle, which has been blessed by a High Priest. It would please me if, wherever you go and whatever you do, you would keep this candle with you as a small reminder of my love." The wife thanked him, assured him that, because she loved him too, she would do as he asked, and, after his death, she kept her word.

### The Crimson Candle, by Ambrose Bierce

A man lying at the point of death called his wife to his bedside and said:

"I am about to leave you forever; give me, therefore, one last proof of your affection and fidelity, for, according to our holy religion, a married man seeking admittance at the gate of Heaven is required to swear that he has never defiled himself with an unworthy woman. In my desk you will find a crimson candle, which has been blessed by the High Priest and has a peculiar mystical significance. Swear to me that while it is in existence you will not remarry."

The Woman swore and the Man died. At the funeral the Woman stood at the head of the bier, holding a lighted crimson candle till it was wasted entirely away. (Bierce 1946)

Both versions of "The Crimson Candle" fit the rhetorical definition of narrative, since both involve a teller and an audience, a progression of instability-complication-resolution (each husband seeks the promise, each wife gives it, and each fulfills it in her own way), and a series of developing responses by the audience. But Bierce's version has a higher degree of narrativity, and it does so for two reasons, only the first of which is typically given a lot of attention: (1) Bierce's version introduces a more substantial instability and resolves it with more ingenuity; and (2) Bierce's version represents and invites two more substantial sets of judgments: one set made by the characters and the other set by the audience. Furthermore—and these are my most basic claims—(1) we experience the story as involving the synthesis of the pattern of instabilities and the sequence of judgments; and, therefore, (2) the set of judgments made by the audience is at least as fundamental to the higher degree of narrativity as the set involving the characters.

In other words, we can't locate the difference between Bierce's version and my version only by pointing to the presence or absence of the progression by instability itself. We get closer to locating the difference by noting that the progression by instability is accompanied by narrative judgments and that those judgments, in turn, significantly affect our emotive, ethical, and aesthetic engagements with the narrative. This point brings me to my second thesis.

Thesis two: readers make three main types of narrative judgment, each of which has the potential to overlap with or affect the other two: interpretive judgments about the nature of actions or other elements of the narrative, ethical judgments about the moral value of characters and actions, and aesthetic judgments about the artistic quality of the narrative and of its parts. This thesis has two corollaries: Corollary 1: a single action may evoke multiple kinds of judgment. Corollary 2: because characters' actions include their judgments, readers often judge characters' judgments.

In Bierce's version of "The Crimson Candle," for example, the man's initial request is based on a so-called religious principle which he interprets in his own way, and our judgment of that interpretation will have consequences for our ethical judgment of him. He interprets the principle to say that the test of whether he has "defiled himself with an unworthy woman" is not his behavior while alive but rather his wife's behavior after his death. Not only do we judge his interpretation as off-base, we can, in retrospect, legitimately wonder whether his wife made a similar judgment and so felt freer to act as she did. In addition, we can see that the husband's interpretation fits with his ethical character as someone who assumes that his wife's role is to serve him in both life and death.

The husband and wife also make different interpretive judgments about the nature of the commitment entailed by her oath, and these interpretive judgments overlap with ethical ones. In fact, their interpretive judgments are about the ethical obligation the wife incurs with her sworn promise. The husband assumes that her promise binds her to remain unmarried indefinitely. The wife finds a loophole in the language of the promise, one that allows her to fulfill its letter at the funeral and then be liberated from it. We readers need to make an interpretive judgment about the characters' judgments; we need, that is, to decide about the validity of the wife's interpretation of her oath.

*The interpretation is the ethical judgment*

*are not one & the same, no?*

Not surprisingly, since the characters' interpretive judgments overlap with ethical judgments, the audience's judgments are also overlapping. Indeed, it is possible that the force of one judgment will determine the other. If, for example, we say that the wife has found a valid loophole in her promise, we may also be inclined to say that it is an ethically just fulfillment of that promise. And the other way around. Similarly, if we say that the wife's interpretive judgment is not valid, we may also be inclined to say that she is guilty of breaking her promise. And, once again, the other way around. However, since it is possible to separate the legal and the ethical, we may also separate the interpretive and the ethical judgments at least to some extent: we may decide that the wife's interpretive judgment is not valid because she knew that her husband would not regard her burning the candle at the funeral as a fulfillment of her promise. But we may also make a positive ethical judgment of her action, because we see it as an appropriate response to the husband's ethically deficient actions of misinterpreting the principle for his selfish ends and of insisting on her promise.

The decisions we make about these ethical questions will have consequences for our aesthetic judgments, by which I mean our assessments of a narrative's quality. Indeed, a large part of the aesthetic difference between Bierce's version and my version of "The Crimson Candle" stems from the relative blandness of the ethical judgments in my version when compared with Bierce's version. I will return to this issue of aesthetic judgments in thesis six; for now I want to say more about ethical judgments.

**3.** *Thesis three: individual narratives explicitly or more often implicitly establish their own ethical standards in order to guide their audiences to particular ethical judgments. Consequently, within rhetorical ethics, narrative judgments proceed from the inside out rather than the outside in. It is for this reason they are closely tied to aesthetic judgments.*

The rhetorical theorist, in other words, does not do ethical criticism by applying a pre-existing ethical system to the narrative, however much he may admire the ethics elaborated by Aristotle, Kant, Levinas, or any other thinker; instead the rhetorical theorist seeks to reconstruct the ethical principles upon which the narrative is built. To be sure, the rhetorical theorist does bring values to the text, but he or she remains open to having those values challenged and even repudiated by the experience of reading.[3] More

*rarely an issue of challenge or repudiation given the author's margin'd presence or desire pov*

---

3. I recognize that there are other valid ways to do ethical criticism, including proceeding from the outside in. The efficacy of such criticism depends on both the soundness of the ethical system upon which it is based and the skill and sensitivity with which that system is brought to the narrative.

generally, then, ethical judgments work through the application of the ethical principles underlying the work to the specific behavior of a character (or narrator). Sometimes the underlying principles will be coherent and systematic, but at others they may be ad hoc and unsystematic, and at still others they may be inconsistent.

In *Living to Tell about It,* I identified four ethical positions, one involving the ethics of the told (the character-character relations); two involving the ethics of the telling (the narrator's relation to the characters, the task of narrating, and to the audience; and the implied author's relation to these things); and one involving the flesh-and-blood audience's responses to the first three positions. In this book, I want to make explicit an ethical relation that I left implicit in *Living to Tell:* the ethics of rhetorical purpose, that is, the ethical dimension of the overall narrative act. Here I will focus on how the narrative guides us to judge the character-character relations. When I discuss thesis four, I will attend to the other ethical relations.

Bierce reveals his underlying ethical principles through his stylistic choices, his use of the narrator, and his management of the progression. The stylistic choices reveal that the husband acts in violation of such basic values as love, generosity, and justice, as a comparison of his speech with that of the corresponding character in my version of the story indicates. To take just one prominent contrast, Bierce's character does not make requests; he issues commands. He "calls" his wife to his bedside and delivers a series of additional imperatives: "give me one last proof"; "swear that you will not remarry." The ethical subtext of his speech, which, as noted above, is also evident in his interpretation of the religious principle he cites, is "because I am your superior and my fate matters more, you should do what I command regardless of the personal consequences for you." All of these elements of the language are reinforced by the inescapable phallic symbolism of the crimson candle. Consequently, we make—tacitly and automatically—a negative ethical judgment of him.

Bierce manages the progression so that we make no significant interpretive or ethical judgments of the woman until the last sentence, when the narrator's simple report of her behavior at the funeral prompts not only the resolution of the instability in this unexpected way, but also our simultaneous interpretive and ethical judgments of her and our aesthetic judgment of the whole. When we read, "The Woman stood at the head of the bier, holding a lighted crimson candle till it was wasted entirely away," we simultaneously recognize and endorse her unexpected interpretive and ethical judgment of her promise. The simultaneity of these responses gives the ending its kick and contributes substantially to our positive aesthetic

*[handwritten top margin: Is this really a loophole. she literally obeys his injunction/request]*

judgment of the story. To put the point another way, given our ethical judgments about the husband, we approve of the wife's insight and her values in finding the loophole and acting upon that finding so swiftly and dramatically; in addition, we find the sudden revelation of her judgments and actions aesthetically satisfying. We may or may not decide that the loophole is technically valid—that is, whether she is fulfilling the promise in a legalistic sense or simply manipulating it for her own ends—but our negative ethical judgment of the husband allows us to leave this question open without detracting from the effect of the story.

*[handwritten left margin: we laugh / grin at / as implied / as intended / ethical / judgment]*

*[handwritten right margin: We don't ponder the matter!]*

The woman's acting out her release from the promise during the husband's funeral is also a telling commentary on her view of this promise (whether she regards the husband's interpretation of the principle as off-base or not) and, we are invited to extrapolate, of the marriage itself. Indeed, the inferences packed into the final sentence are so many that we can't help moving from the wife's manipulation of the promise back to Bierce's management of the narrative. And that move brings me to thesis four.

*[handwritten: 4. ?]*

*Thesis four: ethical judgments in narrative include not only the ones we make about the characters and their actions but also those we make about the ethics of storytelling itself, especially the ethics of the implied author's relation to the narrator, the characters, and the audience.*

This thesis highlights the point mentioned above: there is an ethics of the told and an ethics of the telling, which includes the ethics of rhetorical purpose. In considering the ethics of the telling, we again want to identify the author's implicit ethical principles and apply them to the particular techniques of the telling. With "The Crimson Candle," we can start with Bierce's relation to the narrator. While narrators typically serve three main functions—reporting, interpreting, and evaluating (see Phelan 2005)—Bierce restricts his narrator to the single function of reporting, and relies on his audience's being able to infer interpretations and evaluations through the progression and the style. These inferences here include symbolic meanings of the candle that go beyond its phallic appearance to its long tradition of religious significance. Thus, the wife's burning of the candle at the funeral enhances the subversive and comic quality of her action.

As the sudden flurry of inferences surrounding the last sentence indicates, the technique is at once straightforward—the narrator is a reliable and efficient reporter—and coy: the narrator neither prepares us for the wife's maneuver nor gives us any inside view of her. This technique of restricted narration has consequences for Bierce's ethical relation to his

*[handwritten at top: only the husband speaks!]*

characters and to his audience. He lets the characters speak and act for themselves, and he assumes that, through our inferential activity, we can stand with him and take satisfaction in the interpretive, ethical, and aesthetic dimensions of his narrative. Identifying this assumption brings me to thesis five.

(5.)    *Thesis five: individual readers need to evaluate the ethical standards and purposes of individual narratives, and they are likely to do so in different ways.*

The point here is that rhetorical ethics involves a two-step process: reconstruction and evaluation. That is, it attempts to identify the relevant underlying ethical principles, to apply them to specific behavior of the characters and techniques of the telling, and, ultimately, to determine the ethics of the overall narrative purpose. Then, having done that reconstruction, rhetorical ethics moves to evaluation. Bierce's handling of the characterization and the progression, with its emphasis on the husband's selfishness and the wife's brilliant manipulation of her promise, may receive the total approval of some readers, while it may make others uneasy about the way Bierce treats the husband. For these readers, including me, the issue is not that Bierce may be unfair to his own creation but rather that he delights in exposing the husband's ultimate futility. I discover that this delight borders on a gleeful embrace of the impotence conferred by death that I find emotionally chilling and ethically deficient. At the same time, I can recognize that other readers may not evaluate Bierce's underlying ethical stance in this way and that this difference provides an opportunity for productive dialogue about ethics (what Wayne C. Booth [1988] calls coduction)—why do I evaluate one way and you the other?—rather than an opportunity for me to convince you of the error of your evaluation.

(6.)    *Thesis six: just as rhetorical ethics proceeds from the inside out, so too does rhetorical aesthetics. And just as rhetorical ethics involves a two-step process of reconstruction and evaluation, so too does rhetorical aesthetics.*

Doing aesthetics from the inside out means identifying the nature of the work's narrative project and analyzing the skill with which it executes that project. Just as rhetorical ethics does not start with a particular ethical system or a finite list of approved ethical values, rhetorical aesthetics does not start with a hierarchy of pre-approved aesthetic principles. Instead, it seeks to understand the aesthetic principles upon which the individual work is constructed (including, at times, the work's explicit deviation from a dominant aesthetics) and the particular execution of those principles, and it then moves to make an evaluation of the overall aesthetic achievement. This evaluation can include an idea of relative achievement, one rooted

in the concept of aesthetic ambition: that is, what is finally achieved is
connected not only to the particular execution of the project but also
to where the author sets the bar for the project itself. In "The Crimson
Candle," Bierce sets the bar lower than he does in, say, "An Occurrence
at Owl Creek Bridge," and he sets the bar lower there than, say, Morrison
does in *Beloved*. But even as rhetorical ethics and rhetorical aesthetics can
be distinguished from each other, they also interact, and for that reason I
will defer further comment on the aesthetic achievement of "The Crimson
Candle" until I introduce the seventh and final thesis.

*Thesis seven: individual readers' ethical and aesthetic judgments sig-
nificantly influence each other, even as the two kinds of judgments remain
distinct and not fully dependent on each other.*

We have already seen how the interpretive, ethical, and aesthetic judgments to which Bierce guides us overlap—and reinforce each other—in the
ending of his tale. But I want to emphasize that ethical judgments we make
about storytelling have consequences for our aesthetic judgments and vice
versa—even as the two kinds of judgment remain distinct. In my overall
response to "The Crimson Candle," I find that my ethical judgment about
Bierce's pleasure in the husband's futility detracts from my otherwise positive aesthetic judgment of the narrative. Similarly, aesthetic judgments can
have consequences for ethical ones. If, for example, Bierce had employed
an intrusive narrator who imposed explicit ethical judgments on the characters, he would not only have introduced an aesthetic flaw that reduced
our pleasure in inferring those judgments, but that flaw would also lead
to a negative judgment about the ethics of his telling, since the technique
would communicate his distrust of his audience.

There are nevertheless aspects of narrative ethics and narrative aesthetics that are not adequately captured by focusing solely on their mutual
dependence. If we find the values underlying our ethical judgments of
characters or narrators to be deficient but nevertheless deployed with great
skill, we will judge the aesthetics of the narrative more highly than its
ethics. Similarly, an admirable underlying value structure and ethical purpose may be deployed and achieved well or badly, and the difference will
have major consequences for our overall experience of the work. In addition, individual works may work with relatively simple value structures
but work with them with such skill that they constitute significant ethical
and aesthetic achievements. I shall argue that such a situation prevails in
Sandra Cisneros's "Woman Hollering Creek."

Putting together theses six and seven, I conclude that "The Crimson
Candle" is a relatively slight achievement in both ethical and aesthetic

terms—arguably as valuable for my heuristic expository purposes as for its intrinsic merit. Its value structure is sound but simple: it relies on a conventional, widely accepted set of values and reinforces them rather than explores or challenges them. Its narrative project is also simple—to construct a pleasurable reversal narrative involving tyrannical husband and apparently submissive wife—even as its execution shows Bierce's high level of narrative skill. Though the story packs a lot of satisfying readerly activity into its short space, its ambition is otherwise modest and so, we can say from our vantage point of more than one hundred years after its publication, is its importance. Nevertheless, Bierce's high level of narrative skill, his ability to pack so much readerly activity into such a short space, suggests that his modest achievement here is beyond what many—perhaps even most—of us who are reading this book could accomplish.

## Narrative Progressions: Beginnings, Middles, and Endings

I turn now to relate these theses about narrative judgments to my ideas about narrative progression. In this section, I shall describe a rhetorical model for analyzing progression and shall offer brief illustrations of how the model applies to Edith Wharton's "Roman Fever." In chapter 4, I shall offer a detailed analysis of judgments and progression in Wharton's story as I consider the ethics and aesthetics of her use of a surprise ending. The model of narrative progression I propose here strives to be specific enough to use for analyzing individual narratives but flexible enough for analyzing narrative progressions in all their variety. The model is not designed to predict (or prescribe) how progressions must proceed but rather to give us tools for unpacking how they have proceeded. But there is one important assumption that is worth stating at the outset: while the elements of a progression are themselves key components of our experience of a narrative, they are themselves governed by the overarching purpose(s) of that narrative. Let's then turn to the model and start—where else?—with beginnings.

Previous narrative theory, for the most part, has emphasized the textual rather than the readerly side of narrative beginnings. Aristotle tells us in his wonderfully logical way that a beginning is that which is not itself necessarily after anything else and that which has naturally something else after it. Structuralist theorists, following Propp (1968 [1928]), identify the beginning with the introduction of a lack. Emma Kafalenos's analysis of causality in narrative (2006) identifies the first move as the introduction of disequilibrium. Psychoanalytic critics such as Peter Brooks (1984) view the beginning as the initiation of narrative desire. In my previous work on narrative progression (1989; passim), I have identified the beginning as that which generates the progression of the narrative by introducing unstable relationships between characters (instabilities) or between implied author and authorial audience or narrator and authorial audience (tensions). Local instabilities are those whose resolution does not signal the completeness of the progression; global instabilities are those that provide the main track of the progression and must be resolved for a narrative to attain completeness. (Of course not all narratives seek completeness in this sense.) The first chapter of *Pride and Prejudice,* for example, uses local instabilities—the dialogue between Mr. and Mrs. Bennet about whether Mr. Bennet will visit the new tenant of Netherfield Park—even as it communicates the global instability: the arrival of the single man of good fortune into the neighborhood. The one theorist who has emphasized the readerly side of beginnings, Peter J. Rabinowitz, has been less concerned with identifying beginnings proper than with pointing out that, before reading, we are already equipped with conventional Rules of Notice that mark the initial features of texts—titles, epigraphs, first sentences, first chapters—as deserving special emphasis (1998: 47–75). These different perspectives obviously have much in common and suggest that beginnings not only set the narrative in motion but also give it a particular direction.

Indeed, beginnings do more than initiate the action, as becomes apparent when we look more closely at readerly dynamics. Elements of exposition matter because they influence our understanding of the narrative world, which in turn influences our understanding of the meaning and consequences of the action, including our initial generic identification of the narrative and the expectations that follow from that identification. Furthermore, we need to include in a broadened concept of beginnings narrative discourse and the readerly dynamics associated with it. Sometimes the forward movement of a narrative is generated by the tensions arising in narrative discourse, but even when the forward movement is generated primarily by instabilities, our processing of the narrative discourse is a crucial component of our entry into the narrative world.

Given these considerations, I propose the following conception of narrative beginnings.[4] The initial distinction is between *opening* and *beginning.* I will use *opening* as the general, inclusive term that refers to the first few

---

4. This account of beginnings is a revision and extension of the brief account I offer in my entry on "Beginnings and Ending" in *The Encyclopedia of the Novel.*

pages and the first chapter (or other initial segment) of a narrative, including the front matter. *Beginning* is the technical, precise term, referring to a
segment of a narrative defined by four aspects. The first two aspects focus
on the "aboutness" of the narrative and on the textual dynamics, while the
second two focus on the activity of the authorial audience, what I will call
readerly dynamics.

(1) *Exposition:* everything, including the front matter, that provides
information about the narrative, the characters (listings of traits, past history, and so on), the setting (time and place), and events of the narrative.
The front matter, in addition to the title page, may include such things
as illustrations (as in *Orlando*), epigraphs (as in *Beloved*), preludes (as in
*Middlemarch*), notices (as in *Huckleberry Finn*), and author's or editor's
introductions (such as John Ray, Jr.'s introduction to *Lolita*). Exposition is
of course not limited to an opening but may appear anywhere in a narrative; exposition that is part of a beginning includes anything prior to
or immediately following and directly relevant to what I call the launch.[5]
Wharton's story begins in a fairly leisurely manner because she frontloads
so much exposition. The first paragraph, for example, is entirely given over
to it, introducing the main characters, and something about the time and
place of their meeting:

> From the table at which they had been lunching two American
> ladies of ripe but well-cared for middle-age moved across the lofty
> terrace of the Roman restaurant and, leaning on its parapet, looked
> first at each other, and then down on the outspread glories of the
> Palatine and the Forum, with the same expression of vague but
> benevolent approval. (3)

The expository nature of the paragraph is enhanced by its emphasis on
the similarity between the two ladies: the narrator is describing a stable

5. See Sternberg (1978) for an impressive account of the relation between exposition
and a narrative's handling of time. Sternberg uses the fabula/sjuzhet distinction, i.e., the
distinction between the chronological sequence of events and the order and representation of
those events in the narrative text, to identify exposition as "the first part" of the fabula (14),
and he sees its function as providing the reader "with the general and specific antecedents
indispensable to the understanding of what happens in [the fictive world of the story]" (1).
Sternberg's understanding of exposition informs my own, but my interest in the phenomenon
here is different (and more limited): I want to account for the role of exposition in that part
of the sjuzhet that I am calling the beginning.

rather than an unstable situation. Frontloading this exposition means that Wharton can later let the narrative progress largely through the narrator's reporting of the dialogue between these two American ladies, Alida Slade and Grace Ansley. By starting with an emphasis on the similarity between the two women in this time and place, Wharton also prepares for the dramatic effects of her later revelation of their differences.

(2) *Launch*: the revelation of the first set of global instabilities or tensions in the narrative. This moment in the narrative marks the boundary between the beginning and the middle. The launch may come early or it may come late, but I set the boundary at the first global instability or tension because until then a narrative has not established a clear direction. This way of identifying the launch also means that, from a first-time reader's perspective, the identification will initially be a tentative one, something for which the reader will seek confirmation or disconfirmation in the subsequent progression. The tentative nature of our initial identification helps us recognize that authors can play with the launch, sometimes offering false starts. I'll return to this last point during the discussion of Hemingway's "A Clean, Well-Lighted Place" in chapter 5. In "Roman Fever," the launch is completed at the end of Part I with Grace's thought that "on the whole [Alida] had had a sad life. Full of failures and mistakes; Mrs. Ansley had always been rather sorry for her. . . ." Grace's thought completes the launch because it establishes a global tension about why Grace regards Alida this way and because it complements Alida's thoughts about being superior to Grace, whom she regards as old-fashioned, conventional, and a "nullity." Wharton then uses exposition to underline the launch with her narrator's comment, "So these two ladies visualized each other, each through the wrong end of her little telescope." Thus, at the end of Part I, we have both a significant instability between the characters—each feels superior to the other—and a global tension about the past and its effect on their current estimations of each other.

(3) *Initiation*: the initial rhetorical transactions among implied author and narrator, on the one hand, and flesh-and-blood and authorial audience on the other. Rabinowitz's Rules of Notice (1998: 47–75) are especially relevant to the reader's experience of the initiation. In Wharton's first paragraph, for example, we get introduced to a formal narrator who keeps her emotional distance from both characters, a distance underlined in the comment at the end of Part I about each woman's view through "her little telescope." As we proceed through the beginning, we discover that the narrator more readily offers us inside views of Alida than of Grace; this element of the initiation makes the revelation of Grace's thoughts to complete the launch stand out. More generally, this initiation also keeps the

authorial audience somewhat distant from the characters and encourages us to align ourselves more with the implied Wharton as the designer of the story.

(4) *Entrance:* the flesh-and-blood reader's multileveled—cognitive, emotive, ethical—movement from outside the text to a specific location in the authorial audience at the end of the launch. When the entrance is complete, the authorial audience has typically made numerous significant interpretive, ethical, and even aesthetic judgments, and these judgments influence what is arguably the most important element of the entrance: the authorial audience's hypothesis, implicit or explicit, about the direction and purpose of the whole narrative, what I will call its configuration. This hypothesis about configuration is of course subject to revision in light of developments in the middle and even the ending. In "Roman Fever," we enter with an awareness of a coming clash between the protagonists, with an expectation that the clash will be painful, but with no clear sense of its outcome. Narratives such as "Roman Fever" that offer surprise endings deliberately seek to move our configuration in one direction only to reveal to us in their final moments that a different direction and purpose has been guiding the progression all along.

This conception of a beginning means that it is a unit whose length will vary considerably from narrative to narrative, since some beginnings will include more exposition than others and some will take longer to establish the first set of global instabilities or tensions. In addition, this conception of a beginning naturally leads into similar conceptions of middles and endings, conceptions that also identify four aspects of each, two concerned with textual dynamics and two with reader dynamics.

Middles have the following aspects:

(5) *Exposition:* again, information relevant to the narrative (e.g., chapter titles), setting, characters, and events. In "Roman Fever," the exposition in the middle focuses primarily on the setting, on how the advancing evening affects the characters' views of Rome, and on Grace's handling of her knitting. Both kinds of exposition influence our understanding of the conversational dynamics.

(6) *Voyage:* the development of the global instabilities and/or tensions. Sometimes the initial set of global instabilities or tensions becomes more complicated, as it is in "Roman Fever"; sometimes, as in many picaresque narratives, the global instabilities remain largely as they are or get only mildly complicated as the characters deal with a series of local instabilities. In Wharton's story, as we shall see in more detail in chapter 4, the conflict between the characters in the present escalates as the tensions about the past slowly get resolved.

(7) *Interaction:* the ongoing communicative exchanges between implied author, narrator, and audience. These exchanges have significant effects on our developing responses to the characters and events as well as to our ongoing relationship with the narrator and implied author. In "Roman Fever," the narrator continues to maintain her emotional distance from the characters, and she reverts to giving us inside views only of Alida. We trust the narrator but remain aware that she is not telling us all, and we continue to align ourselves with the implied author, following the sequence of inferences she builds into the story.

—(8) *Intermediate configuration:* the evolving responses of the authorial audience to the overall development of the narrative. During this stage our initial hypothesis about the configuration of the whole will become more fully developed, though that development may either largely confirm or substantially revise the hypothesis formed at the entrance. Although our immediate configuration has the potential to shift with each new sentence of the middle, sometimes the textual and readerly dynamics will collaborate to have a particular configuration—or key elements of it, at least—remain in place for a good stretch (in *Great Expectations,* for example, we're invited to believe for a long time that Pip's benefactor is Miss Havisham) and sometimes those dynamics will give a special emphasis to a particular shape of an evolving configuration. In "Roman Fever," once Alida inflicts on Grace the knowledge that Alida forged the note from Delphin, we have such an emphasis as we infer that the present is repeating the past: Alida is the aggressor and Grace is the victim.

Endings have the following four aspects:

—(9) *Exposition/Closure:* when this information about the narrative, characters, or action includes a signal that the narrative is coming to an end, regardless of the state of the instabilities and tensions, it becomes a device of closure. In "Roman Fever," closure is explicitly signaled when the narrator tells us, after Grace's last line of dialogue, that she "began to move ahead of Mrs. Slade toward the stairway," because that movement signals the end of the conversation. In narratives that are constructed around a character's journey, closure is signaled by the character's reaching the appointed destination. Just as beginnings may include such paratextual material as epigraphs and authors' notes, endings may include epilogues, afterwords, appendixes, and the like.

—(10) *Arrival:* the resolution, in whole or in part, of the global instabilities and tensions. Grace's last line of dialogue, "I had Barbara," constitutes the arrival in Wharton's story because it resolves both the final tensions about the events of the previous twenty-five years and the instabilities in

Grace's and Alida's relationship as revealed and complicated by their conversation. This arrival of course causes us to reconfigure our understanding of the events; I will say more about the details of that reconfiguration in chapter 4.

(11) *Farewell:* the concluding exchanges among implied author, narrator, and audiences. The farewell may or may not involve a direct address to the narratee, but the final exchanges always have the potential to affect the audience's response to the whole narrative. The narrator and Wharton maintain the same stance as they have throughout the beginning and middle, but because they trust us to infer the meaning and consequences of the reconfiguration, we are likely to feel that the last lines actually bring us closer together.

(12) *Completion:* the conclusion of the reader's evolving responses to the whole narrative. These responses include our ethical and aesthetic judgments of the narrative as a whole. I will discuss the completion of "Roman Fever" at some length in chapter 4, since I can do better justice to it after a more detailed look at its progression.

Another way of presenting this model is in rows and columns so that, reading across, one can see how the two aspects of textual dynamics and the two aspects of readerly dynamics develop.

| Beginning | Middle | Ending |
|-----------|--------|--------|
| Exposition | Exposition | Exposition/Closure |
| Launch | Voyage | Arrival |
| Initiation | Interaction | Farewell |
| Entrance | Intermediate Configuration | Completion |

These twelve aspects of narrative progression provide a way to track textual and readerly dynamics, but they do not offer any specific predictions about the specific trajectory of any individual narrative progression or set any strong constraints on what any one beginning, middle, or ending will do. The model does not seek such prediction or constraint because the rhetorical approach contends that the specifics of any given progression are themselves determined by the overall purpose(s) of the individual narrative. Consequently, my analyses of individual narratives will not be directed toward arguing that their beginnings, middles, and endings are representative of all narratives, but rather toward showing how their specific ways of working with these elements of progression serve their individual purposes.

## Progression and Judgment in Lyric Narratives and Portrait Narratives

In Part One of this book, I shall attempt to show how attention to judgments and progressions can help identify and resolve some significant interpretive problems in a range of narrative texts. But in order to expand the scope and usefulness of the rhetorical theory of narrative, in Part Two I take up the different experiences offered by hybrid forms, specifically lyric narratives, which combine elements of narrative with elements of lyric, and what I call portrait narratives, which combine elements of narrative with elements of the character sketch. In order to describe these hybrid forms more adequately, I offer rhetorical accounts of lyricality[6] and portraiture that parallel the rhetorical account of narrativity I offer in the first section of this introduction.

With lyricality, I start with a rhetorical definition of lyric that identifies two main modes: (1) somebody telling somebody else (or even himself or herself) on some occasion for some purpose that something is—a situation, an emotion, a perception, an attitude, a belief; (2) somebody telling somebody else (or even himself or herself) on some occasion about his or her meditations on something; to put it another way, in this mode, the poem records the speaker's thoughts. Furthermore, in both kinds of lyric, the authorial audience is less in the position of observer and judge and more in the position of participant. While we recognize that the speaker is different from us, we move from that recognition toward fusion with the speaker—or, to put it in more measured terms, toward adopting the speaker's perspective without any irritable reaching after difference and evaluation. This element of lyricality also depends on the absence of distance between the implied

---

6. My ideas about lyric and portraiture have been significantly influenced by Ralph Rader. His essay, "The Dramatic Monologue and Related Lyric Forms," offers a highly insightful way to think about the relations among (implied) author, the "I" of the poem, and the (authorial) audience. For a sampling of other good work on lyric and narrative, see Friedman, Gerlach (1989, 2004), and Dubrow (2000, 2006). Friedman seeks to make connections between the two forms and gender. Gerlach seeks to identify similarities and differences among the short story, the prose poem, and the lyric. Dubrow points to the contested nature of the concept of lyric and notes the value of understanding the mode within specific historical contexts. I am especially grateful for conversations with Dubrow about the intersections of lyric and narrative.

author and the "I" of the poem. Furthermore, the standard tense for lyric is the present. Lyricality, then, in contrast to narrativity is neutral on the issue of change for the speaker—it may or may not be present—and invested not in character and event but in thoughts, attitudes, beliefs, emotions, specific conditions. Furthermore, the dynamics of audience response stem from adopting the speaker's perspective without judging it. Thus, the double movement of lyric is toward fuller revelation of the speaker's situation and perspective and, on the audience's part, toward deeper understanding of and participation in what is revealed.

The space between narrativity and lyricality is occupied by what I call portraiture, a rhetorical design inviting the authorial audience to apprehend the revelation of character. Since portraiture is manifest most commonly—though not exclusively—in one form of the dramatic mono-logue, I will draw on that form to illustrate its main principles. In the dramatic monologue, somebody tells somebody else whatever the speaker judges to be relevant in that rhetorical occasion; as the speaker's dis-course progresses, the author gradually reveals to her audience the nature of the speaker's character. In other words, the double movement of the form involves a double logic: the speaker's telling progresses according to the logic of the dramatic situation, while the author's construction of that telling progresses in order to give her audience a gradually deepening knowledge and understanding of the speaker. Thus, portraiture is neutral on both change and stasis, since its point is neither event nor condition but character. Regardless of what is told, however, the implied author and the speaker are distinct figures, and so are the speaker and the authorial audience. Furthermore, as the audience remains in the observer role, that role will typically involve judging the character: the judgment, however, will not be directed toward our developing expectations or hopes that are important for the text's progression but instead will be part and parcel of our coming to know the character. In a sense, the purpose of portraiture is to evoke in the audience a response much like that of Browning's Duke to Fra Pandolf's painting: "There she stands as if alive."

This account of portraiture allows us to recognize the dramatic mono-logue as only one mode in which it occurs. Portraiture can also be achieved through the reporting of a noncharacter narrator to an uncharacterized narratee, who is not part of the dramatic situation, provided that the author designs that reporting to reveal a character whom we observe from the outside.

Now there is no theoretical or practical reason why, in any specific text, the relationships among events, character, attitude/thought/belief/, change, and audience activity need to stay within the boundaries of narrativity, lyricality, and portraiture. Indeed, for more than a century, writers have been combining elements of all three modes in order to create effects that are not possible by remaining within the boundaries of any one. To this point, narrative theory, including rhetorical theory, has only begun to come to terms with these hybrid forms. By devoting Part Two of this book to the way judgments and progressions work in some highly effective experiments in hybridity, I hope to advance our understanding of not only those texts but also of these fascinating forms.

As I noted in the Preface, in the chapters that follow I will use the ideas about judgments and progression I have offered here as a way to identify and approach some significant interpretive problems in a range of fictional narratives (for a sketch of the specifics see pp. xi–xii). In building on the principles outlined here in the analysis of this diverse body of narratives, *Experiencing Fiction* seeks to demonstrate the power of the rhetorical theory of narrative, even as it develops new aspects of that theory such as its accounts of narrativity, the relations between ethics and aesthetics, and of the hybrid genre of portrait narrative. More generally, it attempts to show the myriad ways in which a focus on narrative judgments and narrative progressions can help us understand the links and the distinctions among rhetorical conceptions of form, ethics, and aesthetics.

—— PART ONE ——

Judgments and Progressions:
Beginnings, Middles, Endings

# CHAPTER ONE

# Jane Austen's Experiment in Narrative Comedy

## The Beginning and Early Middle of *Persuasion*

Sir Walter Elliot of Kellynch-hall, in Somersetshire, was a man who, for his own amusement, never took up any book but the Baronetage; there he found occupation for an idle hour, and consolation in a distressed one. . . . (3)

Mr. Shepherd was completely empowered to act; and no sooner had such an end been reached, than Anne, who had been a most attentive listener to the whole, left the room, to seek the comfort of cool air for her flushed cheeks; and as she walked along a favourite grove, said, with a gentle sigh, "a few months more, and *he,* perhaps may be walking here." (25)

This little circumstance seemed the completion of all that had gone before. She understood him. He could not forgive her—but he could not be unfeeling. Though condemning her for the past and considering it with high and unjust resentment, though perfectly careless of her and becoming attached to another, still he could not see her suffer without the desire to give her relief. It was a remainder of former sentiment; it was an impulse of pure, though unacknowledged friendship; it was a proof of his own warm and amiable heart, which she could not contemplate without emotions so compounded of pleasure and pain, that she knew not which prevailed. (91)

These three well-known passages from Jane Austen's last novel represent the first move of exposition, the launch, i.e., introduction of the narrative's global instability, and the culmination of Anne's reflections about Wentworth during the Uppercross section of the novel, at a point I will call its early middle. It is my contention that, in constructing the progression from the opening exposition through the launch to Anne's culminating reflection, Austen develops her most radical experiment with the form of narrative comedy. Indeed, during this section of the narrative Austen *almost* transgresses the boundaries of the form. In this chapter, I shall seek to demonstrate these claims by analyzing the role of narrative judgments in the beginning and early middle of the novel and their consequences for the overall progression, including their relevance to the widely-held view that *Persuasion* is distinctive among Austen's novels for its elegiac,

autumnal quality. I begin, however, with an analysis of Austen's approach
to narrative comedy prior to *Persuasion,* a move designed to allow us to
comprehend the aesthetic innovation she is attempting in her last completed novel.[1]

## Austen and Narrative Comedy

As everyone knows, Austen works with the marriage plot; all her novels
trace the routes that her female protagonists take to the altar. In all cases,
she uses that marriage plot in the service of narrative comedy: that is, she
asks her audience both to desire and to expect the marriage and to take
pleasure in its achievement. From a rhetorical perspective, Austen's use of
the form prior to *Persuasion* has the following main characteristics:

1. Austen asks her audience to make an interpretive judgment that
   the engagement of the female protagonist to the male hero is
   the best outcome available within the world of the novel. This
   interpretive judgment is interdependent with the ethical judgment that the two characters are worthy of both each other and
   happiness. Comparing Austen's handling of Charlotte Lucas's
   story and Elizabeth Bennet's story in *Pride and Prejudice* illustrates the point. Austen guides us to make the interpretive judgment that, in marrying Mr. Collins, Charlotte Lucas has made
   a reasonable though less than optimal choice for a woman in
   her circumstances, even as she emphasizes that Collins is not
   the ethical equal of his wife and that marriage to him is not
   capable of bringing her lasting happiness. On the other hand,
   Austen also guides us to regard Elizabeth Bennet's engagement
   to Darcy as the best possible outcome for her in that world, and
   to regard both Elizabeth and Darcy as ethically deserving of
   the happiness their engagement brings them. In short, though
   both Charlotte's story and Elizabeth's are versions of the marriage plot, their affective force is radically different and only
   Elizabeth's story is a narrative comedy.

1. The dominant mode of Austen criticism for the last twenty-five years or so has been
political, as feminist and other critics have sought to place Austen in the larger historical
and cultural framework of her time. For some strong contributions to this strand of Austen
criticism, see Brown, Johnson, Poovey, and Wiltshire. In the earlier version of this chapter
that appeared in *Partial Answers,* I compared my conclusions with those of Poovey (65–87).
For a feminist narratological approach to *Persuasion,* see Warhol.

   More generally, one way that Austen guides our interpretive and ethical judgments of the characters is by guiding our judgments of their contexts: a social world that puts considerable constraints on women's behavior and within that social world a marriage market that places value on money and rank over and above anything else. Austen, however, never shifts ultimate responsibility for the characters' behavior to those contexts: Austen uses the context to mitigate our judgment of Charlotte's choice, not to make us endorse it wholeheartedly. To put this point another way, Austen does not present the constraints on women's behavior as absolute but instead shows that they still retain some degree of choice. Consequently, our ethical judgments focus on how and what they choose within those constraints.

2. The instabilities faced by the protagonists that drive the progression of the action are both internal and external; that is, the successful resolution depends on the protagonist recognizing and overcoming deficiencies in her own character even as she negotiates or endures various external obstacles, including, at times, temporary deficiencies in the male hero. This dimension of Austen's procedure means that we are often in the position of judging the protagonists' judgments, including their initial misjudgments and their subsequent self-judgments.

3. Throughout the progression of instabilities, even at the point of their greatest complication, Austen guides her audience's interpretive judgment so that we expect the engagement will occur, and she guides our ethical judgment so that we desire it to occur. Consequently, our interest is focused less on *whether* the engagement will occur and more on *how* it will come about. This way of proceeding, then, sets the conditions for our aesthetic judgment. What matters most is whether the particular route that the protagonist takes to her marriage produces in the audience the estimation that the marriage represents a satisfactory outcome for the protagonist and an appropriate fulfillment of the promises of the progression.[2] Our evaluation of the aesthetic achievement is also dependent on the way the route

---

2. Much, though not all, of the debates about the endings of *Pride and Prejudice, Emma,* and *Mansfield Park* revolve, in different ways, around the degree of Austen's success in this effort: in *Pride and Prejudice,* the issue is whether Elizabeth has to curtail her liveliness too much, while in *Emma* and *Mansfield Park,* the issue is whether the husbands are appropriate for the protagonists.

to the marriage allows Austen to explore significant thematic
material and on our estimation of that exploration.

*Pride and Prejudice* provides an excellent example of Austen's approach,
including her skill in juxtaposing judgments by her characters and judgments by the authorial audience. As Austen represents Elizabeth's movement from her initial position as one of the five unmarried Bennet sisters
to her engagement with Darcy, Austen focuses on Elizabeth's interpretive
and ethical judgments. Austen asks us to recognize that (1) Elizabeth initially makes many flawed judgments of both kinds, especially in regard to
Darcy and to Wickham; (2) when presented with the evidence of her misjudgments in Darcy's letter, Elizabeth has the insight and moral character
not only to revise her judgments but also to judge herself rather harshly;
and (3) Elizabeth has the strength to accept what she regards as the consequences of her misjudgments. Austen couples this progression of judgments with another series of engagements and judgments in a range of
thematic issues that Austen's critics have admirably discussed throughout
the history of commentary on the novel.

As Austen asks us to approve of Elizabeth's harsh self-judgment at
the midpoint of the progression, she also gives us grounds for making a
different interpretive judgment from Elizabeth, and, thus, gives us different expectations from hers about the consequences of her misjudgments.
Consider, for example, how Austen handles a key secondary event in the
progression, Lydia's elopement with Wickham.

Elizabeth learns of the elopement during her visit to Pemberley several
months after she has rejected Darcy's initial proposal and realized, through
her reflections on his letter to her, that she has thoroughly misjudged him
and Wickham. During this visit, through her viewing of the grounds, hearing Mrs. Reynolds's testimony about Darcy's character, and spending some
time in his company, both Elizabeth's and the authorial audience's interpretive and ethical judgments of Darcy's character become increasingly
more favorable. Consequently, Elizabeth begins to fall in love with him
and the audience comes to desire more keenly their eventual union. When
Jane's letter tells her of Lydia's flight, however, Elizabeth believes that
nothing can come of her feelings, since, to her mind, the disgrace Lydia has
brought on the family must strengthen Darcy's negative judgment of it:

> He seemed scarcely to hear her, and was walking up and down the
> room in earnest meditation; his brow contracted, his air gloomy.
> Elizabeth soon observed and instantly understood it. Her power was

sinking; every thing must sink under such a proof of family weakness, such an assurance of the deepest disgrace. She should neither
wonder nor condemn, but the belief of his self-conquest brought
nothing consolatory to her bosom, afforded no palliation of her distress. It was, on the contrary, exactly calculated to make her understand her own wishes; and never had she so honestly felt that she
could have loved him, as now, when all love must be vain. (278)

Austen, however, has given her audience a different set of interpretive judgments and thus a different set of expectations. By this point in
the narrative Austen has established a pattern in which the threats to
Elizabeth's happiness always dissipate. Collins's marriage proposal is the
most salient example of this part of the pattern, though Jane's illness
and subsequent return to good health, and Elizabeth's own progress after
receiving Darcy's letter, are also parts of it. Consequently, Austen's authorial audience interprets Lydia's behavior as a significant but temporary
obstacle to Elizabeth's eventual happy union with Darcy. We don't worry
about whether, only about how.

Furthermore, once we see how, we make a very positive aesthetic judgment of Austen's handling of that how. She skillfully and efficiently uses
the obstacle as a means for demonstrating how Darcy has changed and for
bringing the lovers together. Rather than shunning the Bennets, Darcy
takes it upon himself to deal with Wickham and make the best of the
bad situation. Darcy's behavior is the best possible example of the ethical change in his character, and it clinches Austen's exploration of the
difference between proper and improper pride. When Elizabeth expresses
her gratitude for his actions, Darcy feels emboldened to make his second,
successful proposal. The positive aesthetic judgment results from the great
satisfaction we feel in the engagement as the appropriate culmination of
the demonstrable ethical growth of the two characters.[3]

*Persuasion* is so distinctive among Austen's novels because in it she
fully retains only the first of the three essential characteristics of her
approach to narrative comedy. Although Austen clearly signals that marriage to Wentworth is the most desirable fate for Anne, Anne is already
a fully-formed ethical being, a woman who does not need to change in
any substantial way. Anne is a woman who has previously made, with
the advice of Lady Russell, one major interpretive misjudgment—breaking her engagement with Wentworth—but Austen asks us to see that this

---

3. For more on the difference between the heroine's expectations and those of the
audience, see Tave 1973: 17–18.

interpretive misjudgment was done for ethically admirable reasons—that is, done because she believed breaking the engagement would ultimately be better for Wentworth as well as herself. Though Anne regrets her misjudgment, she does not need to undergo the kind of moral maturation that most of Austen's other heroines do. Indeed, at the end of the narrative, after Anne has been reunited with Wentworth and looks back on her decision to reject his first proposal, she offers the same assessment that we do: it was an interpretive misjudgment but an ethically appropriate one:

> I am not saying that [Lady Russell] did not err in her advice. . . . I certainly never should, in any circumstance of tolerable similarity, give such advice [as Lady Russell gave to me]. But I mean, that I was right in submitting to her, and that if I had done otherwise, I should have suffered more in continuing the engagement than I did even in giving it up, because I should have suffered in my conscience. (246)

Furthermore, as I shall attempt to demonstrate, for the first half of the novel Austen gives us a different pattern of interpretive judgments than she ever has before, a pattern that does not provide the usual assurances that the protagonist and the male lead will be united. Consequently, *Persuasion* offers a significantly different reading experience, one associated with a different kind of aesthetic project.

That variation starts with the beginning of the novel, which delays the introduction of the global instability until a relatively late point in the progression, the end of the third chapter. Furthermore, in using the first three chapters for giving us the mini-narrative about Sir Walter and his financial troubles, Austen starts further away from what turns out to be the main action of the novel than she usually does (*Sense and Sensibility* is the only other novel in which the introduction of the global instability is similarly delayed). So, the first questions about Austen's experiment with her form are about those first three chapters: what is the function of the initial focus on the mini-narrative involving Sir Walter, and what is the effect of the shift from Sir Walter to Anne at the end of Chapter III?

To start with the second question, one effect of the shift is to provide a new energy and direction to the narrative; it is as if the engine driving the narrative suddenly switches into a higher gear as the direction of the narrative's movement shifts. To be sure, the pace of the progression quickly slows as the new direction is solidified in the shift to Anne as both the main focus and frequently the focalizer of the narration: Chapter IV presents an unhurried analepsis detailing the history between Anne and the "he" of Chapter III, Frederick Wentworth, and the segment of the narrative between Anne's anticipation of Wentworth's arrival and the events in Lyme contains only intermittent direct interaction between Frederick and Anne, as Frederick pays much more attention to Henrietta and Louisa Musgrove. Indeed, *Persuasion* is a narrative that, at least for its first several chapters, seems to exemplify Peter Brooks's contention that effective plots must delay and defer, must find ways to retard forward progress, must take the reader through arabesques of event and repetitions of various kinds—must, in fact, be much like this sentence—before reaching their endings. But *Persuasion*'s return to a leisurely pace in Chapter IV only strengthens the force of the shift in the progression provided at the end of Chapter III.

But there is more to the effect of the end of Chapter III than what happens to the narrative's textual dynamics: the audience is also actively responding to that shift. Sheldon Sacks, in two essays published a generation ago that offer very insightful, albeit brief, commentary on the novel's form, has made the strongest claim about the audience's response, one that sees the novel as giving us the same kind of assurance about Anne's eventual fate as we have in Austen's previous novels. Sacks puts it this way: if "we," Austen's implied readers, infer that the traitless "he" is to be Anne's future husband, we have not merely guessed correctly but have done so because we have already intuited that the novel has a comic form. Consequently, this intuition acts as tacit knowledge that strongly affects our understanding of every subsequent sentence of the narrative, or in Sacks's words, this intuition enables us "to recognize a fate still to be realized in a fictional future while [we] use that knowledge in the interpretation of present aesthetic experience" (1976: S104). In more concrete terms: because we already know that happiness for Anne can only reside outside the home of Sir Walter and because the combination of Anne's attentiveness, flushed cheeks, and gentle sigh signals her desire for the "he," our intuition of the comic form leads us to infer that her desire will be fulfilled. I find Sacks's description both very helpful and not quite adequate to Austen's experiment with the progression, as I will now try to show in a closer look at the novel's beginning.

## The Beginning of *Persuasion*

*Persuasion*'s beginning has three especially striking features: (1) its surprising length: the beginning takes 3 chapters and about 25 pages or almost 10 percent of the book; (2) a very unusual sequence of exposition, mini-narrative, and then launch; (3) an initiation that establishes the narrator as a strong guide to the events of the narrative. Let us look at the interaction of exposition and initiation and then turn to the mini-narrative and the launch as a way to assess where we are at the entrance.

Here is the opening sentence of the novel:

> Sir Walter Elliot, of Kellynch Hall, in Somersetshire, was a man who, for his own amusement, never took up any book but the Baronetage; there he found occupation for an idle hour, and consolation in a distressed one; there his faculties were roused into admiration and respect, by contemplating the limited remnant of the earliest patents; there any unwelcome sensations, arising from domestic affairs changed naturally into pity and contempt as he turned over the almost endless creations of the last century; and there, if every other leaf were powerless, he could read his own history with an interest which never failed. (3)

The sentence provides exposition and initiation: it gives us a character in a specific location, information about one of his habitual activities, and it gives us an introduction to the narrator and her ways of communicating. In addition, the sentence hints at—we might say it leads us to anticipate—an instability through the references to "a distressed" hour and to "unwelcome sensations, arising from domestic affairs." The sentence also gives us our first exchange with a narrator who is extremely knowledgeable about her characters, and who shares that knowledge through both clear and direct statements and their subtle implications. Consequently, initiation works hand-in-hand with exposition. In describing Sir Walter's attachment to the Baronetage, the narrator also conveys (a) that he is not much of a reader ("a man who, for his own amusement, never took up any" other book), (b) that he uses the book as escapist reading, a way to deny his domestic troubles by converting them into objects of "pity and contempt"; and (c) that his ego is so large that he never fails to tire of reading about himself ("if every other leaf were powerless, he could read his own history with an interest which never failed"). The character is at once amusing and dangerous (in the way that the combination of rank, money, and vanity can be dangerous), while the narrator is at once reliable, direct, and deft. We are initiated into a relationship with the narrator in which our alertness will be rewarded with communication that is instructive, amusing, and serious.

As the first chapter progresses, the exposition continues as we learn key facts about the Elliot family, especially about Sir Walter's two unmarried daughters, Elizabeth and Anne, and the initiation leads to a broader range of communicative relations. Sometimes the narrator can be very direct: "Vanity was the beginning and end of Sir Walter's character; vanity of person and of situation" (4). Sometimes she can mix the literal and the ironic as she swiftly moves from an internal to an external view of a character: "He considered the blessing of beauty as inferior only to the blessing of a baronetcy: and the Sir Walter, who united these gifts, was the constant object of his warmest respect and devotion" (4). And she can move from ironic representation of internal views to extremely serious and sympathetic attitudes: "His two other children were of very inferior value. Mary had acquired a little artificial importance, by becoming Mrs. Charles Musgrove; but Anne, [note the shift to narrator's vision and voice] with an elegance of mind and sweetness of character, which must have placed her high with any people of real understanding, was nobody with either father or sister; her word had no weight; [back to internal view] her convenience was always to give way;—she was only Anne" (5).

Not surprisingly, the exposition and initiation signal neither a comic nor a noncomic form. The exposition does not itself indicate whether this configuration of character and situation is likely to alter for the better or the worse. The comic pleasures of the initiation co-exist with the narrator's taking Sir Walter's vanity and its potential consequences quite seriously. Let us look more closely at the mini-narrative about Sir Walter's financial troubles with an eye toward how it affects the audience's formulation of a hypothesis about the narrative as a whole once we reach the launch.

Sacks's claims about the entrance rest largely on his reading of this mini-narrative, and those claims entail an interpretive judgment leading to an aesthetic judgment. In Sacks's view, Austen uses the mini-narrative to reassure her audience that Anne's desire (and ours) will eventually be fulfilled. Then by showing both Anne's significant suffering throughout the Uppercross section and her moral maturity throughout the narrative, Austen maximizes the audience's satisfaction and pleasure in the moment of comic fulfillment, Anne and Wentworth's final engagement. In essence, Sacks argues that what is aesthetically distinctive about the comic form of *Persuasion* is precisely this representation of suffering within the frame of reassurance that the suffering is only temporary.

Sacks reads the mini-narrative about Sir Walter's financial troubles as a punitive comedy: Sir Walter's moral deficiencies are temporarily allowed to go unchecked until they themselves become the agency by which he gets his comeuppance (1969: 288). Once we see this mini-narrative played out, Sacks argues, we are assured that we are in a world where virtue will be rewarded and vice punished and so we can be confident about Anne's eventual fate. I find Sacks's argument attractive, but not ultimately persuasive because it is finally too schematic. First, Sir Walter's excesses are not represented as a series of choices unfolding in time but rather are summarized by the narrator. That is, Austen focuses our attention less on the narrative of Walter's behavior between the time of his wife's death and the present time of the action and more on the instability in that present. Second, Sir Walter is not punished in any but the mildest sense, so the connection between one's virtue and one's situation is not established. Not only is Sir Walter able to bear the material sacrifice of leaving Kellynch Hall quite easily, but he is also able to go to Bath and be "important at comparatively little expense" (14). Furthermore, in the Crofts, he has found the ideal tenants. Finally, Sir Walter's vanity of person and station remains completely untouched by his financial setback. He remains available as the object of the narrator's delicious irony, precisely because the resolution of this initial instability leaves him largely unscathed.

Furthermore, Anne's role in the mini-narrative does not augur well for her future. In Chapter II, the narrator twice calls special attention to Anne's preferences and both occasions confirm the narrator's observations that "her word had no weight." First, Anne urges Lady Russell to recommend "vigorous measures" for retrenchment to Sir Walter, and though Lady Russell was "in a degree . . . influenced by her" (12), the narrator reports, in another example of her shift from external description to indirect speech, that "How Anne's more rigid requisitions might have been taken, is of little consequence. Lady Russell's had no success at all—could not be put up with—were not to be borne" (13). Second, once it is decided that the family will rent Kellynch Hall, Anne prefers that they move to a smaller house in the neighborhood rather than go to either London or Bath, but this hope is thoroughly dashed: "But the usual fate of Anne attended her, in having something very opposite from her inclination fixed on. She disliked Bath, and did not think it agreed with her—and Bath was to be her home" (14).

Moreover, the sudden shift from the end of the mini-narrative to the launch of the main narrative with Anne's thought that "a few months more, and *he,* perhaps, may be walking here," (25) also works against the establishment of comic reassurance. Since it is not until this moment that the narrative unequivocally establishes Anne as the protagonist, we cannot have inferred much, if anything, about her final happiness. In sum, as we complete our entrance into *Persuasion,* we cannot settle on a definitive hypothesis about the trajectory of the whole narrative. While the initiation and exposition work to establish Anne as a protagonist whose happiness we desire and while the initiation does offer us the pleasures of previous Austen comedies, these two aspects of the beginning and the launch combine to give us material that could be shaped in more than one direction. We have neither the traditional assurances of narrative comedy nor clear signals that only misfortune will follow from this beginning. In light of Austen's past practice, this result is itself noteworthy, offering us grounds to wonder whether for once Austen's version of the marriage plot might fail to end with the engagement of the heroine. In other words, if you confidently conclude, upon reading the end of Chapter III, that "he" will be Anne's future husband, you are relying less on the progression of the first three chapters and more on your sense of what Austen's other novels have done, and thus, what her novels are supposed to do.

## The Early Middle of *Persuasion*

In the next chapter I will offer an extended analysis of *Beloved*'s middle, so here I will just identify the middle as that part of the narrative in which the progression conveys both forward movement and delay. This double nature of the middle is a result of the launch leading to the voyage and the voyage typically leading to initial further complication of the global instability or tension. Similarly, the audience's responses to what's at stake in the voyage also get complicated by means of further interaction with author and narrator. As these complications develop, the audience continues to modify its understanding of the narrative as a whole. With regard to *Persuasion,* I will focus primarily on the exposition, the voyage, and the interaction during the early middle, the section of narrative from Chapter IV through the scene in Chapter XII when Louisa falls from the Cobb in Lyme. After this scene, the progression undergoes another shift as *Persuasion* fits more smoothly into the grooves of Austen's previous narrative comedies: from this point forward, as I shall argue later, Anne and Wentworth's reunion ceases to be a question of whether and becomes a question of how.

Let me start with the exposition of Chapter IV in which the narrator not only solves the local tension about the identity of the traitless "he" whose presence Anne so keenly anticipates, but also gives us the back story about him and Anne: their previous engagement; Anne's decision, under the influence of advice from Lady Russell, to end the engagement;

Wentworth's anger; and the consequences of the whole episode for Anne. From the perspective of judgments and progression, there are four related features of the exposition that are especially salient.

1. The narrator emphasizes the link between Anne's ethical and interpretive judgments when she decides to end the engagement. The narrator starts with Anne's interpretive judgment which itself shades into an ethical judgment: "[Anne] was persuaded to believe the engagement a wrong thing—indiscreet, improper, hardly capable of success, and not deserving it" (27). But then the narrator notes that a stronger, admirable ethical judgment becomes decisive: "But it was not a merely selfish caution, under which she acted, in putting an end to it. Had she not imagined herself consulting his good, even more than her own, she could hardly have given him up. The belief of being prudent, and self-denying principally for his advantage, was her chief consolation" (27–28).

2. Anne subsequently separates her interpretive and ethical judgments as she comes to regard her earlier interpretation of the situation as a misjudgment. "She did not blame Lady Russell, she did not blame herself for having been guided by her; but . . . she was persuaded that under every disadvantage of disapprobation at home, and every anxiety attending his profession, all their probable fears, delays and disappointments, she should yet have been a happier woman in maintaining the engagement than she had been in the sacrifice of it" (29).

3. Austen uses her narrator to align the authorial audience's interpretive and ethical judgments with Anne's at the time of the action. That is, because the narrator authoritatively reports on Anne's other-directed motives in her earlier decision and implicitly endorses Anne's revised interpretive judgment, we also don't find any ethical fault in her ending the engagement even as we share her view that she misread the situation. More generally, because the narrator consistently approves of Anne and her current judgments, we remain strongly aligned with Anne.

4. Chapter IV reveals that Anne still holds Wentworth in the highest regard; consequently, Anne, unlike Austen's other protagonists, does not need to undergo any change of feeling. Furthermore, Anne is not in need of any greater ethical or intellectual maturity,

and, thus, does not need to undergo any change in character. As a result, Austen is working with a progression in which her protagonist has no internal instability that she needs to overcome. The internal instability, we find out in Chapter VII, is in Wentworth, who believes himself ready to marry anyone but Anne. This narrative situation means that Austen has given herself a very difficult task. It is Wentworth who must change, but it is Anne who is the focal character and the one Austen wants her audience to care most about. Furthermore, given the limited agency of women in her world, Anne cannot directly act to bring about any change in Wentworth but can only be herself and wait. Yet the more Austen can give Anne some agency that we will see as contributing to Wentworth's change, the more aesthetically satisfying we are likely to find the progression. Austen's challenge, then, is to respect the constraints she has established and still make Anne a significant agent of her own happiness. With these effects of the exposition in Chapter IV in mind, let us turn to Chapters VIII, IX, and X.

Again Sacks's analysis provides a very helpful way into the details of the progression. Sacks focuses on the scenes at Uppercross and he describes them as paradoxically lyric. He argues that, from the perspective of the events themselves, Anne does not move either closer to or further from Wentworth but rather remains in a static situation, the dimensions of which are gradually revealed to us. At the same time, however, from the perspective of the audience, the effect of the Uppercross section is to reinforce the comic assurances of the beginning by making us feel that the two are moving toward each other (1976, S105). Sacks notes that aspects of the situation are very difficult for Anne: Wentworth's presence at Uppercross with an intention to marry someone other than the woman who rejected his proposal eight years ago continually reminds Anne of what she has lost by that rejection, and those reminders occasionally bring her to tears. Nevertheless, Sacks maintains, because we are reading within the context of our intuition of a comic narrative, we regard this situation as only temporary. Consequently, we interpret the lyric section's revelations of the similarity of Anne's and Wentworth's moral judgment— Sacks's chief example is the famous scene in Chapter VIII in which Anne observes Wentworth's discussion with Mrs. Musgrove about her deceased son Dicky—as material that both reinforces our comic expectations and moves Anne and Wentworth toward their eventual union.

Sacks's discussion of the lyric quality of the Uppercross section astutely identifies something new and remarkable in Austen's handling of the form. Indeed, her adopting some principles of lyricality—the exploration of a character's feelings in a particular situation while also keeping the narrative principles of judgment operating—for this section of the narrative is very much in keeping with the constraints she has chosen to write within: rather than developing new complications between Anne and Wentworth by showing their direct interaction, she focuses on revealing the quality of Anne's situation at this crucial juncture of her life. As insightful as Sacks's discussion is, however, I believe it falls short in two ways. First, because Sacks focuses almost exclusively on the lyric dimension of this part of the novel, he does not give sufficient attention to the developing instabilities surrounding Wentworth's involvement with Louisa Musgrove. Second, Sacks's commitment to the idea that Austen is working within her standard form of narrative comedy leads him to underestimate the effect of those lyric scenes, especially the ways in which they gradually show a separation of our judgments from Anne's.

Consistent with the narrative situation in which it is Wentworth rather than Anne who must change, Austen's approach to the voyage is to show Anne's essentially static situation as she watches Wentworth become increasingly involved with Louisa Musgrove. Furthermore, Austen gives some but less than full credence to the possibility that Wentworth will actually marry Louisa by carefully managing the interaction between narrator and audience. Consider the narrator's comments in Chapter VII on Wentworth's purpose in his visit to Uppercross: "It was now his object to marry. He was rich, and being turned on shore, fully intended to settle, as soon as he could be properly tempted; actually looking round, ready to fall in love with all the speed which a clear head and quick taste could allow. He had a heart for either of the Miss Musgroves, if they could catch it; a heart, in short, for any pleasing young woman who came in his way, excepting Anne Elliot" (61). The passage is in the narrator's voice but it is predominantly in Wentworth's vision. Consequently, the narrator does not commit herself to the position that Wentworth will never marry Anne, even as the passage shows that Wentworth believes that to be the case. Indeed, one possible, though not required interpretive judgment here, is that Wentworth is in denial about his feelings for Anne. Furthermore, the parts of the passage that are from the narrator's perspective also qualify our understanding of how he is likely to act: with "all the speed which a clear head and quick taste could allow"—in other words, not so fast.

In addition, the narrator's remark amplifying his comment to his sister on the qualities that he is looking for in a woman keeps the possibility of Wentworth's reuniting with Anne very much alive without assuring us that the reunion will happen. "Anne Elliot was not out of his thoughts, when he more seriously described the woman he should wish to meet with. 'A strong mind with sweetness of manner,' made the first and last of the description" (62). That the Anne of eight years ago has given him a model does not mean that he regards the current Anne (whom he has judged as "so altered that he would not have known her again" [60]) as the woman he'd like to marry, especially because it is likely that he is thinking of her as a negative model: in his view, Anne's flaw is a weakness of mind that led her to succumb to the persuasion of Lady Russell. Nevertheless, the pairing of "strong mind" and "sweetness of manner" in his thoughts of Anne also suggests that at some level of consciousness he recognizes that she possesses both qualities, and, thus, is still a possible match for him.

I turn now to the lyric segment of the progression that Sacks has insightfully identified, especially to the sequence of interactions between Anne and Wentworth in Chapters VIII, IX, and X. There is a significant qualitative difference between Chapter VIII and what follows in Chapters IX and X, both because Chapter VIII captures Anne at the low point of her situation and because in Chapters IX and X, Austen begins to separate the authorial audience's interpretive judgments from Anne's. Both the events of Chapters IX and X and this separation of judgment constitute some forward movement in the voyage. It is, I believe, this movement from the lyric revelation of Chapter VIII to small steps forward in Chapters IX and X that accounts for what Sacks refers to as the paradox in the lyrical quality of these chapters. In other words, where Sacks sees the prior comic assurances as crucial to the effect of forward movement, I see the qualitative difference—found in both the events and in our judgments of them—between the scene in Chapter VIII and its parallel scenes in Chapters IX and X as creating that effect.

Chapter VIII describes a party at the Musgroves' Great House, at the end of which Anne takes her place at the piano, and occupies herself with thoughts of Wentworth and the attention he is happily receiving from the other young women assembled there. The narrator also tells us that as she sat at the piano "her eyes would sometimes fill with tears" (71). At the end of the scene, Anne and Wentworth engage in a very brief exchange at the Musgroves' piano:

He saw her, and, instantly rising, said with studied politeness,

"I beg your pardon, madam, this is your seat;" and though she immediately drew back with a decided negative, he was not to be induced to sit down again.

Anne did not wish for more of such looks and speeches. His cold politeness, his ceremonious grace, were worse than any thing. (72)

Although Austen has previously shown her heroines in scenes of emotional suffering—think of Elizabeth after she reads Darcy's letter or Emma after Knightley upbraids her for her behavior at Box Hill—she has typically connected that suffering to their own ethical deficiencies; they have, to some degree, brought it upon themselves. Moreover, those moments of suffering have typically been ones in which their characters were being tested; they needed not only to acknowledge their deficient behavior but also to change in ways that make such behavior far less likely. Their ability to respond so well to these situations marks their moral maturation, and, as such, that ability is crucial for the satisfaction we take in their final happiness.

Austen's representation of Anne's emotional suffering here is a significant departure from that pattern. As noted above, she has not brought it on herself as a result of ethically deficient behavior; she is suffering simply because she still loves Wentworth, and seeing him again makes her acutely aware of what she has lost. If I am right that we read this scene of suffering without the comic assurances of Austen's previous narrative comedies, then Austen is offering here a reading experience qualitatively different from any she has created before. It is a head-on representation of undeserved emotional pain, and it carries the implication that there is much more of the same to follow. Furthermore, without the comic assurances, our interpretive judgments remain closely aligned with Anne's. Indeed, the only surefire solution to the suffering is for Anne to stop loving Wentworth. But that solution is out of the question, given Anne's constancy and her renewed sense of his worth.

Our ethical judgments of Anne and our interpretive judgments of her situation make her even more sympathetic and, thus, make us more desirous of what we still cannot expect—an improvement of her situation. As a result, Austen builds a darker element into *Persuasion* than she does into any of her other novels, an element whose effect, as I shall argue below, is felt all the way through to the novel's end. To put all this another way, the aesthetic innovation of delaying the comic assurances and aligning the interpretive judgments of audience and character combines with Austen's representation of unmerited suffering to add a significantly new ethical dimension to her work. Austen is both exploring new ethical territory and offering her audience a different kind of trajectory through that territory, one in which our interpretive and ethical judgments make us feel the suffering acutely. Alternatively, we could say that Austen's interest in exploring new ethical territory led to her aesthetic innovation of pushing the formal envelope of her narrative comedy. I now turn to consider how Austen gradually moves the progression back within the grooves of narrative comedy.

The end of Chapter VIII turns out to be the emotional low point of the narrative—though Anne has much more to endure. In the concluding scenes of the next two chapters, Austen begins to move Wentworth and Anne closer together, albeit by inches rather than leaps. At the end of Chapter IX Wentworth lifts the toddler Walter Musgrove off Anne's back while she is busy tending to young Charles, an event that leaves Anne too agitated to speak:

> She could not even thank him. She could only hang over little Charles, with most disordered feelings. His kindness in stepping forward to her relief—the manner—the silence in which it had passed—the little particulars of the circumstance—with the conviction soon forced on her by the noise he was studiously making with the child, that he meant to avoid hearing her thanks, and rather sought to testify that her conversation was the last of his wants, produced such a confusion of varying, but very painful agitation, as she could not [soon] recover from. (80)

Anne's agitation is clearly "painful," but that pain and her "disordered feelings" stem from what she regards as a double message in Wentworth's behavior: she understands his help as evidence of "his kindness" but reads his preoccupation with Walter as a sign that he does not want to interact with her. In the authorial audience, however, we begin to separate our interpretive judgments from Anne's. We are far less certain about Anne's reading of Wentworth's behavior, since it is just as plausible to infer that he feels awkward in her presence rather than uninterested in her response.

At the end of Chapter X, Wentworth, perceiving Anne's fatigue from the long walk to Winthrop, hands her into the Crofts' carriage, an action that prompts the reflections I quoted at the beginning of the essay and that I will repeat here:

This little circumstance seemed the completion of all that had gone before. She understood him. He could not forgive her—but he could not be unfeeling. Though condemning her for the past and considering it with high and unjust resentment, though perfectly careless of her and becoming attached to another, still he could not see her suffer without the desire to give her relief. It was a remainder of former sentiment; it was an impulse of pure, though unacknowledged friendship; it was a proof of his own warm and amiable heart, which she could not contemplate without emotions so compounded of pleasure and pain, that she knew not which prevailed. (91)

The forward movement between Chapters IX and X is clearly evident through the sequence of action, thought, and judgment. The order of events matters because this gesture of Wentworth's reveals his increasingly greater attentiveness to and solicitousness for Anne. His lifting Anne's nephew from her back is an active response to a situation in which she needs assistance, and Austen clearly contrasts it with Charles Hayter's ineffectual admonishment of the child from across the room. Wentworth's handing Anne into the carriage shows a similarly active response but in a situation in which Anne's distress is far less evident. The progress of Anne's reflections is even greater: she moves from "varying, but very painful agitation" to contemplating the "remainder of former sentiment." Furthermore, Anne's reflections at the end of Chapters IX and X show her to be so much in love with Wentworth and so aware of his developing relationship with Louisa that, when she can control her agitation, she protects herself by reading his behavior in as unflattering a way as possible: his talk with young Charles is a sign that he does not want to listen to her, his kindness with the carriage still signifies that "he could not forgive her." Above all else, Anne struggles to keep from believing that Wentworth's feelings for her might be changing even as she cannot help hoping that they are. There are many signals in Chapter X that Austen wants us to make a different interpretive judgment from Anne; perhaps the clearest is the contradiction in her thoughts in the Crofts' carriage: "though perfectly careless of her . . . still he could not see her suffer without the desire to give her relief" (91). By the end of Chapter X, Austen's authorial audience has more hope for the future than does Anne.[4]

4. For a somewhat different and more extensive discussion of this passage from Chapter X, one that focuses on its stylistic effectiveness, see my *Worlds from Words: A Theory of Language in Fiction* (Phelan 1981: 135–38). For a highly engaging discussion of Austen's representation of intersubjectivity here and elsewhere in her corpus, see Butte's discussion in

However, the sequence of Chapters IX and X does not convert that hope into the clear expectations that accompany comic assurances. First, since each act is itself a small one, and since each occurs in a public space and involves the least direct interaction between the two imaginable, these acts have only a small effect on Anne and Wentworth's current estrangement. Second, as becomes evident earlier in Chapter X when Anne overhears Wentworth's speech to Louisa praising her firmness of character, there is ample reason to expect that relationship to continue to develop. The narrator herself remarks "Everything now marked out Louisa for Captain Wentworth" (90), a statement that neatly encapsulates the stage this element of the voyage has reached while also stopping short of authoritatively predicting the marriage. From this perspective, the sequence of events at the ends of Chapters IX and X does more to demonstrate Wentworth's worthiness for Anne than to promise their eventual union. As a result, this sequence increases the audience's understanding of Anne's sense of loss: the more we see his worth, the more acutely we appreciate Anne's distress. As a result, the demonstration of Wentworth's merit increases our desire and hope for a reunion, without bringing us to the point of expecting it. Consequently, although we do see Anne's situation more fully and clearly than she herself does, we do not have the kind of confidence about the eventual outcome that we do in the middle of Austen's other novels.

This difference means that Austen, in effect, puts Anne in a very different situation than that of any of Austen's previous heroines. Since there are no comic assurances here, the audience must seriously contemplate not only Anne's undeserved suffering during the time of Wentworth's visit to Uppercross but also the unbroken continuation of her life as the unregarded Elliot sister. What we have seen of that life, both at Kellynch Hall and at Uppercross, is quite painful. At home, as we have noted, "her word [has] no weight" (5) with her father and her sister Elizabeth, and at Uppercross she is treated more like an exalted servant than like an equal. Austen has previously shown us heroines who face serious threats of deeply unhappy futures, e.g., Fanny Price confined to living in poverty with her parents in Portsmouth, an unmarried Elizabeth Bennet living with her mother and sisters after her father's death and their eviction from Longbourne by Mr. Collins. But those threats are in a hypothetical future, and they are more real for the heroines than for us readers because the comic assurances in *Mansfield Park* and *Pride and Prejudice* mean that the hypothetical will never become the actual. In *Persuasion,* by contrast, the hypothetical has already been the actual for eight years, and Austen both initially withholds

---

*I Know That You Know That I Know,* 110–14 and passim.

the assurances that Anne's fate will change and continually reminds us of the gap between Anne's merit and her actual fate. These elements of the novel, I believe, contribute greatly to its qualitative difference from Austen's other novels.

## The Late Middle and the Ending

Once Austen brings Anne, Wentworth, and the Musgroves to Lyme, the progression again shifts gears, as Wentworth notices both William Elliot's noticing Anne and Anne's clear good sense in responding to the crisis precipitated by Louisa's fall from the Cobb. As a result, Wentworth's attention to both Anne and Louisa shifts, and the internal instability begins to be resolved. Once Louisa jumps from the Cobb and Wentworth sees both the dangers of her kind of firmness as well as the new evidence of Anne's "strong mind, with sweetness of manner" (62), we have moved comfortably back into Austen's usual world of narrative comedy. At this point, our interpretive judgments diverge from Anne's in the way that they diverge from Elizabeth Bennet's after she learns of Lydia's elopement. Though we don't yet know how, we no longer worry about whether Anne and Wentworth will be reunited.

Austen's specific handling of that how is worthy of a detailed analysis, but since it is less distinctive than her handling of the beginning and early middle, I will offer just a sketch here and then turn to the consequences of the earlier parts of the progression for the ending. The key moves Austen makes in the voyage are the following:

1. To remove the obstacle of Wentworth's entanglement with Louisa by having her transfer her affections to Benwick. While this development is perhaps too convenient, it is consistent with both their characters. It is also fitting that, before it happens, Wentworth has to look at the potential consequences of his flirtation with Louisa, consequences that include his beginning to feel that his carelessness has imperiled his chances of reuniting with Anne.

2. The development of the complication of William's interest in Anne. This move is more important for the anxiety it raises in Wentworth (again it's fitting that not everything come so easily to him) than for any anxiety it raises in the authorial audience. At the same time, with characteristic economy and efficiency, Austen uses William's newfound interest in the Elliot family as

a way to return to the narrative threads involving Sir Walter, Elizabeth, and Mrs. Clay.

3. The use of the disabled Mrs. Smith to reveal the truth about William's past. I find this move to be the one significant blemish in Austen's otherwise brilliant design, and the problem shows the interrelation of the ethical and the aesthetic. The formal problem Austen faces is difficult: how to reveal the information about William while retaining Anne as the focal character and continuing to move the progression of the Wentworth-Anne voyage forward. But Austen's solution is flawed for several reasons. First, it is contrived, far more so than the engagement of Louisa and Benwick. That development follows from their characterization. But if we ask why Anne's friend Mrs. Smith should happen to have both firsthand and secondhand information about William's shady dealings and complete untrustworthiness, the only answer is that Austen needs to have that information disclosed both to Anne and to the authorial audience. Second, there is the ethical problem of Anne's involvement in the chain of gossip from Nurse Rook to Mrs. Smith to herself. Third, the information isn't crucially integrated into the progression. Anne would not have accepted a proposal from William in any case.

I am aware that it is possible to justify Austen's use of Mrs. Smith on thematic grounds, that is, as contributing to Austen's explorations of such things as the precarious position of women, or her implicit commentary on the changing social order. I find these justifications only partially successful, but will defer the reasons for this assessment until chapter 3, when I will look more closely at the practice of doing interpretation by thematizing.

Let me turn then to a brief look at the elements of the ending with an emphasis on how they are influenced by the beginning and early middle. Especially revealing in this connection is a comparison between the arrival in the cancelled chapter and the one Austen wrote to replace it. The major difference is the role that each version assigns to Anne. In the cancelled chapter, Admiral Croft prevails upon Wentworth to speak to Anne to pass on his offer to give up their lease of Kellynch Hall so that Anne and William Elliot can live there after their imminent marriage. When Anne corrects the false report about her engagement to William, "a silent but very powerful Dialogue" (263) ensues and very quickly "all Suspense and Indecision were over. They were re-united. They were restored to all that had been lost" (263). The advantages of this arrival include (1) the nice dramatic irony of William's attentions to Anne being the final means for bringing about her reunion with Wentworth; and (2) the way that Admiral Croft's benevolent intentions temporarily put Wentworth in an extremely awkward position in light of the report that Anne is to marry William. But this arrival is far inferior to the one in Austen's revision.

The revised arrival is superior because it gives Anne much more agency. In the cancelled chapter, Anne must wait for Wentworth, first, to articulate Admiral Croft's message, and, second, to respond to her denial of the report about her engagement. In the revision, Anne is given an opportunity to speak for herself through her conversation with Captain Harville that can be overheard by Wentworth. Her famous speech to Captain Harville on the greater constancy of women is spoken with "a full heart" because she is thinking about her own case: "All the privilege I claim for my own sex . . . is that of loving longest, when existence or when hope is gone" (235). Wentworth must still respond, but his letter makes it clear that now Anne, through this speech and through so many of her previous actions, has been responsible for his renewing the proposal—and in that sense bringing about her own happiness: "I can listen no longer in silence . . . You pierce my soul . . . I offer myself to you again with a heart even more your own than when you almost broke it eight years and a half ago . . . You alone have brought me to Bath. For you alone I think and plan" (237).

The revision is also superior because the gradual unfolding of the arrival—Anne's speech, Wentworth's letter, their meeting on the street first in the company of Charles Musgrove, and finally by themselves—is a more appropriate culmination to their reunion than the very swift and private means Austen uses in the cancelled chapter. Austen and her audience derive more satisfaction from the relatively extended arrival, after the eight-year separation and after Anne's suffering and slow restoration of hope once Wentworth returns to her social orbit. Similarly, bringing the lovers together in a public rather than a private space keeps their expression of feeling muted, something again in keeping with the voyage.

Furthermore, the interaction here also shows the effect of the beginning and the early middle as it asks the audience not only to participate in the joy of the lovers, who are "more tender, more tried, more fixed in a knowledge of each other's character, truth and attachment; more equal to act, more justified in acting" (240–41) than they were eight years ago, but also to remain aware of how that joy is tempered by their awareness of the pain of the last eight years. "There they exchanged again those feelings and those promises, which had once before seemed to secure every thing, but which had been followed by so many, many years of division and estrangement" (240). Indeed, the narrator will say only that Anne and Wentworth are "perhaps" "more exquisitely happy in their re-union than when it had been first projected" (240).

Austen creates a similar dual emphasis on the power of the lovers' feelings and their awareness of what they have lost in a dialogue of exposition that follows soon after the arrival. Wentworth asks Anne whether she would have renewed their engagement if he had written to her "in the year eight," that is, six years previously, when he returned to England after having made a few thousand pounds. Anne's reply is arguably the most powerful expression of desire on the part of any Austen heroine; indeed, the combination of its simplicity and directness and the narrator's remark about her accent makes it sneakily erotic: "'Would I!' was all her answer; but the tone was decisive enough" (247). Wentworth replies in kind: "'Good God!' he cried, you would!," and he soon draws the appropriate inference: If he hadn't been so proud, "six years of separation and suffering might have been spared" (247). Austen moves his reflections back to his current happiness, but even with that move the point remains: "Like other great men under reverses, . . . I must learn to subdue my mind to my fortune. I must learn to brook being happier than I deserve" (247).

This different affective quality of the ending, in which Anne's genuine happiness is tinged with her—and our—awareness of time and opportunity lost, is further reinforced by the closure and farewell of the novel's final sentences: "Anne was tenderness itself and she had the full worth of it in Captain Wentworth's affection. His profession was all that could ever make her friends wish that tenderness less; the dread of a future war all that could dim her sunshine. She gloried in being a sailor's wife, but she must pay the tax of quick alarm for belonging to that profession which is, if possible, more distinguished in its domestic virtues than its national importance" (252).

Rather than looking back, this closure looks ahead, and it does so in a way that is remarkably consonant with the previous progression. Anne and Wentworth's happy reunion faces no threat from matters that they can control, but, for once in Austen, these lovers do face a threat from matters that they cannot control. The manner of the farewell reinforces the affective emphasis: the narrator initially focuses on the reciprocal love and tenderness between Anne and Wentworth, then turns to the hypothetical rather than the actual (what "could" rather than what "will" dim her sunshine) to add the tempering note. Finally, the last sentence puts both sides of Anne's situation together (her pleasure in her identity as sailor's wife and the price of that pleasure). In addition, the final phrases, delivered with the balance and parallelism that we have come to glory in since the narrator's opening description of Sir Walter, give, if possible, more praise to Wentworth as a husband than as a sailor.

This emphasis helps clarify my point about the affective quality of the ending. To say that the mood is bittersweet would be to overstate the point by a large margin. A better way to say it is that the layered rhetorical communications of the progression show Austen, while ultimately committed to her narrative comedy, exploring a deeper sense of pain, loss, undeserved misfortune, and the irrevocable quality of some mistakes than she ever has before. The implied author of *Persuasion* is the woman who, in retrospect, judged *Pride and Prejudice* as "too light and bright and sparkling" (*Letters* 203). More than that, the implied author of *Persuasion* is deeply aware that even for the best of us some choices prove to be so mistaken that, even when we take advantage of a second chance and make things right, they are never the same (Jay Gatsby, I'm sure, never read *Persuasion*). Just as Wentworth's handing Anne into the Crofts' carriage does not erase her painful night at the piano in the Great House, their engagement and marriage do not erase their eight years of estrangement. Furthermore, those eight years are far from being a necessary route to the happy outcome, and Austen implies that, though Anne has not wasted those years, they have *almost* wasted her: they have, at the beginning of the action, "destroyed her youth and bloom" (61). Finally, Austen's new emphasis on these matters that are less than light and bright and sparkling joins with her consistent vision that happiness is both a rare and precarious commodity—here, besides Anne and Wentworth only the Crofts clearly have it—to make *Persuasion* both her most and her least romantic novel. For these reasons, I find it to be the novel that offers her audience the deepest ethical explorations.

As this discussion implies, the affective power and ethical explorations of the narrative are closely interrelated and both of them are also intertwined with Austen's remarkable aesthetic achievement in the novel. The two major dimensions of the formal experiment—dropping the comic assurances in the beginning and early middle, and using Anne, who does not need to undergo any alteration of her character as the chief focalizer—work in marvelous conjunction with the affective and the ethical layers of our experience of the novel. Consequently, despite my dissatisfaction with the Mrs. Smith episodes, I also find *Persuasion* to be Austen's most impressive aesthetic achievement.

# CHAPTER TWO

# Sethe's Choice and
# Toni Morrison's Strategies

## The Beginning and Middle of *Beloved*

### Morrison's Unusual Guidance

Now, too late, [Stamp Paid] understood [Baby Suggs]. The heart that pumped out love, the mouth that spoke the Word, didn't count. They came in her yard anyway and she could not approve or condemn Sethe's rough choice. (180)

"Sethe's rough choice," her decision to kill her daughter rather than have her become a slave at the plantation they called Sweet Home, is at once the most stunning and most important event in Toni Morrison's novel. Stunning for obvious reasons: how can the love of a mother for her child lead her to murder the child? Important because the temporal, psychological, structural, and thematic logic of the novel flows from that event and because Morrison's treatment of it presents her audience with a difficult and unusual ethical problem. In order to appreciate the events of the present time of the narrative—1873—we need to know what happened in the woodshed behind 124 Bluestone Rd. on an August afternoon in 1855. In order to understand the characters of Sethe, Denver, and Beloved in 1873, we need to know that on that afternoon Sethe reached for the handsaw before the schoolteacher could reach for her or her children. In order to come to terms with the novel's progression, its affective power and thematic import—indeed, its aesthetic achievement—we need to come to ethical terms with Sethe's choice to pull the handsaw across the neck of her daughter.[1]

---

1. In the twenty years since its publication, *Beloved* has attracted a great deal of critical attention, becoming the subject of over two hundred books and articles; yet no one, to

Morrison includes some cryptic allusions to the event early in the novel, but it is not until the middle, when the voyage is already well under way, that Morrison represents the event. Indeed, taking advantage of the middle as the place for both forward movement and delay, she represents it multiple times and through multiple perspectives: that of the white slave catchers, that of Stamp Paid, and finally that of Sethe herself. But what especially stands out in these three representations is that Morrison stops short of taking any clear ethical stand on Sethe's rough choice and of guiding her audience to judge it in any definitive way. She presents it instead as something that she, like Baby Suggs, can neither approve nor condemn. This chapter will focus on the consequences of Morrison's formal and ethical choices by (1) considering Morrison's decision to place her representation of Sethe's action in the middle of the progression; (2) contextualizing Morrison's treatment of Sethe's choice in relation to the typical relation between implied author and audience in ethically complex texts; (3) analyzing the narrative strategies Morrison uses to offer some limited guidance to our ethical judgment without clearly signaling her own assessment; (4) examining the consequences of that treatment for our relation to Sethe and, ultimately, to Morrison herself; and (5) considering the implications of Morrison's treatment for the rest of the narrative, including our aesthetic judgment of it.

As my discussions of the ethical dimensions of "The Crimson Candle" and *Persuasion* indicate, my rhetorical approach to ethics assumes that authors typically guide their audiences toward particular ethical judgments about their characters' actions and that the means of their guidance itself invites an additional ethical judgment. Morrison's approach to Sethe's choice is so distinctive because only the second assumption applies. To highlight this point, consider a short survey of other fictions and how their authors guide their audience's ethical judgments of their protagonists. In some cases, the ethical judgments of characters work by clear contrast. In *Tom Jones,* for example, Henry Fielding sets up a sharp opposition between our positive judgments of Tom and our negative judgments of Blifil. In some cases, the key to the narrative progression is the evolution of the

---

my knowledge, has directly addressed the ethics of Sethe's choice. The existing criticism is especially strong on the novel's many thematic components from history and memory to motherhood and identity as well as on its relation to previous American narratives and its mingling of Western and African cultural values. For a sample of this work, see Christian, Handley (on Western and African culture), Armstrong, Moreland, Travis (on relation to previous traditions), Hirsch, Wilt, Wyatt (on motherhood and its related issues), Hartman and Moglen (on history and memory). For essays that focus on issues of song, narrative, narrative theory and technique, see Homans, Rimmon-Kenan, and Wolfe.

protagonists' own ethical judgments and corresponding behavior: as I discussed in the last chapter, in *Pride and Prejudice,* Jane Austen positions us to judge the initial ethical deficiencies of both Elizabeth Bennet and Fitzwilliam Darcy and then shows how each one comes to judge his or her prior behavior and change accordingly. These developments prepare the way for their happy union and for our satisfaction in it. In some cases, authors will present us with characters who face difficult ethical decisions and then guide us to see both the difficulty and their own judgment of the situation: Joseph Conrad, for example, allows Jim to tell the story of how he jumped from the *Patna* but uses characters such as Brierly, who commits suicide because he sees himself in Jim, and the French lieutenant, who clearly states that the sailor's duty is to stay with the ship, to indicate both the depth of Jim's temptation and the unequivocal negative judgment of his action. In some cases, authors will show characters who transgress standard societal and legal norms but nevertheless follow an ethically superior path: in *One Flew over the Cuckoo's Nest,* Ken Kesey, for example, represents Chief Bromden's killing of the lobotomized McMurphy not as a horrible murder but rather as an act of both mercy and courage. Even in situations where authors have written famously ambiguous narratives, the ethical positions within each side of the ambiguity may be clearly delineated: Henry James in *The Turn of the Screw,* for example, has sketched a portrait either of a heroic governess who risks her own safety in order to protect the children in her care against evil ghosts or of a psychotic woman whose delusions constitute a serious threat to those children.

Of course no inductive survey can establish that authors must imply ethical judgments of their characters' central actions, and, indeed, I do not want to argue for that "must." Furthermore, we can also readily see that an author might want to move to a kind of meta-ethical position and guide us to the conclusion that no clear and fixed ethical judgment of a central action is possible. But my point here is twofold. (1) The default expectation for reading fiction is that authors will take ethical stands on the events and characters they represent and will guide us explicitly or implicitly, heavy-handedly or subtly (or, indeed, in any way in between) to adopt those stands. Indeed, this default expectation helps us recognize that the default ethical relation between implied author and authorial audience in narrative is one of reciprocity. Each party both gives and receives. Authors give, among other things, guidance to their particular value systems and to the ethical judgments that follow from those systems; they expect to receive in return their audiences' interest and attention. Audiences give that interest and attention and expect to receive in return, among other things, reinforcements, challenges to, or disagreements with their own value systems. As noted above, the default assumption of course need not always be in place, but deviating from it necessarily entails certain risks. Audiences who place their own interests (ideologies, politics, ethics) at the center of their reading risk turning reading into a repetitious activity that misses the ways in which authors can extend their vision of human possibility and experience. Authors who flaunt their power and take aggressive stances toward their audiences risk alienating them to the point of losing them.

(2) When authors do not provide guidance and do not overtly signal that they are not providing it, they put their audiences in a highly challenging situation, one that also entails certain risks for the authors. As authors shift responsibility for the ethical judgments—or for the decision that no clear judgments are possible—to their audiences, the ethics of their telling, the means by which they represent the characters and actions without judging them, become more prominent. Audiences may decide that the lack of guidance is an abdication of authorial responsibility. Given what I have been arguing about the interrelations among interpretive, ethical, and aesthetic judgments, audiences may also decide that the lack of guidance leaves a hole at the center of the narrative project. On the other hand, effectively executing the transfer of responsibility for ethical judgment to the authorial and flesh-and-blood audiences can not only challenge those audiences but provide them with extremely rich reading experiences. In the rest of this chapter, I shall argue that Morrison's execution allows *Beloved* to offer its audience such an experience. More specifically, I will analyze the novel's beginning, showing how it provides the crucial context for our responses to Morrison's strategy of transferring ethical responsibility to the audience through her multiple narratives about Sethe's choice in the middle.

## The Beginning: Front Matter and First Chapter

Morrison does not number the sections of her novel, leaving it to us to notice that Part One has 18 sections, Part Two 7 sections, and Part Three 3 sections, which, when combined, give us 1873, the year of the narrative's present action. The first section of Part One, which I shall call the first chapter, constitutes the beginning of the novel: by its end the various unstable situations and tensions introduced in the previous pages coalesce around an event that launches the narrative forward. The first chapter also provides us with an excellent initiation into the ways of the implied author and her relations to both the protean narrator and her authorial audience. But even before we get to the first sentence of the novel, "124 was spiteful," we encounter some important paratextual front matter.

In addition to the title, the paratexts include a dedication, an epigraph, and two illustrations. Together these expository materials provide a complex backdrop against which to begin reading, a set of thematic associations that provides a context within which to understand the rest of the narrative. The dedication to "Sixty million and more" who died on the Middle Passage makes a link between this narrative and the genocide accompanying the slave trade, and as such it suggests that Morrison sees herself as taking on an ambitious project, something that would be worthy to dedicate to those sixty million and more. The epigraph, from Romans 9:25, not only makes a reference to the title, but it also foregrounds the idea of paradox and suggests that it will be a significant element of the narrative:

I will call them my people
which were not my people; and her beloved
which was not beloved

On the title page the reader is confronted by an illustration of an angelic female figure with curly hair, a black, frowning face, and wide eyes staring directly out from the page. That stare conveys a challenge to the viewer, a challenge mixed with the sorrow in the face. On the page announcing Part One, there is another black figure, this one hairless so that the head seems more like a skull. Like the first figure, this one has a frown and big, round staring eyes. The angelic quality is preserved in the appearance of wings behind the face. The illustrations call forth themes of race, death, angels, and unhappiness, and in so doing they reinforce the effect of the dedication and of the epigraph. The paratexts, in short, announce an ambitious narrative about difficult, potentially horrific, subjects in American history and culture.

The first paragraph of the novel continues the exposition but does so in a way that calls attention to the remarkable quality of the initiation.

124 was spiteful. Full of a baby's venom. The women in the house knew it and so did the children. For years each put up with the spite in his own way, but by 1873 Sethe and her daughter Denver were its only victims. The grandmother, Baby Suggs, was dead, and the sons, Howard and Buglar, had run away by the time they were

thirteen years old—as soon as merely looking in a mirror shattered it (that was the signal for Buglar); as soon as two tiny hand prints appeared in the cake (that was it for Howard). Neither boy waited to see more; another kettleful of chickpeas smoking in a heap on the floor; soda crackers crumbled and strewn in a line next to the doorsill. Nor did they wait for one of the relief periods: the weeks, months even, when nothing was disturbed. No. Each one fled at once—the moment the house committed what was for him the one insult not to be borne or witnessed a second time. Within two months, in the dead of winter, leaving their grandmother, Baby Suggs; Sethe, their mother; and their little sister, Denver, all by themselves in the gray and white house on Bluestone Road. It didn't have a number then, because Cincinnati didn't stretch that far. In fact, Ohio had been calling itself a state only seventy years when first one brother and then the next stuffed quilt packing into his hat, snatched up his shoes, and crept away from the lively spite the house felt for them. (3)

This paragraph is, above all, disorienting. Although the narrator gives us a lot of expository information, the relation between all of it is murky at best—especially because the narrator withholds some very important information from us. The narrator moves the audience in and out of *medias res,* starting there early in the paragraph, but, by the end, signaling her own temporal distance from the action. Concurrent with her movement in time and space is the movement of her voice. Sometimes she is distant, formal, and authoritative, "by 1873, Sethe and Denver were its only victims." Sometimes, she is more intimate and informal, but she always retains the authoritative tone: "Nor did they wait for one of the relief periods: the weeks, months even, when nothing was disturbed. No." This initiation is one that requires the audience to stretch, even struggle, to keep up with the narrator and the implied author, as a closer look at the paragraph will reveal.

"124 was spiteful. Full of a baby's venom. The women in the house knew it and so did the children. For years each put up with the spite in his own way, but by 1873 Sethe and her daughter Denver were its only victims." The narrator does not say what sort of entity 124 is, though by the third sentence and certainly by the end of the paragraph, we can identify it as a house. Establishing this fact calls attention to Morrison's use of personification. The house has a life apart from the people who live in it, a life very much linked with the baby's venom. Indeed, the metonymic relation established between house and baby in the first two sentences becomes metaphoric by the middle of the paragraph, when the narrator tells us that Howard and Buglar flee "the moment *the house* committed . . . the one insult not to be borne or witnessed a second time." By establishing this metaphoric relation, Morrison underlines the alienation of Sethe and Denver from their own house. This underlining suggests, in turn, that any resolution of that alienation will depend on some resolution of their relation to this venomous baby. What's striking about the situation revealed here is that it appears to be a kind of fixed instability, that is, an unstable relationship that is now a constant in the lives of the women in the house. In that sense, this information is part of the exposition rather than the launch. For the narrative to get launched, the energy will need to come from some source that has the potential to alter this static disequilibrium.

Furthermore, the interpretive and ethical judgments we make in the first three sentences incline us to align our sympathies with Sethe and Denver. They seem to be not foolish victims but people with staying power. Of course this initial alignment must be tentative until we get more information, but it also signals the potential importance of persistence in the value structure of the story.

The phrase "baby's venom" evokes other responses. It is disorienting because it has the ring of an oxymoron: we don't typically associate babies with venom. It is also disorienting because it seems initially related to Baby Suggs and then later to a ghostly presence. Once we infer that the baby is a ghost, the phrase makes more sense, but the initial disorientation has some ongoing effects. The narrator's casual use of the phrase sends a strong signal about the distance between the narrative world and that of many flesh-and-blood readers. If baby's venom is a matter of course, something that can be casually invoked to explain a spiteful house, then it is part of a reality that many flesh-and-blood readers (including me) are not familiar with. Of course ghosts are not unheard of in gothic fiction, but this first paragraph does not contain other signals that we are in the realm of the gothic. The absence of such signals suggests that Morrison wants many members of her audience to be taken aback by the matter-of-factness of her introduction of the ghost and to think about the distance they must travel to enter her narrative and her authorial audiences.

Indeed, one of the radical moves Morrison makes in the narrative is to ask her authorial audience to believe in ghosts. Again, although the first paragraph does not definitively settle the issue of the authorial audience's belief in the supernatural, the matter-of-fact tone and the lack of distance between implied author and narrator in the paragraph point toward such belief. As the narrative progresses, Morrison more clearly establishes the authorial audience's belief in ghosts, especially in the possibility that Beloved is the ghost of this first paragraph. What's radical about Morrison's move, however, is that she does not use this belief to move the narrative firmly into the genre of the gothic, but instead uses it in conjunction with her insistence that she is writing a historical narrative. Thus, in the authorial audience we come to accept the idea that the historical slave trade, not the conventions of gothic fiction, generated ghosts such as Beloved.

At the same time, not all flesh-and-blood readers will feel that they are traveling far in order to share the authorial audience's belief in ghosts. For some readers, including some segments of Morrison's African American audience, a belief in ghosts is the norm, not the exception. This recognition does not alter the fact that Morrison's narrative and authorial audiences can take a matter-of-fact attitude toward the presence of ghosts in the world, but it does indicate that different flesh-and-blood readers will have different relations to that audience. Some readers will feel the comfort of having their beliefs confirmed by Morrison's narrative, whereas others, like me, will have to adopt new beliefs to participate fully in that narrative.

This dimension of Morrison's approach to audience reveals an ethical dimension to the initiation she offers. Morrison uses her narration to convey both authority and pride. With neither apology nor explanatory introduction, she implicitly says, here is my narrative world; deal with it. In other words, the burden of establishing a satisfactory rhetorical relationship between author and audience here falls largely on the audience. This strategy also entails some obligations on Morrison's part or it will end up working against her. The obligation is simply to reward the audience that meets her challenge with a rich reading experience, one commensurate with the effort it takes to enter her world.

Reading on, we discover that "baby's venom" is not so virulent: it gets manifested in a shattered mirror, hand prints in a cake, spilled chickpeas, crumbled soda crackers. Faced with such venom, I might find courage enough to qualify for a Medal of Honor. But not so the two young males in the story. Indeed, the main action summarized in the paragraph is the fleeing of Howard and Buglar, and the narrator's report emphasizes that they abandoned the women of 124: "Within two months, in the dead of winter, leaving their grandmother, Baby Suggs; Sethe, their mother; and their little sister, Denver, all by themselves in the gray and white house on Bluestone Road." As a result, 124 gets clearly established here as a distinctly female space, and the issue of gender relations gets established as a potentially significant one for the whole narrative.

These sentences about Howard's and Buglar's flights also form part of the paragraph's disorienting discourse on time. In the fourth sentence, we have two temporal references: "for years" and "by 1873." In the fifth sentence we learn that in 1873 Baby Suggs was dead, and that Howard and Buglar had run away by the time they were thirteen. The two sentences I have just discussed tell us that they left within "two months of each other" and that when they left Baby Suggs was still alive. So we can't tell what year they left, but it must have been before 1873. But then the last two sentences, which shift the narrator's location in time, say that they left seventy years after Ohio became a state (1803), which means 1873. What is going on? Clearly, Morrison wants to foreground the importance of time, history, and the interrelation of events in this narrative but also wants to suggest that in this world time is a jumble; that past, present, and future easily get mixed up. Nevertheless, I judge Morrison's contradictory messages about when the boys left as a mistake, because there is no way to resolve the contradiction and the rest of the narrative does not contain similar contradictions but rather allows us to reconstruct the chronological order of most events. Some readers may find Morrison's mistake here to be evidence that she is overdoing her effort to disorient her audience initially, but I take it as a small flaw in otherwise masterful first paragraph.

The last two sentences of that paragraph significantly complicate exposition and initiation in other ways as well. "It didn't have a number then, because Cincinnati didn't stretch that far. In fact, Ohio had been calling itself a state only seventy years when [Howard and Buglar left]." First, these sentences underscore how important the number 124 must be to the narrative. "124 was spiteful. Full of baby's venom. The women in the house knew it and so did the children." This expository discourse seems to be describing a particular moment when the action will begin, and consequently, it suggests that all the things named in that discourse are as they were at that moment—the venom, the women, the children, the house. But since the house was not then numbered, this discourse must be heavily retrospective. The narrator has not stepped all the way back into the moment in 1873, when the story will begin. Furthermore, the next sentence suggests that she is located in the 1980s, because it is only from a perspective considerably after 1873 that one would say "Ohio had been calling itself a state *only* seventy years" (my emphasis). I say that the narrator's perspective is the 1980s because, in the absence of evidence to the contrary, a narrator's present will be an author's present and Morrison published the book in 1987.

These matters of temporal perspective combine with the specific information about the numbering and location of the house in Cincinnati to emphasize the way that this narrative is very much interested in locating itself in the larger history of America. So, in conjunction with the front matter, especially the dedication, 1873 becomes important as a time shortly after the end of slavery. The narrator's location in the 1980s implies a yet-to-be revealed relevance of the events of 1873 to those of the 1980s.

By the end of the first paragraph then, the authorial audience has had to work hard simply to understand the expository moves Morrison is making; it has developed a sympathetic disposition toward the women of 124; and it has begun to feel, despite some minor bumps, both challenged and rewarded in its developing relation to Morrison.

The move from the exposition and initiation of the first paragraph to the launch and entrance does not come swiftly or easily. As I noted above, the first paragraph reveals a fixed instability, a static disequilibrium that needs to be disrupted by some new force before any significant alteration in the characters' lives will be possible. That force is Paul D Garner, who knew Sethe during the time that both were slaves on the Kentucky plantation called Sweet Home, and who has now, eighteen years after Sethe fled the plantation, made his way to 124 Bluestone Rd. Paul's arrival is a major instability for several reasons: it introduces an adult male into the female space of 124; it signals an opportunity for Sethe to confront the past; it holds out some promise for a future different from the dismal present. But Paul D's role in the launch cannot be understood apart from the whole series of instabilities and tensions established in the first chapter.

Indeed, the progression of the first chapter depends at least as much on tensions of unequal knowledge between Morrison and the narrator, on one side, and the authorial audience on the other, as it does on instabilities. Morrison's narrator continues the exposition by giving us pieces of the past and present, but because those pieces raise more questions than they answer, the exposition allows us to establish only an insecure foothold in this narrative world. The greatest tension surrounds the ghost: how did the baby die? Morrison alludes to the death in Sethe's memory of how her powerful love for the baby led her to trade sex for the engraving of the word "Beloved" on her tombstone: "Not only did she have to live out her years in a house palsied by the baby's fury at having her throat cut, but those ten minutes she spent pressed up against dawn-colored stone studded with star chips, her knees wide open as the grave, were longer than life, more alive, more pulsating than the baby blood that soaked her fingers like oil" (5). The glimpse, however, does not allow us to see who cut the baby's throat or the circumstances under which Sethe was able to feel the blood soaking her fingers. At the same time, the implied Morrison clearly guides our affective and ethical responses: we deepen our sympathy for Sethe as we learn about the measures she took on her dead daughter's behalf, and we condemn the conditions that lead her to this particular bargain.

There are numerous other tensions as well. Once Paul D arrives, we learn pieces of the story of Sweet Home, pieces that create tensions about other parts of that story. Sethe was the only female slave among five black men; she chose to marry one called Halle and had four children in four years, the last, her daughter Denver, shortly after escaping from the plantation. Just before she left, she was assaulted by white men; first, they "held [her] down" and "took [her] milk," then when she told Mrs. Garner, they came and whipped her until they left scars in the figure of a tree on her back. The affective and ethical consequences here are similar but not identical to those in the passage about Sethe's trading sex for the engraving on the tombstone. Our sympathy once again deepens for her, and our negative ethical judgments are directed strongly at the white men who assault her, a little less strongly at Mrs. Garner who is unable to intervene, and most strongly at the system of slavery that authorizes the behavior of the white men.

Although some tensions about Sweet Home get resolved as the chapter continues, many others remain and new ones get introduced. These tensions reinforce the first paragraph's emphasis on the importance of time and memory in this narrative. By the end of the chapter, we know that any positive progression forward in 1873 depends in part on some working through of Sethe's past experience at Sweet Home.

The first chapter also opens the narrative out beyond the story of Sethe and Paul D by introducing instabilities and tensions involving Sethe's daughter Denver. The narrative discourse switches to her perspective and shows us that Paul D represents an overt threat and a covert hope for Denver. He makes her mother act differently, like a flirtatious girl instead of "the quiet, queenly woman Denver had known all her life" (12). Paul and Sethe with their talk of Sweet Home and her father seem to share a world in which she has no place. And so she acts out, then breaks down crying in a way that she had not for nine years. The crying is not just about being shut out of the intimacy between her mother and Paul D but also about the life she is forced to have:

"I can't live here. I don't know where to go or what to do, but I can't live here. Nobody speaks to us. Nobody comes by. Boys don't like me. Girls don't either."

"Honey, honey."

"What's she talking 'bout nobody speaks to you?," asked Paul D.

"It's the house. People don't—"

"It's not! It's not the house. It's us! And it's you!" (14)

Again the new information we learn here also opens up new tensions: what is it about Sethe, what is it about all of them that makes nobody want to interact with them? At the same time, even as this dialogue shows Denver's opposition to her mother, Morrison uses it to generate sympathy for and positive ethical judgments of each of them: of Sethe because she is genuinely concerned for Denver here, and for Denver herself because her complaint is fair, and her mother's concern does not change her isolation.

Paul D's own sympathy with Sethe, and the glimpses we get of his past, position us in a similar sympathetic relation and generally positive ethical relation to him, even as the narrative continues to mark the importance of gender difference. Consider the dialogue that follows Sethe's narration of how she came to get the "tree" on her back.

"Men don't know nothing much," said Paul D, tucking his pouch back into his vest pocket, "but they do know a suckling can't be away from its mother for long."

"Then they know what it's like to send your children off when your breasts are full."

"We was talking 'bout a tree, Sethe."

"After I left you, those boys came in there and took my milk. That's what they came in there for. Held me down and took it. I told Mrs. Garner on em. . . . Them boys found out I told on em. Schoolteacher made one open up my back, and when it closed it made a tree. It grows there still."

"They used cowhide on you?"

"And they took my milk."

"They beat you and you was pregnant."

"And they took my milk!" (16–17)

Where Paul focuses on what seems to him the greater physical violation of Sethe's body—the white men's beating her—Sethe emphasizes the violation to her role as mother, first in having to send her children off without feeding them, second, in having her milk taken by the white men. Again Morrison asks us to judge each character's position as ethically sound, though her giving the last word to Sethe suggests that Sethe's position trumps Paul D's. More than that, the dialogue itself reinforces the significance of gender difference for the narrative and its underlying ethical values. I shall return to this passage later in the chapter.

As the source of the greatest tensions, the ghost is both a powerful magnet for our interest and a great mystery, something we do not know yet know how to respond to: she is obviously a disruptive force, but she is the ghost of a baby who had her throat cut, and so a creature who deserves our sympathy. Denver is the character whom we can interpret and judge most readily, even as the narrative's move to her concerns and interests certainly complicates our response to Sethe, especially in adding the tension about how Sethe could be the reason that nobody will come to the house. In short, as the chapter develops, it introduces so many tensions, so many instabilities and it offers so much competition for our attention, interest, sympathy, and understanding that it heightens the disorienting effect of the first paragraph.

In the final pages of the chapter, the narrative focus returns to Sethe and Paul D and then shifts to Paul D and the ghost as Morrison pulls things sufficiently together to provide the launch. Sethe tells Paul the story of how she got the tree on her back, and he begins to comfort her physically, putting his mouth on the scars of her back and holding her breasts in his hands, an action which prompts Sethe to wonder:

> Would there be a little space . . . a little time, some way to hold off eventfulness, to push busyness into the corners of the room and just stand there a minute or two, naked from shoulder blade to waist, relieved of the weight of her breasts, smelling the stolen milk again and the pleasure of baking bread? (18)

Because of our sympathy for Sethe and our positive ethical judgments of her, we share the hope underneath her wondering. But Sethe's pleasure in this moment arouses the jealous resentment of the ghost, who exhibits a venom far greater than anything mentioned in the first paragraph. The ghost makes the whole house pitch, until Paul D, seizing a table that has been flung at him and bashing it about while screaming for the ghost to leave, succeeds in chasing the ghost from the house. The chapter ends not with a focus on Paul D and Sethe, but rather with Denver missing her brothers and Baby Suggs, and thinking, "Now her mother was upstairs with the man who had gotten rid of the only other company she had. Denver dipped a bit of bread into the jelly. Slowly, methodically, miserably she ate it" (19).

With the elimination of the ghost, the static disequilibrium revealed in the first paragraph is significantly altered. This alteration constitutes the launch because it significantly complicates rather than resolves that initial unstable situation. Although the ghost is "gone," the narrator also tells us that after the battle, while "Sethe, Denver, and Paul D breathed to the same beat, like one tired person," "[a]nother breathing was just as tired" (18–19). The implicit promise of this sentence—and, indeed, of the magnetic interest surrounding the ghost throughout this section—is that she will return. Furthermore, that magnetic interest and Denver's regret over losing the ghost's company complicates any judgment that Paul D's driving the ghost away is a wholly positive move. After all, from the sympathetic Denver's point of view, the house was better with the ghost and without Paul D.

By the end of the chapter, then, we have sufficient information to complete our entrance into the narrative world. We are temporally oriented toward the present of 1873, the past at Sweet Home, and the future of Morrison's time of writing. Our ethical judgments of Sethe, Paul D, and Denver are generally positive, and we feel substantial sympathy for each of them—even as we recognize the unstable relations between them. We desire that Paul D's arrival at 124 will make life better for Sethe, but we don't want an improvement for Sethe that will come at the expense of her daughter. We are also aware that the ghost remains a threat to disrupt whatever positive changes Paul D might help to bring about. And we are very cognizant of the multiple thematic threads introduced into the narrative, especially the ones about slavery, death, unhappiness, time and memory, and gender. This entrance does not allow us to predict the trajectory of the narrative for either the characters or the thematic issues, but it does take us inside a compelling and difficult narrative world. Indeed, the beginning shows us that Morrison's aesthetic ambitions are significant: she is taking on challenging themes, employing a protean narrator, a complex temporality, and a progression with multiple dimensions.

## The Middle

In the voyage, the global instability of the beginning gets complicated by the ghost's return as Beloved (although, as I and others have argued,

"returned ghost" is only one of Beloved's identities and meanings).
Beloved's arrival complicates the situations of Sethe, of Paul D, and of
Denver, individually and collectively, and these complications make the
tension about what happened between Sethe and the baby all the more
important to resolve. The voyage continues to highlight the tension in
the early parts of the middle. In a conversation with Paul D about Denver
in the third chapter, Sethe makes reference to the events of August 1855
without telling the whole story:

> "And when the schoolteacher found us and came busting in here
> with the law and a shotgun—"
>    "Schoolteacher found you?"
>    "Took a while, but he did. Finally."
>    "And he didn't take you back?"
>    "Oh, no, I wasn't going back there. I don't care who found who.
> Any life but that one. I went to jail instead. Denver was just a baby
> so she went right along with me. Rats bit everything in there but
> her."
>    Paul D turned away. He wanted to know more about it, but jail
> put him back in Alfred, Georgia. (42)

There are other cryptic allusions such as this one in the ninth chapter,
which skips over any explanation of *why* the baby ghost took up residence
at 124 Bluestone Rd: "Years ago—when 124 was alive—she had women
friends, men friends from all around to share grief with. Then there was no
one, for they would not visit her while the baby ghost filled the house, and
she returned their disapproval with the potent pride of the mistreated" (95–
96). This tension creates an aura not just of mystery but also of privilege
around the mystery; each reference increases the audience's sense of its
importance and the audience's desire to resolve the tension. The strategy
of deferral establishes an ethical obligation on Morrison's part to provide
some resolution to the tension, even as it compliments the audience on
its abilities to register the various hints and to wait for the resolution. In
the meantime, Morrison is providing careful ethical guidance through the
exposition, the interactions, and the voyage.

Although that guidance is carefully nuanced, its broad outlines are
clear. First, Morrison uses her protean narrator to give us a wide range of
interactions: the narrator continues to offer us inside views of the major
characters—Sethe, Paul D, Denver, and Baby Suggs—and she also continues

to comment directly in her own voice on the action and the characters. As she did in the first chapter, Morrison uses this range to multiply the number of valorized ethical perspectives. For example, Sethe and Denver have very different feelings and judgments about Beloved's entering the house at 124 Bluestone Rd. In this early part of the middle, Morrison does not privilege either character's judgment but instead asks us to enter into each character's consciousness and to recognize the validity of her feelings and judgments.[2] Second, Morrison establishes slavery not just as an abstract evil or an historical evil but as something that has continuing and profound negative effects on Sethe and Paul D in 1873—and thus, on Denver and every one else in their circle. Indeed, Morrison's representation of slavery guides us to recognize the historical validity of Baby Suggs's conclusion that "there is no bad luck in the world but whitefolks" (89). This ethical position is all the more compelling because the exposition shows that slavery at the Garners' Sweet Home plantation was *relatively* benevolent. Third, Morrison identifies Sethe's habit of "beating back the past" (73), her efforts to repress the events of 1855, as both impossible and dangerous; the consequence of her emphasis on this instability is to increase the pressure on the revelation of those events—Sethe's future will be determined by what happens when she faces rather than beats back that past.

While establishing this context, Morrison builds toward the revelation of Sethe's choice by providing enough information about 1855 for us to understand what is at stake for Sethe when schoolteacher arrives at 124 and by taking the instabilities of 1873 forward to the point where Paul D asks her to have his child. The resolution of the tension, then, not only provides the audience with crucial information that makes the situation in 1873 intelligible but also provides a major turning point in the ongoing development of that situation. Each of the three tellings—and the triangulation of all three—contribute to the resolution and especially to the ethical guidance Morrison does and does not provide. As noted above, the first telling is focalized through the white men who come to return Sethe and her children to slavery; the following passage, in which the focalization begins with the slave catcher and then shifts to schoolteacher, is a representative example:[3]

---

2. I don't mean to suggest that Morrison never exposes the limits of some values and beliefs held by the main characters. For example, she asks us to recognize both the immaturity of Denver's view of Paul D as an unwelcome intruder and the reasons why she clings to it so strongly.

3. "Representative" in the sense that it provides an appropriate focus for my discussion

Inside two boys bled in the sawdust and dirt at the feet of a nigger woman holding a blood-soaked child to her chest with one hand and an infant by the heels in the other. She did not look at them; she simply swung the baby toward the wall planks, missed and tried to connect a second time, when out of nowhere—in the ticking time the men spent staring at what there was to stare at—the old nigger boy, still mewing, ran through the door behind them and snatched the baby from the arch of its mother's swing.

Right off, it was clear, to schoolteacher especially, that there was nothing there to claim. . . . [S]he'd gone wild, due to the mishandling of the nephew who'd overbeat her and made her cut and run. Schoolteacher had chastised that nephew, telling him to think—just think—what would his own horse do if you beat it to beyond the point of education. Or Chipper, or Samson. Suppose you beat the hounds past that point thataway. Never again could you trust them in the woods or anywhere else. You'd be feeding them maybe, holding out a piece of rabbit in your hand and the animal would revert—bite your hand clean off. . . . The whole lot was lost now. Five. He could claim the baby struggling in the arms of the mewing old man, but who'd tend her? Because the woman— something was wrong with her. She was looking at him now, and if his other nephew could see that look he would learn the lesson for sure: you just can't mishandle creatures and expect success. (149–50)

By unraveling the mystery by means of a new mode of interaction, Morrison provides a highly unsettling experience for the authorial audience. After seeing Sethe from the inside or from the perspective of the narrator for so long, we feel emotionally, psychologically—and ethically— jarred by seeing her from what is such an alien perspective, one that thinks of her as "a nigger woman" and as a "creature" equivalent to a horse or a hound. The previous interactions of course provide a context that reinforces our active negative judgment of this vision—indeed, our repudiation of it. When we see schoolteacher regarding Sethe as a dog who no longer trusts its master, and when we see that his concern is ultimately with himself and his loss, not at all with Sethe or her children, our judgments of his vision are quick, clear, and harsh. Strikingly, however, Morrison's strategy of moving away from Sethe's perspective and describing her actions from

---

of the ethical dimension of the first telling, but not "representative" in the sense that all sections of the telling work exactly the way this one does.

the outside highlights not only the ethical deficiency of the slave catcher's and schoolteacher's racist perspectives but also the horror of what Sethe is doing: "holding a blood-soaked child to her chest with one hand and an infant by the heels in the other . . . she simply swung the baby toward the wall planks, missed and tried to connect a second time." If the shift in perspective is jarring, the revelation of Sethe's action is shocking, especially because it is rendered as a straight physical description, focused primarily on Sethe's action and secondarily on its main adjective: "blood-soaked." The physical description is not pretty, and it is not possible to find a way to make it pretty. This description is from the slave catcher's angle of vision, but there is no sign that the angle distorts his view of the physical action. Thus, when we separate perceiver from perceived, we have no direct guidance to judge the perceived. Morrison leaves us to judge Sethe's action ourselves.

Morrison does, however, also leave space for us to defer that judgment. Since this first telling picks up the story after the white men have entered the shed, it does not explain how or why Sethe went there with her children. In the second telling, Morrison partially addresses those aspects of the story, with particular attention to the how. The perspective here belongs to Stamp Paid; the telling occurs as part of a recollection he is prepared to share with Paul D but does not because Paul insists that the woman in the newspaper story Stamp gives him cannot be Sethe:

> So Stamp Paid did not tell him how she flew, snatching up her children like a hawk on the wing; how her face beaked, how her hands worked like claws, how she collected them every which way; one on her shoulder, one under her arm, one by the hand, the other shouted forward into the woodshed filled with just sunlight and shavings now because there wasn't any wood. The party had used it all, which is why he was chopping some. Nothing was in that shed, he knew, having been there early that morning. Nothing but sunlight. Sunlight, shavings, a shovel. The ax he himself took out. Nothing was in there except the shovel—and of course the saw. (157)

Because Paul D holds fast to his belief that the woman in the story was not Sethe, Stamp wonders "if it had happened at all, eighteen years ago, that while he and Baby Suggs were looking the wrong way, a pretty little slavegirl had recognized a hat, and split to the woodshed to kill her children" (158).

Stamp Paid, too, sees Sethe from the outside, and though he also compares her to an animal, he does not reduce her to one. Indeed, the comparison of Sethe with a hawk on the wing works to illuminate the how and why: because Sethe senses danger, she instinctively reacts, fiercely and swiftly gathering her children into the shed. Because Stamp Paid does not have access to Sethe's mental state and because his narration emphasizes her instinctive reaction, Morrison's technique again stops short of rendering a full account of the why and any clear ethical judgment. But the end of the passage recalls the horror of the physical action not only in its naming of the instrument Sethe uses to cut her baby's throat but in the delayed disclosure of its presence. We go from "nothing" being in the shed to "Sunlight, shavings, a shovel" and, after the notation that Stamp had removed the ax, to the revelation that "of course the saw" was also there. Stamp Paid's final thought more directly foregrounds the horror of what Sethe is doing: "a pretty little slavegirl . . . split to the woodshed to kill her children." The contrast between the condescending description, "pretty little slavegirl," and the plain statement of her purpose, "to kill her children" has complex ethical effects. The plain statement, when juxtaposed to the description of Sethe swinging her baby toward the wall, may initially move us toward concluding that Sethe's instinctive reaction is ultimately wrong—however instinctive, it's a frightening overreaction. But the condescending description, in combination with the power of our previous sympathy for Sethe and the absence of an internal view of Sethe, gives us space to defer any final conclusion yet again. If Stamp Paid is wrong about who Sethe is, perhaps he's also wrong about her purpose. But even as we defer a final judgment, we continue to contemplate the almost unbelievable horror of what Sethe has done. We may wish to adopt Paul D's attitude of denial but, with this second telling through a more sympathetic focalizer, Morrison has effectively eliminated that coping strategy from our repertoire.

Sethe's own telling to Paul D—with occasional further commentary by the narrator—is, not surprisingly, the longest version of the story and the one that most fully addresses her motives. Sethe circles the room as she talks, much as the novel has circled the event up until these three tellings. Sethe begins not with the day that the four horsemen rode into the yard but rather with her arrival at 124 twenty days earlier, the pride and love she felt as a result of that accomplishment, and its consequences for her behavior when schoolteacher returned:

> "We was here. Each and every one of my babies and me too. I birthed them and I got em out and it wasn't no accident. I did that. . . . It felt good. Good and right. I was big, Paul D, and deep and wide and when I stretched out my arms all my children could get

in between. I was *that* wide. Look like I loved em more after I got
here. Or maybe I couldn't love em proper in Kentucky because they
wasn't mine to love. But when I got here, when I jumped down off
that wagon—there wasn't nobody in the world I couldn't love if I
wanted to.

"...I couldn't let her nor any of em live under schoolteacher."
(162–63)

With Sethe's words to Paul D about the relation between freedom and
her expanded mother love as background, Morrison shifts to Sethe's
thoughts:

Sethe knew that . . . she could never close in, pin it down for any-
body who had to ask. If they didn't get it right off—she could never
explain. Because the truth was simple. . . . [W]hen she saw them
coming and recognized schoolteacher's hat, she heard wings. Little
hummingbirds stuck their needle beaks right through her headcloth
into her hair and beat their wings. If she thought anything it was
No. No. Nono. Nonono. Simple. She just flew. Collected every bit of
life she had made, all the parts of her that were precious and fine
and beautiful, and carried, pushed, dragged them through the veil,
out, away, over there where no one could hurt them. Over there
outside this place, where they would be safe. . . .

"I stopped him," she said, staring at the place where the fence
used to be. "I took and put my babies where they'd be safe." (163–
64)

Sethe's version is obviously a strong counter to the earlier two: her purpose was not to kill but to protect, her motivation was unselfish love, and
the action was a success. She does act instinctively, but the instincts are
those of mother love and her aim is to keep her children safe from slavery.
The animal imagery here does not suggest anything about her agency but
rather about an association between schoolteacher and a feeling in her
head—a matter I will return to below.

Thus, the progression of the stories gives us a progression of possibilities for ethical judgment: Sethe has committed a subhuman action; Sethe
has done the wrong thing but done it instinctively and understandably;
Sethe has done something difficult but heroic because it is done for the best
motives and it turns out to be a success. Since the progression of the narrative perspectives, from outside to inside, from the white men's to Stamp

Paid's to Sethe's, is a progression toward increasingly sympathetic views, we might be inclined to conclude that Morrison is guiding us toward judging Sethe's version as the one we should endorse. Furthermore, if we stay inside Sethe's perspective, her account is very compelling: "Collected every bit of life she had made, all the parts of her that were precious and fine and beautiful, and carried, pushed, dragged them through the veil, out, away, over there where no one could hurt them" (163). But the triangulation of all three stories indicates that Morrison doesn't want Sethe's story to be the authoritative version by calling attention to what Sethe leaves out of her account: the handsaw, the slit throat, the blood, the swinging of the baby toward the wall, its death at her hands. In short, Sethe's telling isn't definitive because it erases the horror of her action under its talk of motivations (love) and purpose (safety).

Furthermore, before the third telling concludes, Morrison uses Paul D to provide an internal counter to Sethe's perspective. Paul D, of course, is the most sympathetic audience Sethe could find within the world of the novel, someone who knows first-hand the evils of slavery and someone who loves her. But Paul D immediately rejects Sethe's judgments and imposes his own, much harsher ones. Morrison's narrator shows that he immediately thinks, "what she wanted for her children was exactly what was missing in 124: safety" (164). His experience, in other words, makes him question Sethe's claims for the success of her action. Morrison also has Paul D say to Sethe that "your love is too thick," that "what you did was wrong, Sethe," and that "you got two feet, Sethe, not four" (163–65).

Of these responses, the first resonates most with the authorial audience. Our own experience of the narrative to this point shows that 124 has not been a safe place—literally haunted by the ghost of the dead baby and her return as Beloved, metaphorically haunted by the consequences of Sethe's rough choice for her and her other children. Howard and Buglar felt compelled to leave, Denver felt deeply frustrated by her isolation before Beloved's arrival. Furthermore, Sethe's own constant work "of beating back the past" indicates that her narrative does not accurately capture the complexity of her choice. If her story were adequate to the events, then she would not need to work so hard at repression. Part Two will give further evidence, in Sethe's extreme efforts to expiate her guilt toward Beloved, that she herself does not fully believe that her choice was the right one.

But Morrison also gives us reason not to endorse the rest of Paul's negative judgments. His remark that Sethe has "two feet not four" clearly links his assessment with schoolteacher's, and that link affects our judgment of their judgments. On the one hand, Paul D's seeing Sethe's action in the same terms as schoolteacher reminds us of the horror of the physical description of what schoolteacher saw. But on the other, Paul D's adopting schoolteacher's terms is strong evidence that Paul's judgment is deficient. Again, Morrison's technique leads us to rule out certain ethical responses—schoolteacher's racist one, Sethe's own heroic one, Paul D's more conventional assessment—without leading us to a clear judgment.

Morrison places Sethe's telling to Paul D right at the end of Part One, and she shows that the telling and Paul D's response radically disrupts their developing relationship, and, in that way, seriously complicates the major instabilities. While the progression to this point has emphasized that Sethe must work through her relation to the past in order to resolve the instabilities of her present situation, this moment in the voyage only complicates those instabilities. As soon as Paul D says, "You got two feet, Sethe, not four," "a forest sprang up between them; trackless and quiet" (165). Shortly thereafter, he leaves without saying "goodbye," but Sethe knows that he is not coming back and she murmurs "So long" . . ."from the far side of the trees" (165). Morrison's narrative logic is impeccable here: as she resolves some significant tensions of unequal knowledge, she also shows that Sethe has not resolved her relation to the past but has only articulated her partial and defensive understanding of it. Again, as noted above, if Sethe were totally convinced by her own narrative, she would not have to work so hard at repressing the past. Moreover, because Sethe has articulated her narrative of the past to Paul D, who takes such a very different view of her actions, her voyage forward is now going to be that much more difficult. Indeed, Paul's departure and Sethe's lingering guilt lead to her dangerous obsession with and subservience to Beloved, and it is not until the community acts to break her from that relationship that Paul can return and the instabilities begin to be resolved.

## Connections and Configurations

Morrison's complex handling of temporality has rightly been compared to that of Faulkner. Like Faulkner's experiments with temporal order—and indeed, like that of many other modernist novelists—Morrison's technique requires the authorial audience to be very active not only in piecing the fabula together but also in recognizing implied connections between elements of the progression. That is, a particular scene will have resonance not only for other scenes that are close to it in the fabula order but also for scenes that may be at some distance both in the fabula and in the

progression itself. In this section, I would like to look at two such connections to the representations of Sethe's choice, one from later in the middle,
and one from the beginning, and at how they affect our configuration of
the narrative as a whole. The first passage is Sethe's account to Beloved
in section 1 of Part Two about what happened when she overheard one of
schoolteacher's lessons:

> This is the first time I'm telling it and I'm telling it to you because
> it might help explain something to you although I know you don't
> need me to do it. To tell it or even think over it. You don't have to
> listen either, if you don't want to. But I couldn't help listening to
> what I heard that day. He was talking to his pupils and I heard him
> say, "Which one are you doing?" And one the boys said, "Sethe."
> That's when I stopped because I heard my name, and then I took a
> few steps to where I could see what they was doing. Schoolteacher
> was standing over one of them with one hand behind his back. He
> licked a forefinger a couple of times and turned a few pages. Slow. I
> was about to turn around and keep on my way to where the muslin
> was, when I heard him say, "No, no. That's not the way. I told you
> to put her human characteristics on the left; her animal ones on the
> right. And don't forget to line them up." I commenced to walk back-
> ward, didn't even look behind me to find out where I was headed.
> I just kept lifting my feet and pushing back. When I bumped up
> against a tree my scalp was prickly. One of the dogs was licking out
> a pan in the yard. I got to the grape arbor fast enough, but I didn't
> have the muslin [to cover you in your basket]. Flies settled all over
> your face, rubbing their hands. My head itched like the devil. Like
> somebody was sticking fine needles in my scalp. I never told Halle
> or nobody. (193)

The retrospective light of this passage aids our configuration of the
narrative by providing further illumination to the tellings of Sethe's choice
from schoolteacher's perspective and from hers. The passage shows that his
conception of her behavior as like a horse or a hound does not derive from
that behavior itself but rather from his a priori racist assumptions. Furthermore, in combination with Sethe's telling, it shows that his explanation of
her behavior is incomplete. It is not just the abuse Sethe has received from
the nephew who beat her, but even more the verbal abuse she has received
from his intellectual authority that affects her choice. We now understand
why the very sight of schoolteacher at 124 Bluestone Rd. makes Sethe feel

as if hummingbirds are sticking their "needle beaks" in her scalp. The passage also adds another significant dimension to our understanding of Sethe's response to Paul D's comment that "you got two legs not four." No wonder that a forest springs up between them when he uses schoolteacher's categories to judge her. In sum, the retrospective light of this passage shines most brightly on Sethe's telling, giving us greater insights into her instinctive choice. I will discuss the significance of this effect after looking at the second connection.

This connection involves Sethe and Paul D, and particularly their discussion in the beginning after she tells him about how she came to get the "tree" on her back. The passage is worth quoting again:

> "Men don't know nothing much," said Paul D, tucking his pouch back into his vest pocket, "but they do know a suckling can't be away from its mother for long."
>
> "Then they know what it's like to send your children off when your breasts are full."
>
> "We was talking 'bout a tree, Sethe."
>
> "After I left you, those boys came in there and took my milk. That's what they came in there for. Held me down and took it. I told Mrs. Garner on em. . . . Them boys found out I told on em. Schoolteacher made one open up my back, and when it closed it made a tree. It grows there still."
>
> "They used cowhide on you?"
>
> "And they took my milk."
>
> "They beat you and you was pregnant."
>
> "And they took my milk!" (16–17)

Paul D's failure to understand that Sethe felt more violated by the white men's taking her milk than by their whipping her back links with his judgments that "her love is too thick" and that she has "two legs not four." These later judgments are similarly inadequate because they discount the distinctive quality of Sethe's experiences as a mother. Although Paul D knows the evils of slavery, he does not know what it is like to be both parent and slave let alone both mother and slave. As in the first chapter, Paul D is once again thinking like a man without children rather than like a mother.[4] Again the effect of the connection is to deepen our sense of why

---

4. There is one more very suggestive consequence of following the connections between Schoolteacher's lesson and his and Paul D's judgment of Sethe. These connections, along with a few other moments in the text, suggest that Morrison wants to question the distinction—or at

Sethe acts as she does and why she views her action the way she does. Nevertheless, this deepened understanding increases our sympathy for Sethe without leading us clearly to endorse Sethe's self-judgment. It is one thing to expose the extent of schoolteacher's racism and the limits of Paul D's judgments, but quite another to move from that exposure to Sethe's view of her choice. Neither connection actually addresses the recalcitrance Sethe's narrative encounters—the horror of child murder, the lack of true safety in her life, the repression she practices and the guilt she feels—and neither one can eliminate the physical description we've taken in from the first telling. Morrison sets up these connections with the crucial elements of the narrative middle not to sway us in favor of Sethe's choice but to help us maintain sympathy for Sethe once she discloses the events of August 1855.

## Consequences

To summarize, Morrison clearly designates some positions that we ought *not* occupy—Sethe deserves Paul D's harsh judgment; Sethe's own account should be endorsed—without positively establishing her own ethical assessment. As we have seen in the epigraph, Morrison incorporates this attitude into the narrative through the character of Baby Suggs, a source of knowledge and wisdom throughout the novel, who is finally unable either to approve or condemn Sethe's choice. The larger effects of Morrison's ethical stance here are best seen in the context of the larger progression.

---

least to question the usual assumed hierarchy of the distinction—at the heart of schoolteacher's lesson, that between the human and the animal. The inversion of the hierarchy is, of course, very much a part of the passage describing the lesson: Sethe has a kind of self-consciousness that we don't usually attribute to animals, whereas Schoolteacher has lost all sense of what we usually think of as humanity in his assumptions about Sethe as subhuman. But Morrison goes further than that in the way in which the distinction operates in the larger narrative. First, as A. S. Byatt points out in her review of the novel, Sethe's giving birth to Denver depends on her going on all fours, on her acting as if she has four legs not two. Indeed, the symbolic forest that springs up between Sethe and Paul D after he renders his judgment may very well be the forest through which Sethe crawled on the night of her flight from Sweet Home, the night before Denver was born. Indeed, if Paul D's comment applies to Sethe's murder of Beloved, it also applies to Sethe's most unambiguous demonstration of motherly love and devotion.

Paul D's remark also is complicated by his own past actions that might suggest that he has four legs not two, particularly his finding sexual release by rutting with cows. Schoolteacher's lesson, Morrison's suggestions about inverting the usual hierarchies, Paul D's comment to Sethe about how many legs she has, the Sweet Home men's sexual practices: all these elements of the narrative suggest that Morrison is very much interested in questioning the boundaries of the human, very much trying to suggest that the lines between the human and the animal are not as clear and clean as some one such as Schoolteacher would like his pupils to believe.

Morrison resolves the instabilities with a series of arrivals that hold out hope after the traumatic events of both 1855 and 1873. Denver escapes from the increasingly oppressive environment created by Sethe's guilt and Beloved's neediness at 124 and begins to work at the Bodwins; as noted above, the community, which had ignored Sethe since August 1855, comes to rescue her from Beloved's insatiable needs; and Paul D eventually realizes that he wants to "put his story next to hers" and so returns to assure her that she is her own "best thing" (273). Morrison then juxtaposes these arrivals with the extraordinary farewell of the last two pages. This farewell, as I have argued in *Narrative as Rhetoric,*[5] is spoken by the narrator from her position in 1987, and it insists that the hopeful arrivals of the previous narrative should not erase the trauma of the narrative and what it signifies about the history of slavery in America. "This is not a story to pass on" (275) in the sense of "pass by." We must remain conscious of those who, like Beloved, are otherwise "disremembered and unaccounted for" (274). The last word of the novel, at once a summary comment and an address from the narrator to the reader, encapsulates both the challenge of the farewell and the hope of the arrival: "Beloved" (275). But the effect of the arrival and farewell becomes clearer when we consider some further consequences of Morrison's decision not to make an explicit judgment about Sethe's rough choice for the readerly dynamics of the progression.

Unlike Baby Suggs, we in the authorial audience cannot simply withdraw from the ethical demands of the narrative and give our days over to the contemplation of color. Instead, we need first to recognize Morrison's point that Sethe's choice is somehow beyond the reach of standard ethical judgment—an action at once instinctive and unnatural, motivated by love and destructive to life. Consequently, we can neither settle on a clear and fixed judgment nor opt out of judging Sethe's act altogether. In my own experience as a flesh-and-blood reader seeking to enter the authorial audience, I find my judgments of Sethe fluctuating—sometimes the horror of the murder dominates my consciousness and I judge Sethe as having gone beyond the pale; at other times, Sethe's desperation, motivation, and purpose mitigate my judgment and make her choice seem not just comprehensible but something approaching defensible.

This inability to fix a position on the central action complicates our relation to Sethe as the central actor without disrupting our sympathy for

5. See chapter 9 of *Narrative as Rhetoric,* available on-line at www.ohiostatepress.org. More generally, that chapter is a complement to the analysis presented here, one that focuses on the textual and readerly dynamics connected with Morrison's representation of Beloved as character and with the novel's extended farewell.

her. Sethe becomes a character who was once pushed beyond the limits of human endurance and reacted to that pushing in this extraordinary way. Consequently, we turn our judgment on the institution that pushed her beyond the limits: slavery. It is of course easy to say that slavery is evil but it's another thing for readers in the twenty-first century—especially white readers—to *feel* the force of that statement, to comprehend the effects of slavery on individual human lives. Morrison's treatment of Sethe's rough choice moves readers toward such comprehension: in the space where we wrestle with the ethical dilemma presented by Sethe's choice, we must imaginatively engage with Sethe's instinctive decision that, when faced with the prospect of slavery, loving her children means murdering them. Such engagement transforms slavery from an abstract evil to a palpable one. Such engagement is also crucial to the effects of the arrivals and the farewell. Those arrivals allows us to finish the narrative with a sense of hope rather than despair, and though it would be an overstatement to say that without such hope, the narrative would be unreadable, that overstatement gets at both the painful quality of this novel and our desire for something positive to happen to these characters. The same deep engagement is what makes Morrison's challenge to her audience in the farewell so effective. Having participated in the past and present of these particular characters, having felt on our pulses the range and depth of their emotions, we are far more likely to attend to Morrison's injunction about coming to terms with slavery's continuing legacy in the United States.

As this discussion suggests, the aesthetic consequences of Morrison's formal and ethical choices are profound. At the level of form, Morrison is working with multiplicity rather than singularity. She offers multiple perspectives, multiple tensions, multiple instabilities; she works with an extremely complicated temporal schema. Her formal choices require her audience to be working at the top of their powers. As we have seen, Morrison's unusual treatment of Sethe's choice creates an unusual ethical relationship with her audience, one that challenges us to have the negative capability to refrain from any irritable reaching after ethical closure while also signaling her faith that we will be equal to the task of grappling with the difficult ethics of Sethe's choice. Morrison's treatment retains the basic reciprocal relation between author and audience that underlies the ethical dimension of their communication, but it gives a new twist to that reciprocity, one that has significant aesthetic consequences. By limiting her guidance, Morrison gives up some authorial responsibility and transfers it to the audience. By accepting that responsibility—and attending to the parameters within which Morrison asks us to exercise it—we have a more difficult and demanding but also richer reading experience. By guiding us less, Morrison gives us more. By exercising the responsibility Morrison transfers to us, we get more out of what she offers. *Beloved* becomes, if not "our own best thing," a narrative that is simultaneously deeply unsettling and deeply rewarding—and that combination is the key to its aesthetic power.

# CHAPTER THREE

# Chicago Criticism, New Criticism, Cultural Thematics, and Rhetorical Poetics

In this chapter I want to build on the theoretical work of the Introduction by taking a broader view of my project, one that places it more explicitly within the neo-Aristotelian tradition of work on narrative and considers its relation to the current widespread practice of what I call *cultural thematics*. By cultural thematics I mean that branch of cultural studies that views literary texts as in dialogue with other cultural discourses and interprets texts through the lens provided by one or more key concepts from those discourses. In placing the project within the neo-Aristotelian tradition, I will also glance at the rivalry between the first generation neo-Aristotelians and the New Critics as a way to clarify both the tradition and my relation to it. But I start with the neo-Aristotelian approach itself.

One plausible, though highly selective, narrative about the neo-Aristotelian movement has two main chapters (though the timeframe of the first chapter extends past the beginning of the second).[1] Chapter 1: A group of critics at the University of Chicago in the mid-twentieth century, led by R. S. Crane and Elder Olson, sought to fashion a mode of criticism superior to the then dominant mode of New Criticism. They based their

---

1. To counter slightly the selectivity of the narrative, I note that the manifesto of the first generation, *Critics and Criticism, Ancient and Modern,* included the philosophical work of Richard McKeon and literary critical contributions by W. R. Keast, Norman Maclean, and Bernard Weinberg as well as those by Crane and Olson. Among the other members of the second generation are James L. Battersby, Richard Levin, Norman Friedman, and Homer Goldberg. And members of the third generation include Mary Doyle Springer, Peter J. Rabinowitz, David H. Richter, Harry Shaw, Elizabeth Langland, Marshall Gregory, William Monroe, Janet Aikins, and Michael Boardman. For some other accounts of the tradition, see Richter's "The Second Flight of the Phoenix" and his entry on the Chicago School in the *Routledge Encyclopedia of Narrative Theory.*

approach on Aristotle's *Poetics,* but they sought to go beyond its discussion of a single genre of Greek drama, since they wanted to account for the variety of literature that had been produced throughout history. They proposed, among other things, to identify the structural principles of the different literary genres. For any one genre that task involved identifying the objects (plot, character, and thought or what Aristotle would view as the formal cause), manner (the relevant techniques or efficient cause), means (language, performance, song or material cause), and the overall end (final cause) into which these various elements would be synthesized. Although this generation did not succeed in their efforts to supplant the New Criticism as the reigning critical orthodoxy, they did establish the worth of their overall project, and they offered insightful and influential contributions to both literary theory and practical criticism. The work of the first generation was continued by a second generation of neo-Aristotelians, especially Sheldon Sacks, Wayne Booth, and Ralph W. Rader, and then by a much more diverse, loosely affiliated third generation.

Chapter 2: When Wayne C. Booth, a student of Crane's, began working on a defense of overt narratorial rhetoric in fiction against those who contended that such "telling" was aesthetically inferior to "showing," he began a shift from the primarily poetic concerns of the first generation to more rhetorical concerns, a shift from a primary focus on textual structures and techniques to a primary focus on author-audience relations. In *The Rhetoric of Fiction* (1961), Booth demonstrates not just that one must assess overt rhetoric by its contribution to the larger ends of its work rather than by abstract rules, but also that every part of a novel has a rhetorical function. In other words, telling, showing, and every other novelistic strategy are means that authors have at their disposal to influence readers to respond to characters and events in one way rather than another. In a sense, Booth breaks down the distinction Aristotle himself makes between poetics as the art of constructing imitations of action and rhetoric as the art of using all the available means of persuasion. For Booth the art of constructing imitations of actions is crucially dependent on the art of persuading audiences to view the characters in those actions in one way rather than another. And once the focus shifts to the art of persuasion, then the agents who meet through the text (implied author and audience) become as important as that text. As Booth develops this position over the course of his career, he becomes less concerned with the rigorous differentiation of generic kinds and the analysis of the structural particularity and formal power of individual texts that characterizes work by the first generation and, indeed, by his contemporaries Sacks and Rader.

Instead, Booth becomes more convinced that the queen of the disciplines is rhetoric, and over time he becomes more of a rhetorical theorist than an orthodox neo-Aristotelian. When Booth turns to literary interpretation after *The Rhetoric of Fiction,* he typically retains a commitment to means-ends reasoning, but his rhetorical orientation leads him to expand the concept of "end" so that it includes not just meanings and emotions but also values—with all of these being subsumed under the larger end of the shared communication between implied author and authorial audience.

In a sense, *Experiencing Fiction* is an effort to write a third chapter to this narrative of the neo-Aristotelian movement by putting the poetic and the rhetorical strands of the tradition back together in the construction of a rhetorical poetics. Like the first generation and like Sacks and Rader, I want to explain as systematically as the data allow both the dynamics of the individual works and the principles on which those dynamics are based. Like Booth, I want to take a broader view of those dynamics and to include a central place for ethics. I also want to give more explicit attention to aesthetics than others in the tradition have done, and, thus, to give a clearer account of the interrelations of and differentiations among form, ethics, and aesthetics. (See chapter 6 of this book for my expanded discussion of rhetorical aesthetics.) To further situate this rhetorical poetics in relation to the tradition, I find it helpful to return to Chapter 1 and review the rivalry between the first-generation and the New Critics.

The neo-Aristotelians objected so strongly to the principles underlying the work of such New Critics as William Empson and Cleanth Brooks because the Chicagoans believed that the New Critics seriously misunderstood the role of language in literature and that this misunderstanding led to an impoverished practice of interpretation.[2] For the New Critics literature was a special form of language, a distinct arena of discourse in which authors exploited language's potential for conveying connotation, ambiguity, and irony. This conception of literature allowed the New Critics to argue that it gave access to truths and meanings that were distinct from—and as valuable as—the truths and meanings offered by science and its commitment to denotative and univocal uses of language. Since literature is a special kind of language and language's function is to communicate meaning, then interpretation is the task of identifying such meanings or themes. Furthermore, since literature's distinctive capacity is to show ambiguity or meanings in some kind of tension, then interpretation should

2. See the attacks on Empson and Brooks in *Critics and Criticism* by Olson and Crane respectively. See also William Wimsatt's critique of the Chicago School in *The Verbal Icon.* For a longer analysis of Olson on Empson, see my discussion in *Worlds from Words.*

focus on binary themes (or sets of binary themes) (e.g., human vs. animal; nature vs. culture; freedom vs. constraint) and show how these pairs play off one another.

The Chicagoans argued that the New Critics' conception of literature mistook its means or material cause (language) for its end or final cause (the representation of human actions in an artistic form designed to affect an audience in a particular way) and that this mistake meant that they could at best give only a partial account of the formal power of any work. In more specific terms, the Chicagoans saw the fundamental mistake as leading to two related problems with the New Critics' interpretive method. (1) The commitment to binary themes means that just about every element of a work has to be grouped under one theme or the other and that requirement means that the themes have to be general enough to accommodate just about any element. (2) Consequently, a wide range of possible themes could be made to fit (in this very loose fashion) any work, which is another way of saying that the interpretations sacrifice precision and nuance for coherence and comprehensiveness.[3] The Chicagoans suggest the alternative practice of focusing interpretation on the synthesis of events, characters, and techniques in the service of producing a particular emotional or intellectual effect. Indeed, the neo-Aristotelians were so dissatisfied with basing interpretation on binary themes that they developed a distinction between mimetic and didactic works, that is, works designed primarily to affect an audience's emotions and works designed primarily to affect an audience's beliefs or thoughts about the world. Mimetic works could have themes; but rather than being central to those works and thus a key to interpretation, they were subordinate to what those works were doing with the representation of characters and events. That is, the function of themes (or elements of thought) in mimetic works is to enhance our understanding of characters, their choices, and their situations and, thus, enhance the emotional power of these elements. To put the point most polemically, for the neo-Aristotelians, themes were just the inevitable side effects of the author's effort to move his or her audience in a particular way.

Together the neo-Aristotelian attack on the New Critics' view of the relation between language and literature and the mimetic-didactic distinction provide a clear window on a sometimes productive but at other times troubling friction in the Chicagoans' work. This friction arises from their

---

3. Among several fine discussions of the limitations of thematizing, see especially W. R. Keast, "The New Criticism and King Lear" in *Critics and Criticism* and Richard Levin, *New Readings v. Old Plays*. I discuss what I regard as the limitations of Levin's position and the mimetic-didactic distinction more generally in Chapter 1 of *Reading People, Reading Plots*.

relation to the *Poetics*. On the one hand, Crane, Olson, and the others were acutely aware that Aristotle's treatise was inevitably tied to Greek epic and drama and that critical dicta derived from that corpus would not necessarily fit the literature produced under different cultural circumstances. When teaching Aristotle, Crane typically posed the following question: "How would the *Poetics* be different if it were based on Shakespeare's tragedies rather than Sophocles'?"[4] This line of thinking led to a reading of the *Poetics* that emphasized what the Chicagoans regarded as its inductive or a posteriori method. Although Aristotle is hardly shy about offering unqualified pronouncements on his subject (e.g., the hierarchy among the parts of tragedy, the best kind of tragic plot, the superiority of probable impossibilities to possible improbabilities), his frequent references to "what works on the stage" signal that he bases these conclusions on his experience in the theater. Indeed, in this view, Aristotle's definition of tragedy and most of his other dicta arise from his effort to reason back from the effects of tragic drama on its audience to the causes of those effects in the drama itself. This line of thinking ends in the conclusion that Aristotle's a posteriori method of reasoning from effects to causes is far more important than any of his specific positions.

On the other hand, as the attack on the New Critics shows, the Chicagoans took some of Aristotle's conclusions as incontrovertible truths, and they were not themselves at all averse to formulating unqualified across-the-board pronouncements. The case against the New Critics ultimately rests on their conviction that what Aristotle said about where diction ranks among the parts of tragedy (below plot, character, and thought) is true not just for Greek tragedy but for literature in general. No doubt their rivalry with the New Critics encouraged them to harden their position. Faced with what they regarded as an impoverished critical theory that was nevertheless in the ascendancy, they would naturally focus on what was lacking in that approach rather than testing Aristotle's conclusion according to the a posteriori principle. If they had tested it, they would not have had to abandon it, but they would have had to modify it. Working in an a posteriori manner from a broad survey of texts, they would conclude that language can be both a means and an end in a given work, and, more generally, that language's importance relative to other elements can vary from one work to the next.[5]

4. Booth's essay on *Macbeth*, now available in *The Essential Wayne Booth*, is one answer to this question. Crane built on Booth's analysis in his discussion of *Macbeth* in *The Languages of Criticism and the Structure of Poetry*.

5. For a detailed working out of this argument, including a critique of Elder Olson's attack on William Empson, see my *Worlds from Words*.

The mimetic-didactic distinction reflects this friction in the first gen-eration's relation to Aristotle in the following way. On the one hand, the distinction depends on the recognition that the main effect of many works is on our intellects rather than our emotions, that, in other words, what Aristotle called "thought" is in many works more important than plot or character. Reasoning back from these main effects, we can recognize that both the overall structuring principles of such works and the rela-tions among their parts are significantly different from what we find in tragedy and other mimetic genres. In addition, within the large category of didactic works, other worthwhile distinctions of kind can be made: a satire is different from an allegory is different from a didactic poem. On the other hand, the tendency to prefer fixed truths that then function as a priori principles is evident in the sharp binary of the distinction and in the concomitant fierce objections to thematic interpretations of what the first generation regarded as mimetic works.

Furthermore, the distinction, like the friction that underlies it, is both productive and troubling. The distinction's sharp, synoptic view of the broad literary landscape also characterizes much neo-Aristotelian work on smaller portions of it, including both genres and analyses of individual works. Here are just three of many possible examples of the productive side of the distinction and the friction. Crane's essay on "The Concept of Plot and the Plot of *Tom Jones*" lays out not only a neo-Aristotelian idea of plot but also a sketch of comic plots and a detailed account of the workings and effects of Fielding's plot. Sacks's first chapter in *Fiction and the Shape of Belief* develops an account of two kinds of didactic novels (satires and apologues) and three kinds of mimetic novels (tragedies, comedies, and serious actions), with illuminating commentary on a range of examples; Rader's article on "The Dramatic Monologue and Related Lyric Forms" offers productive distinctions among the dramatic monologue, the mask lyric, and the dramatic lyric and first-rate analyses of Browning's "My Last Duchess," Tennyson's "Ulysses," and Hopkins's "The Windhover."

Nevertheless, the neo-Aristotelians sometimes pay a price in the cur-rency of oversimplification for the stark clarity of their vision. They make both individual works and generic categories neater than they actually are. Sacks's reading of the mini-narrative in Chapters 1–3 of *Persuasion* is one example of this problem. He offers a sharp reading of these chapters as a miniature punitive comedy (with Sir Walter as protagonist) because that fits with his equally sharp synoptic view of the novel as a comedy of fulfillment (with Anne as protagonist), a genre that depends on assuring its audience very early on that the heroine will achieve an ultimately happy fate. The trouble is, as I've tried to suggest, that some salient details of Chapters 1–3 prove strongly recalcitrant to the hypothesis that Austen is designing them as a punitive comedy.

More generally, I have already suggested the oversimplification in the neo-Aristotelian view of the relation between language and literature. Something similar happens with the mimetic-didactic distinction. While the insight that some works are built primarily on mimetic principles and others are built primarily on didactic ones is sound, there is no necessary reason to postulate that all works clearly fall on one side of this divide or the other. Furthermore, the distinction itself, particularly if one is strongly invested in it, may obscure one's vision of how significant the thematic component can be in a primarily mimetic work and how significant the mimetic component can be in primarily didactic work.[6]

This reading of the first and second generation leads me to the following principles.

1.  The a posteriori principle should be the foundation of a rhetorical poetics and should therefore always trump any competing principles. Reasoning back from effects to causes grounds the approach in a respect for the concrete details of its objects.

2.  This commitment in turn leads to the recognition of the feedback loop among readerly response (effects), textual phenomena (their causes), and authorial agency (the causes of the textual causes). Working to discover the textual causes of effects often leads one to refine one's understanding of those effects and that, in turn, leads one to refine one's understanding of and relation

6. To their credit Sacks, Rader, and Booth were all working on this insight, albeit in very different ways. For Rader this work grew out of his effort to link the idea of transhistorical form with particular historical and cultural pressures on the execution of the form. See "From Richardson to Austen." In Booth's case, it is striking that he begins the Preface to the first edition of The Rhetoric of Fiction by locating his book as on one side of the mimetic-didactic divide: "In writing about the rhetoric of fiction, I am not primarily interested in didactic fiction, fiction used for propaganda or instruction" (xiii). By 1983, however, when he was writing the Afterword to the second edition, he had completed his shift from the primarily poetic concerns of his teacher Crane to the primarily rhetorical concerns of the rest of his career, and that shift meant he was far less invested in the distinction and more open to the interrelations of the mimetic and didactic. Thus, he notes in the Afterword that he need not have ruled out so-called didactic works. Sacks did not publish anything on the interrelation between the mimetic and the didactic, but I know from sitting in his seminar that he was very interested in it—though he was not yet willing to give up the distinction. David H. Richter's *Fable's End: Completeness and Closure in Rhetorical Fiction,* which began as a dissertation written under Sacks's direction, takes up the issue of how authors can use our mimetic interests in characters in the service of didactic ends.

to the implied author. And then the whole process can begin again.

3.  At the same time, the commitment to a posteriori analysis does not mean that all generalizations are suspect and all works sui generis. Instead, it means that one can both emulate and resist the impulse toward the sharp synoptic views of both individual works and genres achieved by Crane, Olson, Sacks, and Rader. The emulation involves retaining a prominent place for purpose in a rhetorical definition of narrative (somebody telling somebody else on some occasion and some purpose[s] that something happened) and in the work of practical criticism. The concept of purpose is what authorizes the analysis of means in relation to ends, and it is what allows us to recognize the principles underlying a given progression. But the resistance comes, as noted above, from a broader conception of purpose, one rooted in the interrelations of form, ethics, and aesthetics and often not easily reducible to a synoptic view of a single end. At the same time, the a posteriori principle means that the rhetorical critic is as open to the incoherencies and other formal imperfections of a work as she is to its coherence and formal achievements. To put the point another way, sometimes works are built on multiple purposes that turn out to be incompatible, and sometimes the means chosen to advance the progression can be ineffective. Needless to say, fictions with muddled progressions or unsatisfactory means generally do not receive a lot of attention from literary critics (though in some cases incompatible purposes can generate increased critical interest; Oliver Goldsmith's *The Vicar of Wakefield* and Mark Twain's *Adventures of Huckleberry Finn* are just two of many possible examples of this phenomenon).

4.  Most important to my mind, commitment to the a posteriori principle means that rhetorical poetics, however richly stocked with terms and concepts, has a minimal interest in prediction. So far I have been working with twelve aspects of progression, five kinds of audience, three kinds of judgment, three components of character and of readerly interest, three kinds of rhetorical ethics, and two kinds of dynamics in narrative progression. In *Living to Tell about It,* I introduce, among other things, six types of unreliable narration, distinctions among unreliable, restricted, and suppressed narration as well as a dis-

tinction between disclosure functions and narrator functions. All these conceptual tools are designed to be substantial enough to do productive work across a great expanse of narrative variety and flexible enough to be responsive to the distinctive qualities of individual narratives. They are not meant to determine the boundaries within which authors must work or to predict what readers will inevitably find as they experience new narratives. The test of their utility, then, is not whether they apply to every real or conceivable narrative but whether they help us achieve an understanding of the experiences offered by a good range of existing ones. The consequence of this position is that rhetorical poetics is always under construction, subject to revision through its interaction with both old and new narratives and with other developments in narrative theory. Rather than requiring our experiences with texts to squeeze into the spaces already carved out by our conceptual tools, we adjust those tools or invent new ones to account for those experiences.

The battle between the neo-Aristotelians and the New Critics—and especially its outcome—is also relevant to two other issues relevant to the task of situating rhetorical poetics in the critical landscape: (1) the relation of rhetorical poetics to what I call cultural thematics, the currently widespread interpretive practice of reading literary works as participating in dialogues with other cultural discourses; and (2) the existing critical vocabulary for talking about the affective and ethical dimensions of literary experience. Again it will be helpful to recount a selective but plausible (and indeed, fairly standard) narrative of a period in our critical history. Although the New Criticism successfully withstood the attacks from the shores of Lake Michigan in the 1950s, its dominance began to fade in the late 1960s. Indeed, by 1980, the New Criticism had become a favorite whipping boy for theorists of many different stripes. Like any shift in intellectual paradigms, this one had many causes, but prominent among them was a growing conviction that New Critical doctrines mistakenly cordoned literature off from the rest of culture, treating it as an autonomous realm concerned with the production of complex verbal meanings when its connections with other cultural arenas, especially politics, were both undeniable and significant. This conviction, initially expressed and developed in different ways by feminists, New Historicists, postcolonialists, racial and ethnic critics, and others eventually led to the emergence of the larger interpretive practice we know as cultural studies. Its chief principles are fundamentally anti-New Critical: literature, rather than being a realm apart from the rest of culture, is deeply interwoven with it, both influenced by and influencing it. The task of literary criticism, then, is to explore the intersection of literature with one or more other elements of culture (politics, technology, law, science, business, other arts, etc.), and the tools for that exploration can be borrowed from any discipline (sociology, psychology, economics, accounting, legal studies, and so on), including the theory associated with that discipline.[7]

Despite its sharp break with the New Criticism's assumption about the autonomy of literature, much work in cultural studies continues the New Critical practice of generating thematic interpretations. I hasten to add that I am not claiming that this work is the New Criticism gussied up in the style of today's hottest buzzwords from social and cultural theory: its healthy interdisciplinarity guarantees the difference. But I do want to suggest that the interpretive practice of cultural thematics often works by (a) identifying a small number of thematic concepts, often derived from a source other than the literary text, and (b) using those concepts to analyze that text and to make connections between the literary and the cultural realms. There are two reasons why this phenomenon is less surprising than it may at first appear. The first I have just expressed in other terms: the abstractions that are the stock-in-trade of thematizing uncover the necessary common ground to connect the discourses of literature with those of culture. For example, if I want to investigate the relation between *Beloved* and 1980s political discourse about civil rights in the United States, I can choose my terms from either sphere provided that they are general enough to cover significant quantities of data from the novel and from the political discourse. The second reason that the methodology of cultural thematics is not surprising is the hegemony of the New Criticism itself. After years of New Critical practice, thematizing evolved from one way to do interpretation into a virtual synonym for interpretation itself.[8]

In light of this continuity between the New Criticism and cultural studies and in light of the influence of the neo-Aristotelians on rhetorical poetics, what is the relation between cultural thematics and rhetorical poetics? In one respect, they are simply friendly neighbors, both engaged in worthwhile work but pursuing different kinds of knowledge. Because cultural studies has so much to do in its explorations of the interconnec-

---

7. Of course much work cultural studies, even in literature departments, takes up issues that have little or nothing to do with literature and literary interpretation. My comments about cultural thematics do not apply to this work.

8. For a fascinating analysis of some negative consequences of this phenomenon, see Rabinowitz's "Lolita: Solipsized or Sodomized?; or Against Abstraction in General."

tions of literature and culture, it does not concern itself with the experience of reading. Consequently, I see no reason to complain that cultural thematics often neglects one or more of the affective, the ethical, or the aesthetic dimensions of texts. Similarly, because rhetorical poetics has so much to do in its efforts to understand the varieties of literary experience, it does not give substantial attention to cultural thematics. Thus, judging rhetorical poetics according to what its analyses yield about the intersection of literature and culture is to judge it by criteria it does not try to meet.

Nevertheless, because rhetorical poetics shares cultural studies' rejection of the assumption that literature exists in an autonomous realm and because rhetorical poetics regards the thematic as one component of textual dynamics and readerly interest, cultural thematics and rhetorical poetics can sometimes converge. But the outcomes of this convergence can vary across a wide spectrum. Sometimes the convergence provides mutual reinforcement as when the terms and concepts of each mode help the other see the same textual phenomena more clearly. Sometimes the convergence produces complementary results, as when cultural thematics highlights the importance of a particular feature of a work's thematic component that rhetorical poetics may have neglected and rhetorical poetics illuminates the work's dynamics in way that sharpens the cultural thematic analysis. Sometimes the two modes will lead to conflicting views of the work, and then it becomes a matter of assessing the power of each one's claims. In cases when someone working in the mode of rhetorical poetics finds fault with cultural thematics, he typically will, like the earlier neo-Aristotelians, point to the problems with thematizing. But here the objection will often be to the execution of the method and some of its risks rather than to fatal flaws in the method itself. One common problem in execution is the identification of themes, usually derived from another discipline or another cultural discourse, that do not correspond very closely to the concerns raised by the textual and readerly dynamics. By the same token, rhetorical poetics is subject to its own set of problems in execution. The most common of these is a tunnel vision about the details of the text's language and techniques, a vision that occludes attention to the text's implicit dialogues with other cultural discourses.

To illustrate these points, I return to my argument in chapter 1 that in *Persuasion* Austen does not successfully integrate Anne Elliot's visits to Mrs. Smith into the overall progression and attempt to counter it by way of an analysis based in cultural thematics. By the time Austen is writing *Persuasion,* the rigid class structure of British society is beginning to break down, and she includes signs of that breakdown in her narrative. Among

other changes, men can gain wealth and consequence not just by inheri-
tance, but, as Wentworth does, by their own efforts. We can find evidence
of Austen's at least partial approval of the change not only in her choice
of Wentworth as the partner for her protagonist but also in the Mrs. Smith
episodes. Mrs. Smith's information about William Elliot, Sir Walter's "heir
presumptive" and thus a member of the next generation of landed gentry,
itself points toward the decline of the old order. Austen's decision to juxtapose William and Wentworth as potential husbands for Anne and to show
the clear superiority of the naval commander over the knight-to-be allows
her to use the novel to express a stance in favor of the new order. This
account also has the advantage of explaining why Austen doesn't have
Anne more in danger of falling in love with William—she is less interested
in him as a potential obstacle to the reuniting of her lovers than she is in
him as a device for her thematic point. Similarly, Austen needs Mrs. Smith
to get the information about William's past into the novel as efficiently
as possible, and her decision to make Anne the focal character limits her
options. Using Mrs. Smith allows Austen not only to disclose the information but to underline Anne's kindness in visiting her invalid friend and to
buttress another of her thematic points, namely, that unselfishness often
brings unexpected rewards.

From the perspective of rhetorical poetics, this account of Mrs. Smith's
role in the cultural thematics about the changing social order adds something useful to our understanding of Austen's narrative, especially in
what it suggests about the pairing of William and Wentworth as potential
mates for Anne. But a problem remains: the account does not address the
objections I noted in chapter 1, namely, that the disclosures about William
Elliot are contrived, that they put Anne in an ethically problematic chain
of gossip, and that the disclosures are not well integrated into the main
line of the progression, since Anne was not in danger of marrying William.
In this way, Austen's implicit thematic commentary on the changing social
order comes at the expense of other ethical and affective issues that her
progression has defined as more central to her narrative project. My point,
in other words, is not that the results of the cultural thematic analysis are
off-base, but that they do not solve the problem the rhetorical analysis
points to. Furthermore, although one can see why Austen chose to use Mrs.
Smith for the disclosure, one can also recognize that Austen could have
found other means for it, means that would not have interfered with the
affective and ethical dynamics in the way that her choice does.

Since this analysis is intended to be illustrative, I want to round it off
by acknowledging that I get nervous when I find fault with Austen and

that I can well imagine a reader of this book (or one of my future students) convincing me that I have misread Mrs. Smith's role. But even if that happens, I want to hang on to my general point here. One of the important practical consequences of rhetorical poetics is that, while it is committed to the importance of the thematic component of narrative, it does not assume that thematizing is at the center of the interpretive enterprise; rather it wants to place the thematic component of narrative experience alongside the affective, the ethical, and the aesthetic.[9] Consequently, the relation between rhetorical poetics and cultural thematics is not one of direct rivalry or perfect complementarity. Instead it is one that can range across the broad spectrum between those poles.

As I noted above, because the New Criticism emerged with no major damage from the attacks by the Chicago critics (in effect, the New Critics remained broadcasting on a national network while the Chicagoans continued on a cable channel with a narrower distribution), the practice of interpretation never took the turn away from thematizing that the Chicagoans so strongly recommended. Instead, thematizing became even more firmly entrenched as the literary interpreter's stock-in-trade. This outcome has another important consequence for rhetorical poetics. At the present time, we have a far richer inventory of ways for talking about the thematic meanings of narratives than we do for talking about the affective and ethical dimensions of them, especially in relation to readerly dynamics. We can of course draw on the fairly extensive vocabularies we have for talking about emotions and for talking about values, and when we are referring to the emotions and values of characters, these vocabularies serve us well. But when we want to talk about the affective and ethical dimensions of our audience response, we end up relying on a convenient shorthand, or perhaps better, a set of preliminary and partial descriptions that, while generally serviceable, does not adequately capture the complexities and nuances of these elements of our experience.

With regard to the affective dimension of response, I have been using a vocabulary, derived in part from the first- and second-generation neo-Aristotelians, that refers to the consequences of our judgments and of our immersion in progression. Among these terms are *sympathy, desire, hope, disappointment, sorrow, happiness, expectation, anticipation, suspense, frustration,* and *satisfaction.* Another set of terms straddles the border between the affective and the cognitive realms of our response:

9. Two valuable studies that are different from mine and from each other but that also share this interest in attending more to the affective than to the thematic are Charles Altieri's *The Particulars of Rapture* and Robyn Warhol's *Having a Good Cry.*

*uncertainty, puzzlement, understanding* are a representative sample. I call these sets of terms preliminary and partial for two reasons. The first is that they are insufficiently precise—they do not allow us to discriminate as finely as we would like to among our affective responses. For example, we can say the wife in "The Crimson Candle," Anne Elliot, and Sethe are all characters for whom we feel sympathy, but there are significant differences in our affective response to each that are lost if we stop there. We can of course refine our descriptions both by adding adjectives ("partial," "deep," "unusual") and by showing how they connect with other elements of our affective response, but these measures will not always close the gap between our affective experience and our account of it. To some extent, this gap is an inevitable consequence of interpretation itself, since interpretation involves the movement from the particular and the concrete to the more general and the abstract. But since rhetorical interpretation wants to tighten the connection between experience and interpretation, it also would like to decrease that gap.

The second reason that the terms are only partial is that they do not cover a wide enough range of affective response. When we make a negative ethical judgment of a character such as William Elliot, what is the affective consequence? Terms such as *antipathy* and *hostility* seem too strong. *Distrust* is better but it runs the risk of erasing the synthetic component of his character. Distrusting him is different from distrusting a new acquaintance since we know that his fate is fixed even if we do not know how. So perhaps we need a new term or a new phrase such as "our negative judgment of William Elliot *generates misgivings* about him." But of course our affective response to William Elliot is much more straightforward than, say, the response we have to Paul D after Sethe shares her narrative of what she did in the woodshed the day Schoolteacher tracked her down at 124 Bluestone Rd. My point is not that we cannot do a serviceable job of describing that more layered affective response but that there is considerable room for improvement. I see improving this vocabulary as one of the important future tasks in the rhetorical theory of narrative.

The example of *distrust* as a possible candidate for describing our response to William Elliot points to one of the larger issues involved in this task, specifically the relation between the range of emotions characters can feel (the same as the range any of us can feel) and the range that readers feel in relation to those characters. Do we ever feel "distrust" toward characters, given that their fates are fixed and they must act as they have been written to act? On the other hand, our sympathy for Anne Elliot, whose fate is equally fixed, is not qualitatively different from the sympathy we feel for our good friends. Furthermore, are there some emotions that are generally outside the range of what we feel toward fictional characters? Jealousy? Cynicism?

With ethics, the emphasis on judgment and progression leads us to a vocabulary about consequences for our understanding of characters and about our relations with authors. The vocabulary for talking about relations between authors and audiences is not itself a problem, since it involves a relationship between human beings and (in the case of the implied author and authorial audience) projections of human beings. But when we try to describe the consequences of the way the text mediates that relationship, we again come up against some limits of our customary ways of talking. Common terms here are *trust, respect, freedom, reciprocity, responsibility,* but precisely because these terms can be applied to so many different kinds of textual mediations, we need to remain aware that they too are shorthands. And we also want to remain open to the relevance of other ethical categories to the author-reader relation. Such openness is one consequence of doing ethics from the inside out.

The limits of our preliminary terms for ethical responses are more evident when we consider negative ethical judgments of characters. As a consequence of such judgments, we see, in the language of our preliminary terms, the characters as "ethically flawed" or "ethically deficient." The trouble with this formulation is that it too readily becomes a blunt instrument rather than a sharp tool, one that lends itself to summary judgments of characters and, indeed, to lumping different characters together. We make "negative ethical judgments" of the husband in "The Crimson Candle," Elizabeth Elliot in *Persuasion,* and Schoolteacher in *Beloved,* but our actual assessments of each are much more refined and nuanced, and we internally register very significant differences in the nature of each character's ethical failings. Although we can overcome some of the limits of the shorthand by more extensive descriptions of those failings (Schoolteacher's smug racism, the husband's demanding egocentrism, Elizabeth's self-absorbed vanity), there nevertheless remains an appreciable and perhaps insuperable gap between our ethical experience and our ways of talking about it.

At least since Martha Nussbaum advanced her case in *Love's Knowledge* for fictional narrative as an alternative to analytic philosophy's inquiries into ethics, theorists of literary ethics have stressed narrative's ability to explore the ethical dimensions of human behavior through the concrete particulars of characters in action. Fiction's advantage, in other words, is that it can get beyond the abstract meanings and black-and-white implications of ethical categories to the complexities and nuances of ethical choices within the detailed contexts of human lives. In short, the very nature of fiction's ability to offer a significant ethical dimension to our reading experience also makes the task of adequately accounting for that dimension an especially challenging one. Again, I regard finding better ways to meet this challenge an important future task in the rhetorical theory of narrative—even if the gap between our reading experience and our critical language can never be fully closed.

# CHAPTER FOUR

# Progressing toward Surprise

## Edith Wharton's "Roman Fever"

Edith Wharton's "Roman Fever" is a story whose rhetorical effectiveness depends in large part on its surprise ending, Grace Ansley's revelation to her antagonist Alida Slade that the father of Grace's brilliant daughter Barbara was not her own husband but Alida's. Surprise endings provide strong evidence of the interrelation of ethical and aesthetic judgments, as a quick look at the classic example of the ineffective surprise will show. A story that puts the protagonist in peril and then ends with the sudden and unprepared-for revelation that the protagonist has been dreaming is ethically and aesthetically flawed. Such a story is ethically flawed because its implied author asks the audience to invest themselves in the protagonist's actions while knowing all along that those actions are merely illusions even within the world of the fiction. Such a story is aesthetically flawed because the sudden revelation requires the audience radically to reconfigure their understanding of the story for no benefit other than the surprise itself. In short, such a story is built on the aesthetics of the cheap trick.

This negative example leads me to postulate that for a surprise ending to be ethically and aesthetically appropriate at least two conditions should be met: (1) the author includes material in the progression that can retrospectively be understood as preparing the audience for the surprise; or to put this point another way, the audience can recognize that the necessary reconfiguration caused by the surprise actually fits well with the beginning and the middle of the progression; and (2) the audience's emotional and other investments in the characters are rewarded—deepened, used in the service of meaningful instruction, or otherwise enhanced—rather than undermined by the surprise.

My question about the ethics and aesthetics of surprise in "Roman Fever" stems from the observation that Wharton's narrator begins the telling with full knowledge about the characters' secrets, but Wharton restricts the narration so that this knowledge is only alluded to but not disclosed to any audience until the characters reveal it in the climactic moments of the story. From this perspective, Wharton has clearly and carefully manipulated the audience through her tight control of the disclosure. What are the ethics and aesthetics of this control? Or to put the issue in more general terms, I am interested in two main questions that emphasize the relation among technique, ethics, and aesthetics: (1) How does Wharton shape our overall response to the characters and their situations from beginning to end? (2) What are the ethics and aesthetics of that shaping, especially of the delayed disclosure that produces the surprise ending? Wharton's story is also worthy of attention in this study of judgments and progression because she chooses to work with character-character relations that, abstracted from her specific treatment of them, are at best ethically ambiguous. Indeed, without considering Wharton's specific shaping of our responses, we might regard both protagonists as seriously deficient: as a young woman, Grace knew that Alida was engaged to Delphin Slade but pursued him anyway; Alida forged a letter from Delphin in order to lure Grace into a nonexistent nighttime rendezvous with him in the Colosseum in the hope that Grace would contract an illness. In the narrative present, the main action is the contest between Alida and Grace that arises in their conversation. In this narrative present, Alida seeks to injure Grace and establish her own power over Grace by telling her about the forgery. Grace retaliates by telling Alida that Delphin fathered her child, a daughter whom Alida regards as superior to her own. I shall argue, however, that as Wharton constructs her narrative out of this material, she guides her audience to different and determinate ethical judgments of each character. Indeed, as I noted in the Introduction, Wharton's initial exposition emphasizes the apparent similarity of the two women, but, as the narrative progresses, this similarity gives way to a revelation of significant differences between them, differences that are closely connected to our interpretive and ethical judgments of them.

In one respect, Wharton and her narrator have a relation to their audiences similar to the relation Grace Ansley and Alida Slade have with each other: they know something that their audiences do not and they save the revelation of that knowledge until the right moment. However, Wharton and her characters have significantly different motivations for their revelations. Wharton's motivation is to conclude her narrative as effectively as possible (though just exactly what this means must wait for further analysis), while Alida's and Grace's motivations—well, their motivations merit extended discussion, but for now suffice it to say that Alida wants to triumph over Grace and Grace wants to counter Alida's claim that Grace had nothing from Delphin "but that one letter he didn't write" (20). The differences in Wharton's motivation and in her characters' point to the importance of the relation between two different ethical situations: that between the characters and that between Wharton and her audience. More specifically, Wharton's relation to her audience includes the issue of how she treats the ethical dimensions of the Alida-Grace interaction. But before we can do justice to Wharton's relation to her audience—and its consequences for our aesthetic judgment of the story—we need to look more closely at the overall progression of the narrative and at how we're invited to configure it both before and after the ending.

Because Wharton shows us, as the narrative develops, that the moves in the conversation between Grace and Alida are related to the history of the women's relationship, we configure our understanding of the events occurring on two different temporal planes—that of the present action and that of twenty-five years ago—but ultimately our configuration involves the relationship between the two sets of events. The story, in effect, shows the lingering effects of the past on the present. More specifically, as the tensions surrounding the events of twenty-five years ago slowly get resolved, we also recognize that both Alida's and Grace's knowledge of those events has been partial. Indeed, in keeping with the double dynamics of progression, the ending is a surprise for both Alida and the authorial audience just as, during the voyage, the revelation that Alida forged the letter from Delphin that brought Grace to the Colosseum is a surprise for both Grace and the authorial audience. The progression is complete only at the moment when everyone's knowledge—Alida's, Grace's, and the authorial audience's—is equal, and that moment occurs only with Grace's final line, "I had Barbara" (20). Nevertheless, the same knowledge leads to different reconfigurations of both past and present for Grace, Alida, and the authorial audience. In other words, Wharton's major technique for maintaining the element of surprise is to control the disclosure of information so that we remain actively involved in configuring the events of both the present and the past right until the very end of the narrative when the surprise revelation requires us to undertake a substantial reconfiguration, one that encompasses the different necessary reconfigurations of Alida and Grace. To substantiate this point, I turn now to analyze some of the specific details of the progression in a way that builds on the sketch of the progression I have offered in the Introduction.

Part I of "Roman Fever" constitutes its beginning, because our entrance isn't complete until the last sentences of Part I. The somewhat leisurely exposition in Part I, which locates the two American women in their Roman setting and sets the stage for the quicker pace and multiple twists of Part II, is divided between the narrator in her comments on the present and the characters in their references to the past. As noted in the Introduction, the narrator's formal, distant treatment of the characters is a significant part of our initiation into the story. Here we can go further into the kind of readerly dynamics the initiation generates by looking more closely at a typical passage. After Alida comments that she and Grace might just as well stay on the terrace, as their daughters fly off to Tarquinia with some eligible Italian bachelors, because "after all, it's still the most beautiful view in the world," the narrator gives Grace's reply, "It always will be, to me" (4) and comments that she assented "with so slight a stress on the 'me' that Mrs. Slade, though she noticed it, wondered if it were not merely accidental, like the random underlinings of old-fashioned letter-writers" (4).

Even as the narrator keeps her distance from the characters (she always refers to them as "Mrs. Slade" and "Mrs. Ansley"), Wharton invites our closer collaboration with her by restricting how much the narrator discloses at any one point and inviting us to read beyond that restricted narration.[1] In this case, the narrator notes the stress that Grace puts on the word "me," but rather than having the narrator disclose the reason for that stress, Wharton maintains the tension about its significance by shifting to Alida's focalization. That move, furthermore, invites us to infer the unstable situation between the two women. The shift to Alida's focalization shows not only that she is as in the dark about the reason for Grace's intonation as Wharton's audience but also that Alida's particular way of being in the dark is one that does not give Grace much credit. Rather than thinking that Grace has had some experience with the view that makes it special to her, Alida wonders whether Grace's stress on "me" is "merely accidental," "random," and a sign of her being, as Alida says explicitly in her next judgment of Grace, "old-fashioned" (5).[2] In other words, Alida assumes

---

1. For more on the technique of restricted narration see chapter 2 of *Living to Tell about It*.

2. Sweeney points out that Alida's metaphor of the old-fashioned letter is itself not accidental but rather a result of her association between Grace and the letter Alida wrote twenty-five years ago. Petry offers an insightful close reading of Grace's knitting during her conversation with Alida.

that she is superior to Grace, that she has good reasons for condescending to her. Wharton neither endorses nor fully undercuts Alida's interpretive judgment at this point, but she does expect her audience to register both her ways of communicating and the instability being communicated. In addition, she invites us to make a negative ethical judgment of Alida's condescension and, as a result, to cast some doubt on her interpretive judgment (condescension goeth before an underestimation) without yet giving us firm evidence that the judgment is mistaken.

The next significant moves of the progression involve the narrator's revelation of a paradox, which adds a tension and points to further instabilities underlying the two women's conversation, and the disclosure of their mutual assessments. The narrator remarks that "the two ladies, who had been intimate since childhood, reflected how little they knew each other" (6). The paradox of course is the combination of intimacy and ignorance, and the tension involves the explanation for that paradox—and more generally, a question about the precise nature of their relationship. In turning to their judgments of each other, the narrator develops Alida's sense of superiority at some length as she interweaves exposition with instability. Alida regards Grace as a charming young woman who had grown up to be a respectable "nullit[y]" (6), a good match for her respectable nullity of a husband, Horace. Alida judges her own marriage as having been a great success, since her husband Delphin had been a brilliant man with a brilliant career and her presence at his side had won both of them much praise. Currently, however, she is feeling superfluous; her daughter Jenny, "an extremely pretty girl who made youth and prettiness seem as safe as their absence" (8), takes care of her rather than the other way around.

For her part, Grace paints a "slighter" mental portrait of Alida, one with "fainter touches." Grace regards Alida as "awfully brilliant; but not as brilliant as she thinks" (8), and Grace believes that "on the whole [Alida] had had a sad life. Full of failures and mistakes" (9); indeed, Grace "had always been rather sorry for her" (9). Grace's attitude adds another tension to the developing progression: what does she know about Alida that we need to learn; why should she be sorry for Alida? As noted in the Introduction, this completed revelation of the mutual feelings of superiority constitutes the launch: the major instability has now been revealed. The most telling comment of all, because it delivers a direct judgment of the women's interpretive judgments, is the narrator's statement at the end of Part I, a statement that also completes our entrance. "So these two ladies visualized each other, each through the wrong end of her little telescope" (9).

By juxtaposing the characters' mutual assessments and then following them with the narrator's comment, Wharton uses the launch and entrance to underline similarities and differences between the women. Each judges herself superior to the other, but the affect associated with that judgment is different for each. Alida's judgments of her superiority are marked by her condescension, whereas Grace's judgments of Alida carry a certain sympathy. The narrator's metaphor of looking through the wrong end of a telescope guides us not to take either character's interpretive judgments about the other as wholly trustworthy, but at the point of entrance we have stronger reason to suspect Alida's judgments of Grace. Wharton has shown that the values by which Alida judges Grace and, indeed, her own life are superficial: Alida, in effect, applies a scale of "brilliance" to Grace and finds her wanting; she cares less about how much she, Delphin, and Jenny loved and cared for each other than about how well she looked in the eyes of Delphin's business associates and how Jenny's virtue has left little for her to do. We have seen Grace far less clearly, but we know both that there is more to her than Alida thinks and that her own view of Alida is deficient in some way. More generally, Wharton has positioned us in a complex relation to Alida because the narrator's general reticence keeps our knowledge about the past so limited that we must rely, however provisionally, on what we learn through Alida's perceptions as the focal character. We move forward into the voyage, then, caught up in the tensions and instabilities, aware of the women's inadequate interpretive judgments, ethically judging Alida negatively, withholding ethical judgment about Grace, and depending on the narrator's descriptions, the characters' dialogue, and Alida's focalization for the disclosures that will lead to a resolution of the tensions and instabilities.

In Part II, the dynamics of the conversation during the voyage follow a clear pattern: Alida becomes the aggressor against Grace, and Grace is initially reluctant to be drawn in to Alida's competition but eventually replies with disclosures that she knows will hurt Alida. Alida first goes on the offensive by, in effect, politely insulting Grace. After admitting to Grace that her own daughter Jenny will have no chance against Barbara in any competition for the Marchese with whom they have flown to Tarquinia,[3] Alida remarks: "I was wondering, ever so respectfully you understand . . . , wondering how two such exemplary characters as you and Horace had

---

3. I agree with Mortimer that Wharton does not encourage her audience to see the rivalry between Alida and Grace continued into the next generation. Such a rivalry does not fit with the portraits that we get of Jenny and Barbara, and Alida herself says that their daughters need not fear Rome or Roman fever.

managed to produce anything quite so dynamic" (11). Grace, however, does not rise to the bait, but "at length" simply says, "I think you overrate Babs, my dear" (12). Although Alida silently asks herself, "Would she never cure herself of envying [Grace]?," she can't stop baiting Grace, excusing herself with a thought that further heightens the tension about the past: "Perhaps she had begun too long ago" (13). Alida's behavior here even more clearly marks her as ethically deficient, and Grace's gentle responses lead us to judge her more positively and to sympathize with her.

As Alida pushes on to her revelation that she wrote the note that Grace thought was from Delphin, the first set of tensions about the past begins to get resolved. Our knowledge starts to catch up with Alida's—and so does Grace's. The immediate effect of this partial resolution of tension, however, is to complicate the instabilities of the conversation. Alida's revelation is, in effect, an attack on Grace, and it is one that initially succeeds in drawing blood. After Alida explains, "Well, my dear, I know what was in that letter because I wrote it" (16), Grace drops back into her chair, buries her face in her hand and cries. When she speaks again, a new tension gets introduced. In response to Alida's interpretation of Grace's tearful silence, "I horrify you," Grace starts to explain: "I wasn't thinking of you. I was thinking—" and Wharton uses the dash to indicate that Grace does not complete the thought but instead shifts to a new one: "it was the only letter I ever had from him!" (16). Alida presses the attack and begins to justify herself: "And I wrote it. Yes, I wrote it! But I was the girl he was engaged to. Did you happen to remember that?" Grace speaks truthfully: "I'm not trying to excuse myself. . . . I remembered . . ." and then underlines Alida's accusation "And still you went?" with another concession, "Still I went" (17).

Peter J. Rabinowitz's development of the concept of "path" (2005) sheds further light on the progression here. Rabinowitz defines path as a "character's order of experience," and he notes that this order may or may not correspond with the order of events in the fabula or in the sjuzhet. In this case, Alida of course experiences her writing of the note to Delphin at the same time that it occurred in the fabula, but Grace, in a sense, experiences this event twenty-five years later as the instabilities in the current conversation are getting complicated. In the audience, we experience the event at the same time as Grace; however, the event means very different things for Grace than it does for us. For us, it begins to resolve narrative tension even as it complicates the instabilities between Grace and Alida. For Grace, as we shall see, this event now links up with others that make her significantly revise her understanding of her previous path to the conversation.

These exchanges surrounding Alida's revelation deepen our existing emotional and ethical responses with one twist. Alida's attack heightens our awareness of her envy, hatred, and cruelty, while Grace's response has the character of an open admission of her transgression, one that she neither apologizes for nor defends. This admission does not change our sympathy for her, but it reminds us of the narrator's remark at the end of Part I that Alida's view of her is not reliable, and it underlines Grace's own remark that "The most prudent girls aren't always prudent" (15). Consequently, we need to remain open to further revelation of and further judgments about her character, even as we seek a resolution to the new tension about what Grace was really thinking. At the same time, Grace's pain at Alida's revelation shows Grace herself one of the ways in which she has misperceived Alida: she has not previously realized how effectively malicious Alida has been (in forging the letter) and still is (in telling her about it now).

Despite the success of Alida's attack, she remains jealous of Grace because she makes an interpretive judgment that Grace's strong response is a sign of how much Grace "must have loved [Delphin], to treasure the mere memory of [the letter's] ashes!" (18). But Alida goes on, making excuses for her revelation on the grounds that she

> had no reason to think you'd ever taken it seriously. How could I, when you were married to Horace Ansley two months afterward? As soon as you could get out of bed your mother rushed you off to Florence and married you. People were rather surprised—they wondered at its being done so quickly; but I thought I knew. I had an idea you did it out of pique—to be able to say you'd got ahead of Delphin and me . . . your marrying so soon convinced me that you'd never really cared. (18)

Again, Grace chooses not to escalate the current conflict and assents, though we are again invited to infer an edge to her remark that Alida would not catch, an edge reflecting a gap between what actually happened and Alida's understanding of it: "Yes. I suppose it would" (18).

At this juncture of the voyage, the progression has invited us to develop the following intermediate configuration: twenty-five years ago, Alida adopted the strategy of Grace's Great-aunt Harriet, who sent her younger sister, her rival for a man's love, on an errand to pick a night-blooming flower with the result that her sister contracted Roman fever (malaria) and died. Although Alida claims that she only wanted Grace "out of the way" for "just a few weeks" (17), we can infer that Alida's willingness to adopt Great-aunt Harriet's strategy includes her willingness to accept its result: the death of the victim. Although we have reason to question Alida's interpretation of Grace's sudden marriage, we have no clear alternative explanation for it, especially since our limited knowledge of the past and Grace's apparent acceptance of Alida's explanation invites us to assume that Grace did go to the Colosseum and contract some illness. In the present, Alida's continued resentment of Grace's past love for Delphin and her own current unhappiness as a widow and a mother of a daughter who does not need her lead not only to this new effort at injury but also to this assertion of her power over her rival: "I manipulated you in the past to serve my interests, and in telling you about that now, I want to hurt you again." For her part, Grace did not regard Alida's engagement to Delphin as sufficient reason not to pursue him herself, and, in the present, she has lost one of her fondest memories of his expression of love and gained a new understanding of how much ill will Alida bears toward her. In short, we seem to be moving toward the end of a narrative in which we watch the past repeat itself through Alida's manipulative assertion of her power over Grace.

But this understanding becomes substantially revised after two significant developments in the present-time conversation. First, after Alida lingers over her past manipulation by saying, "I suppose I did it as a sort of joke. . . . I remember laughing to myself all that evening at the idea that you were waiting around there in the dark, dodging out of sight, listening for every sound trying to get in" (19), Grace finally changes tactics by making her first crucial revelation about the past: "But I didn't wait. He'd arranged everything. He was there. We were let in at once." Grace goes on to explain that she "answered the letter. I told him I'd be there. So he came" (19). At this point, then, more tensions about the past begin to be resolved. We begin to understand the stress in Grace's earlier statement that to *her* the view from the terrace will always be the most beautiful in the world. Furthermore, we see that Alida is now the character whose path does not conform to the order of events, the character who has to revise her understanding of her path to the present. And she struggles to do so. Her first move is denial, "You must be raving!," and her second is despair at her own blindness: "Oh God—you answered! I never thought of your answering. . . . I was blind with rage" (20).

The second development comes when Grace moves to end the conversation, saying that they should go inside and that "I'm sorry for you" (20). Alida can't bear this sympathy from the rival to whom she is in the habit of condescending, and so seeks to regain the upper hand by discounting the fact of Grace's meeting with Delphin: "After all, I had everything; I had him for twenty-five years. And you had nothing but that one letter he didn't write." Grace is "again silent," but "at length" she turns toward the door of the terrace, stopping to turn and face Alida in order to retaliate with her trenchant exit line, "I had Barbara" (20). As I noted above, the line constitutes the arrival because it resolves the last of the tensions about the past—now Grace, Alida, and the authorial audience know the whole story—and completes the working out of instabilities by permanently changing the power relation between the two characters: Grace not only delivers the trump line in the conversation, but she also announces that she has been the beneficiary of Alida's past manipulation. Once again, Alida's path is remarkably different from the order of events. To appreciate the full sense of completion this ending offers, we need to consider the reconfiguration it requires us to make. The narrator's additional report provides both farewell and closure: Grace "began to move ahead of Mrs. Slade toward the stairway" (20). Grace's movement signifies that the conversation is over—indeed, it is hard to imagine that Alida could have any satisfactory comeback and Grace has nothing more to say. The narrator's cool report of the action is in keeping with her relation to both characters and to the narratee throughout the story: it reinforces her distance from the characters and their vicious conflict and her willingness to let the narratee draw his or her own conclusions. While Wharton uses the narrator's cool detachment to signal her distance from the characters, she also uses it as a means to invite her audience's collaboration with her: she invites us to see the complex dynamics underneath the narrator's cool reports of the characters' words and actions.

## Completion, Ethics, and Aesthetics

To appreciate the full effect of the ending we need to consider the reconfigurations it invites us to make and their ethical and aesthetic consequences. First, we need to recognize the reconfigurations that Grace and Alida themselves must make now that each has revealed her secret to the other. Since Wharton's technique has given us more access to Alida's consciousness, her reconfigurations are more apparent. She must now view Delphin, Grace, and especially herself in a new light—and all three new visions are painful to her. She must recognize that Delphin regarded their engagement so lightly that, when presented with the opportunity for the clandestine meeting with Grace, he seized it. This recognition must lead, in turn, to doubts about Delphin's love and fidelity after their marriage. Indeed, Alida must question whether she is justified in saying, "I had everything. I had him for twenty-five years" (20). Alida must also abandon her view of Grace as her inferior, since she must admit that Grace has outdone her at so many crucial turns: in the past by innocently responding to her forgery and then not so innocently sleeping with Delphin; in the present by silencing her with her secrets of greater import. Even more galling to her, Alida must admit that Grace and Delphin have produced the more brilliant daughter. Finally, Alida must recognize that her own efforts to defeat her rival have actually wreaked far more havoc upon herself than upon Grace: her forgery did not, as she thought, lead to Grace's illness but rather to her conception of Barbara; her revealing her secret about the forgery, though it does injure Grace, prods Grace into giving her even more painful knowledge.

For her part, Grace now understands the irony that her rival inadvertently brought about the sexual encounter that gave her Barbara. And she also realizes that she has herself underestimated Alida, has viewed her with sympathy from her superior position, while Alida was actually both more malicious and more dangerous than Grace realized. Although Grace must take some satisfaction in the irony of Alida's role in making her Barbara's mother, she also pays a high price, as her tears over Alida's revelation reveal. What she was thinking as she cried, and what she chose not to tell Alida, is that knowing about the forgery must alter her understanding of Delphin's role in their nighttime encounter. Rather than thinking of him as its only begetter, the active agent who brought it about, she must consider whether he was only an opportunist, someone willing to take advantage of a situation that others have set up for him. This consideration, in turn, must shake her confidence that Delphin actually loved her. Without knowing that he was the author of the summons to meet in the Colosseum, Grace must wonder whether his actions that night were motivated by an interest in an easy sexual conquest, especially since their encounter did not alter his plans to marry Alida. Wharton encourages us to perceive this reconfiguration by the way Alida's forgery allows (though it does not require) the inference that Grace and Delphin's sexual encounter that night was their first: "Things cannot go on like this. I must see you alone" (15). These sentiments are appropriate for (albeit not exclusively belonging to) the domain of pre-consummated desire; note how different our inferences would be if the note read "I must see you alone again."

Of course as Alida composes the note, she is only guessing about the exact nature of the relationship, but the effect produced by the note— it gets both parties to the Colosseum—indicates that she guessed right.

Consequently, though Grace's "I had Barbara" does trump Alida's claim that "you had nothing but that one letter that he didn't write" (20), it does not overturn Alida's earlier declaration that "You tried your best to get him away from me. . . . But you failed; and I kept him" (18). As we have seen, Alida needs to recognize that she has been wrong to conclude the declaration by saying "That's all," but Grace now has new cause to think that the first part of the declaration is very much on target. Indeed, as we recognize Grace's reconfiguration, we also recognize that Grace's exit line—and, indeed, Barbara herself—must have another layer of meaning: she can no longer be confident that Barbara is the continuing sign of Delphin's love but only that Barbara is her consolation for having given herself to him in a vain effort to win him away from Alida. As a result, we may conclude that Grace may no longer find the view from Rome the most beautiful one in the world. In this regard, the story is one in which there are no winners.

That both Alida and Grace emerge from their conversational conflict with significant wounds should not obscure the way our reconfiguration underlines how different they are—and thus, how the progression has altered our initial understanding of them as similar. Losing her sense of superiority over Grace, her smug satisfaction about her youthful stratagem, and her confidence about what she meant to Delphin hurts Alida so much because these things are all serious blows to her pride and pride is the key component of her self-image. Losing her belief that Delphin loved her hurts Grace so much because it injures her heart. No doubt Grace, too, took pride in her illusion about Delphin's love, but we still recognize that Grace is capable of love in a way that Alida is not. Nevertheless, there is more to our reconfiguration of Grace and her participation in the past and present competition.

That reconfiguration also yields a deeper understanding of Grace's decision to tell Alida her secrets. It is clear that Alida's persistence in asserting her superiority contributes to Grace's retaliation. But more important is that Alida's revelation has robbed Grace of her construction of the past. She becomes determined to take something from Alida as well. At first, Grace is content just to tell Alida that she met Delphin and that, therefore, she feels sorry for her. But Alida's insistence that Grace "had nothing but the one letter that he didn't write" (20) leads her to what she knows, given Alida's earlier question about Barbara, will be the most damaging revelation.

As I have been suggesting, our sense of completion includes all of Grace and Alida's new understandings, but it also goes beyond them to recognize that the coincidence of the resolution of tensions about the past and of the instabilities in the present also makes the story both a repetition and a resolution of the past. It is a repetition because Alida's aggression against Grace in the conversation has similar unexpected results. Just as Alida's scheme to have Grace contract an illness in the Colosseum led to Grace's pregnancy, Alida's scheme to wound Grace by revealing the forgery leads to Grace's greater wounding of her through the revelation of that pregnancy. Both women have acted under the influence of a metaphoric Roman fever both in the past and in the present. The present is also a resolution of the past because the competition, if not the feeling of rivalry, must now be over. It is hard to imagine that either one would want to take on the other once again, especially now that the mutual revelation of secrets means that they know the worst of each other.

Our sense of completion also includes our final understanding of the ethical relations between the characters. Our reconfiguration helps us recognize that Wharton has taken Grace, a character who, by the measure of conventional morality, has acted very dishonorably—pursuing her friend's fiancé to the point of sleeping with him—and presented her as more sinned against than sinning. Wharton's treatment of the present is crucial here: she uses the focalization to reveal that Alida continues to be motivated by envy, hatred, and the desire for dominance—the feelings that led to her own past dishonorable action of luring Grace into a situation in which she might become deathly ill—whereas she uses the external descriptions of Grace along with her dialogue to suggest that Grace not only is capable of love but also would have been content to take her secret to her grave. Consequently, we judge Alida more harshly than we judge Grace, and we find Alida's necessary reconfigurations an appropriate comeuppance, a fit punishment for her behavior toward Grace. At the same time, we also regard Grace's revised understanding about Delphin's behavior as a kind of punishment for her past pursuit of her self-interest, and we recognize that, though she is provoked by Alida's aggression and condescension into revealing her secrets, those revelations are designed to wound. Furthermore, our new view of Grace leads us to understand that Alida's envy has not been at all irrational: Grace was a genuine threat, albeit not one that justified Alida's behavior. To repeat, there are no winners in this story, but given our emotional and ethical attachments, the fact that Grace's retaliation to Alida's attack comes from her injured pride and turns out to be more damaging than the attack itself makes the ending both appropriate and disturbing. In "Roman Fever," Wharton has asked us to collaborate in her portrayal of a subtle and very nasty power struggle that ends up diminishing both competitors.

We are now in a position to come to terms with the ethics of the telling. We can recognize that Wharton's tight control of the disclosure of information is both aesthetically and ethically satisfying, even admirable. First, we can see that it would be misleading to read the ethics of Wharton's surprising her audience as analogous to the ethics of Grace's surprising Alida because the nature and consequences of the disclosure are vastly different. Second, Wharton has carefully set us up for the surprise ending: the signals about Alida's underestimation of Grace, about Grace's attachment to Rome, and, indeed, about Grace's response to Alida's revelation function in retrospect as preparations for the surprise ending—even as these signals take on new significance in light of the surprise. Third, the surprise ending, in simultaneously resolving the tensions and instabilities of the progression and in leading to the reconfigurations we have just examined, deepens our involvement with the characters and their situations: the surprise opens up dimensions of the narrative that have largely been hidden until that point.

These last two points can also be approached from another direction, one that reveals another dimension of Wharton's successful handling of the surprise. For the surprise to work, Wharton obviously needs to restrict our access to Grace's consciousness throughout the narrative. By making Grace's revelation so well-motivated within the dramatic situation and by making it the chief means to resolve the tensions and instabilities, Wharton converts the restriction on her narration from an obstacle to an advantage.

Fourth, and most important, all these features of the surprise ending intensify our collaboration with Wharton herself. In the Preface to her volume of short stories, *Ghost,* Wharton wrote about her awareness of "a common medium between myself and my readers, of their meeting me halfway among the primeval shadows, and filling in the gaps in my narrative with sensations and divinations akin to my own" (x). "Roman Fever" also asks us to share sensations and divinations with her, and that sharing leads us to admire her insight into the power of the past to influence the present and to the psychological and ethical dynamics of a polite power struggle. Collaborating with Wharton also means working at or near the peak of our cognitive, emotive, and ethical powers, and because it requires and rewards such work it is a significant aesthetic achievement. We cannot help but end the narrative grateful for the opportunity to participte in Wharton's beautifully designed, powerful, and disturbing narrative.

# CHAPTER FIVE

# Delayed Disclosure and the Problem of Other Minds

## Ian McEwan's *Atonement*

As its title suggests, Ian McEwan's *Atonement* (2001) focuses on its protagonist's transgression and her effort at making amends for its disastrous
consequences. In this respect, it is a novel that all but cries out for attention to readerly judgments. Furthermore, as a brief description of its progression indicates, it is a novel in which the interrelations of interpretive,
ethical, and aesthetic judgments—by and of its protagonist, Briony Tallis,
and of the implied McEwan's performance—are central to its effects. On a
hot July day in 1935 Briony misidentifies her sister Cecilia's lover, Robbie
Turner, as the man who has sexually assaulted her cousin Lola, and then
years later tries to do what she can to atone for her error. McEwan then
throws a startling twist into the progression in its last twenty pages. These
pages, Briony's diary entry on the night of her seventy-seventh birthday,
reveal that the previous 330 pages have been her novel as well as part of
McEwan's. In other words, Briony's "Atonement," a straightforward and
fascinating modernist novel, is Parts One, Two, and Three of McEwan's
*Atonement*. McEwan's novel continues for this fourth section, "London,
1999," which, among other things, suddenly reveals that his *Atonement* is
a self-conscious, self-reflexive novel employing a character narrator who
is herself a novelist. Furthermore, Briony's diary entry reveals that her
novel has mixed a factual account of her transgression with a fictional
account of her atonement even as she now regards the novel itself as her
major effort at atonement.

   In teaching the novel, I have learned that flesh-and-blood readers are
often sharply divided in their ethical and aesthetic judgments of McEwan's
performance, especially in this ending, with some finding it to be brilliant
and admirable and others finding it to be a cheap trick or cheat, one that

delights in unfairly jerking its audience around. Although I am a member of the first group, I think one test of a rhetorical analysis of the novel is its ability to identify the sources of both responses. Consequently, when I come to discuss the ending I shall take up this division among flesh-and-blood readers. But I begin with two broad questions and a strategy for answering them. How do we judge—formally, ethically, and aesthetically—(1) Briony's embedded novel and (2) McEwan and his novel, especially his springing so much on us so suddenly? I propose to address these questions by looking, first, at the progression in Part One, especially the nature of the instabilities at the time of the entrance and the role of judgments in the representation of Briony's transgression, and, second, at the reconfigurations of the overall progression required by "London, 1999," reconfigurations that will necessarily lead us to consider the functions of Parts Two and Three in the novel's design.

## The Beginning of *Atonement*

The major event of the progression, Briony's misidentification of Robbie as Lola's assailant, occurs near the end of Part One, in the thirteenth of its fourteen chapters. Much like Sethe's choice in *Beloved,* this event is a central node of the progression, something to which and from which everything flows for both characters and audience. Everything else in Part One carefully contextualizes it. Part Two recounts Robbie's experiences as a consequence of it—he is a soldier in the retreat to Dunkirk in 1939, having joined the military in order to escape his prison sentence. Part Three narrates Briony's experiences as a nurse in the war and the direct steps she takes to atone (her crime and the war combine to make her choose nursing rather than the university); and "London, 1999" offers Briony's reflections on her struggle to come to narrative terms with her error and its consequences.

The beginning consists of the title, the epigraph, and the first three chapters of Part One; these chapters introduce two global instabilities and suggest at least a potential connection between them. The first instability involves Briony and her aspirations to be a great writer, and the second involves the relationship between Cecilia and Robbie. I shall return later to the issue of how the delayed disclosure that McEwan's beginning is also the beginning of Briony's novel leads us to reconfigure our judgments and our understanding of the novel's progression.[1]

1. It is worth asking whether the paratexts of McEwan's *Atonement* are also the

The epigraph is the passage from Jane Austen's *Northanger Abbey* in which Henry Tilney calls Catherine Morland to task for her erroneous gothic suspicions about General Tilney's mistreatment of his late wife. The passage reads in part:

> Dear Miss Morland, consider the dreadful nature of the suspicions you have entertained. What have you been judging from? Remember the country and the age in which we live. Remember that we are English: that we are Christians. Consult your own understanding, your own sense of the probable, your own observations of what is passing around you. . . . Dearest Miss Morland, what ideas have you been admitting?
>
> They had reached the end of the gallery; and with tears of shame she ran off to her room. (n.p.)

While the title signals that McEwan's narrative will involve some effort at making amends for a transgression, this epigraph invites us to expect that the transgression will involve a misjudgment like Catherine's, the product of an overactive imagination under the influence of certain kinds of literature. At the same time, the title itself suggests that McEwan's novel will have a different emphasis from Austen's, if only because Catherine's misjudgments do not have consequences so serious that atonement becomes a major issue in *Northanger Abbey*.

The paratexts clue us to recognize the first chapter's exposition about thirteen-year-old Briony's ambitions to be a writer of fiction as the basis for significant instabilities. The chapter itself then gives some specificity to those instabilities, and Chapter Two, which switches from Briony to Cecilia as the primary focal character, introduces instabilities between Cecilia and Robbie, instabilities that are especially evident in their struggle at the fountain over the Tallis family's heirloom vase, which they manage to break. Chapter Three then returns to Briony's perspective and establishes the potential connection between the two sets of instabilities, as it reveals Briony's reflections on the scene at the fountain between Cecilia and Robbie.

The textual dynamics of Chapter One proceed through the introduction and complication of the local instabilities surrounding the difficulties Briony faces in trying to get her cousins, Lola, age fifteen, and the twins

---

paratexts of Briony's, and, thus, whether the beginnings are precisely the same. Obviously the title page with its designation of McEwan as author and Doubleday as publisher belongs only to McEwan's novel, but I take the epigraph from *Northanger Abbey* and the page denoting "Part One" as parts of both novels.

Jackson and Pierrot, age nine, to help her perform her new (and first) play, *The Trials of Arabella*. The play is a highly romantic affair complete with a heroine who endures many hardships before being rescued by a disguised prince. But these local instabilities about staging the play are framed by passages such as the following that combine exposition, initiation, and hints at a global instability:

> writing stories not only involved secrecy it also gave her [Briony] all the pleasures of miniaturization. A world could be made in five pages, and one that was more pleasing than a model farm. The childhood of a spoiled prince could be framed within half a page, a moonlit dash through sleepy villages was one rhythmically emphatic sentence, falling in love could be achieved in a single word—a *glance*. The pages of a recently finished story seemed to vibrate in her hand with all the life they contained. Her passion for tidiness was also satisfied, for an unruly world could be made just so. A crisis in a heroine's life could be made to coincide with hail-stones, gales, and thunder, whereas nuptials were generally blessed with good light and soft breezes. A love of order also shaped the principles of justice, with death and marriage the main engines of housekeeping, the former being set aside exclusively for the mor-ally dubious, the latter a reward withheld until the final page. (7; emphasis in original)

In addition to the exposition about Briony's character and her interests, the passage initiates us into a particular kind of rhetorical exchange. The narration in this passage is primarily from Briony's vision, but it is pri-marily rendered in the narrator's voice. The technique, common in mod-ernist novels, allows us both to enter with some sympathy into Briony's attraction to writing stories and to recognize the potential dangers of that attraction. The most telling sentence is: "The pages of a recently finished story seemed to vibrate in her hand with all the life they contained" and the most telling phrase is "seemed to vibrate," because the sentence and the phrase dramatize the difference between Briony's interpretive judg-ments and ours. Briony understands her stories to be much more than words on a page, to be something closer to a container vibrating with life itself. But we interpret "seemed to vibrate" as double-voiced and double-visioned: for Briony it is an innocent metaphor, but for the narrator and the authorial audience it points to Briony's failure to recognize the cost of making "an unruly world . . . just so." In making the world conform to her romantic desires and tastes, including a penchant for the pathetic fallacy, her stories suck the life out of unruly reality. What's vibrating in the pages is not life itself but her romantic imagination and her belief in the power of the verbal formulas she has learned. At this point in the narrative, there is no significant ethical consequence to Briony's interpretive misjudgment, though there are aesthetic consequences for her stories, since they are all melodramatic, romantic, and formulaic. Our awareness of the gap between her interpretive judgment and our own sets up the potential for ethical and aesthetic consequences within McEwan's novel.

Chapter Two continues the pattern of Chapter One's initiation but shifts the focus to Cecilia and her unstable situation, and toward the end of the chapter, also includes Robbie's perspective. Cecilia, having recently graduated from Cambridge, is feeling uneasy during her summer at home. She feels that she should move on soon but is reluctant to:

> Lingering here, bored and comfortable, was a form of self-punishment tinged with pleasure, or the expectation of it. If she went away something bad might happen or, worse, something good, something she could not afford to miss. And there was Robbie, who exasperated her with his affectation of distance, and his grand plans which he would only discuss with her father. They had known each other since they were seven, she and Robbie, and it bothered her that they were awkward when they talked. Even though she felt it was largely his fault—could his first have gone to his head?—she knew this was something she must clear up before she thought of leaving. (21)

The instability with Robbie gets immediately complicated as the two of them meet by the fountain on the estate, have an awkward conversation, and end up struggling over Uncle Clem's vase, which Cecilia had been planning to fill with water. The struggle leads to their breaking the vase and some of the pieces falling into the fountain. When Robbie begins to unbutton his shirt in preparation for going in after those pieces, Cecilia acts more swiftly:

> Immediately she knew what he was about. Intolerable. He had come to the house and removed his shoes and socks—well, she would show him then. She kicked off her sandals, unbuttoned her blouse and removed it, unfastened her skirt and stepped out of it and went to the basin wall. He stood with hands on his hips and stared as

she climbed into the water in her underwear. Denying his help, any possibility of making amends, was his punishment. The unexpectedly freezing water that caused her to gasp was his punishment. She held her breath, and sank, leaving her hair fanned out across the surface. Drowning herself would be his punishment. . . .

Her movements were savage, and she would not meet his eye. He did not exist, he was banished, and this was also his punishment. He stood there dumbly as she walked away from him, barefoot across the lawn, and he watched her darkened hair swing heavily across her shoulders, drenching her blouse. (29)

The technique focuses on Cecilia's interpretive and ethical judgments and allows us to recognize that the only accurate one is her recognition that Robbie intends to enter the fountain. Her interpretation that her self-punishment in the freezing water is actually his punishment is far off the mark, though his visual pleasure in her disrobing and acting the part of the "frail white nymph" from whom water cascades "far more successfully than it does from the beefy Triton" in the fountain (29) is no doubt leavened by her anger. More than that, the ethical judgment that he deserves punishment is off the mark. Each of them insists on handling the vase, and each is responsible for its breaking. But what the whole scene—their awkward conversation, the struggle over the vase, Cecilia's impetuous plunge into the fountain before Robbie's eyes—reveals is that Cecilia can't leave because of her desire for Robbie, a desire that she has only partially repressed. That repression is revealed in the scene in her overt anger at Robbie and her covert anger at herself, and its partiality is revealed in her stripping to her underwear. The anger provides the cover under which she can display her body before him, and it's striking that the triggers for that display are his beginning to unbutton his shirt and her thought about his removing his shoes and socks in the house: "well, she would show him then." Show him, that is, how to strip right.

Our interpretive judgment about the workings of repression contextualizes our ethical judgments of Cecilia and, thus, our emotional responses to the scene. Cecilia's interpretive and ethical misjudgments are more significant as indicators of her unstable situation than of her permanent character, and, as a result, we regard her with considerable sympathy. Though the chapter ends before we learn a lot about Robbie, our developing responses to Cecilia lead us to desire positive developments in their relationship.

Chapter Three establishes the potential connection between the instabilities about Briony's writerly ambitions and those about Cecilia and Robbie

as the narration returns to Briony's perspective and eventually moves to
her reflections after she witnesses the scene at the fountain. But first the
narrator shows us some of Briony's other thoughts about writing:

> a story was a form of telepathy. By means of inking symbols onto
> a page, she was able to send thoughts and feelings from her mind
> to her reader's. It was a magical process, so commonplace that no
> one stopped to wonder at it. Reading a sentence and understanding
> it were the same thing; as with the crooking of a finger, nothing lay
> between them. There was no gap during which the symbols were
> unraveled. You saw the word *castle,* and it was there, seen from
> some distance, with woods in high summer spread before it, the air
> bluish and soft with smoke rising from the blacksmith's forge, and
> a cobbled road twisting away into the green shade. (35)

The technique here moves from the vision of Briony and the voice
of the narrator to the vision and voice of Briony herself. The distance
between the narrator's interpretive judgment and Briony's is again significant: the naiveté about the relation between life and her stories that affects
her thoughts in Chapter One comes through here in her view of language
as a transparent medium. The passage itself enacts the problem with her
view by means of the word *castle.* When we encounter the clause "You
saw the word *castle,*" we are likely to imagine a castle, but we are highly
unlikely to imagine the highly embellished image of a castle that Briony
believes we can't help imagining. It's revealing—and consistent—that Briony's image is of a setting for some romantic tale.

The juxtaposition of this passage with Briony's reflections on how she
could take a different approach to writing and represent the scene at the
fountain shows Briony caught between significantly different ideas:

> Even as her sister's head broke the surface—thank God!—Briony
> had her first, weak intimation that for her now it could no longer
> be fairy-tale castles and princesses, but the strangeness of the here
> and now, of what passed between people, the ordinary people that
> she knew, and what power one could have over the other, and how
> easy it was to get everything wrong, completely wrong. . . .
>
> She could write the scene three times over, from three points of
> view [the two at the fountain and herself as observer]; her excite-
> ment was in the prospect of freedom, of being delivered from the
> cumbrous struggle between good and bad, heroes and villains.

None of these three was bad, nor were they particularly good. She need not judge. There did not have to be a moral. She need only show separate minds, as alive as her own, struggling with the idea that other minds were equally alive. It wasn't only wickedness and scheming that made people unhappy, it was confusion and misunderstanding; above all, it was the failure to grasp the simple truth that other people were as real as you. And only in a story could you enter the different minds and show how they had an equal value. That was the only moral a story need have. (37–38)

Briony "need not judge," but this passage invites us to, and we make the interpretive judgment that these reflections present a major step forward in Briony's thinking about the relation between writing stories and life. To go from the black-and-white worlds of her previous stories to this one in which judgment drops out except to show the "equal value" of multiple minds is to move a long distance. The passage underlines Briony's in-between status, her having one foot in the world of childhood and another, more tentative one in the world of adulthood. Briony's understanding of judgment itself reflects this in-between status. At this stage she can recognize the limitations of the blunt judgments associated with "good versus bad" and "hero versus villain," but she cannot do better than oppose that option to another stark alternative, that is, no judgment at all. The more nuanced judgments McEwan invites us to make in Chapter Two—and indeed, of Briony herself in this passage—are not yet options for her.

Our interpretive judgment about Briony's in-between status also carries with it a recognition of Briony's potential for more sophisticated aesthetic achievements. But our understanding of her in-between status also means that the ethical dimension of such achievements will depend on how she develops that potential. On the one hand, showing the equal value of multiple minds can itself be a substantial ethical achievement, since it requires, among other things, acts of sympathetic projection into those other minds. On the other hand, because the previous narration has invited us to judge the actors in the scene at the fountain, McEwan as implied author suggests that, within the terms of this narrative, representation without judgment is a less desirable ethical and aesthetic achievement than representation with nuanced judgments. In sum, even as the progression directs us to recognize Briony's insight as a significant breakthrough, it also invites us, on ethical and aesthetic grounds, to stop short of fully embracing Briony's new aesthetic principle of not judging.

Thus, by the end of Chapter Three, McEwan has launched his narrative with three global instabilities: (1) will Briony be able to achieve this new vision in her writing? It's telling that Briony does not immediately try to execute her ideas because her thirteen-year-old sense of order asserts itself: "she must complete what she had initiated, there was a rehearsal in progress, Leon was on his way, the household was expecting a performance tonight. . . . The writing could wait until she was free" (39). (2) If Briony does achieve her new vision, will it be ethically satisfactory? (3) How will the progress of Briony's quest relate to the development of the relationship between Cecilia and Robbie? Will one influence the other, and, if so, how? At this point of entrance, we have no clear expectations about the ways in which these instabilities will get complicated or resolved.

## Readerly Judgments of Briony's Misjudgment

Let us now move forward into the key event in the voyage, and examine the role of judgment in the representation of Briony's misidentification of Robbie as Lola's assailant. In this section, I will look at the judgments we make when we assume that Part One is only McEwan's novel and then, in the next section, will consider how those judgments get modified—if at all—once we learn that Part One is also Briony's novel. The voyage between Chapter Four and the key event is devoted to providing the context for the transgression, a context that shows it to be overdetermined.

In addition to Briony, Cecilia, their mother Emily, Robbie, and the cousins, the Tallis household is host on this July day in 1935 to Briony and Cecilia's older brother, Leon, and to his friend Paul Marshall. Leon is a key member of Briony's intended audience for *The Trials of Arabella*. Marshall remains in the background in Part One as the narrative primarily moves its focus from Briony to Cecilia to Robbie, with a few excursions into Emily's consciousness and into Lola's. Marshall is seen in the nursery with the children through Lola's perception and again through Emily's interpretation of his voice when she hears it from another part of the house. At dinner Robbie notices a two-inch scratch on Marshall's face, shortly after Lola has shown Briony scratches and bruises of her own.

Briony's hopes for a grand performance of *The Trials of Arabella* are dashed by the nonromantic realities of everyday life. Cecilia and Robbie, however, break through their repression after Robbie inadvertently gives Cecilia the wrong draft of a note, one containing the spontaneous overflow of his powerful feelings: "In my dreams I kiss your cunt, your sweet wet cunt. In my thoughts I make love to you all day long" (80). What's more, Robbie asks Briony to deliver the note, and she reads it before passing it on; a little later, Briony interrupts Cecilia and Robbie in the library where they are on the verge of consummating their newly discovered love.

Briony, in an effort to ingratiate herself with her fifteen-year-old cousin, tells Lola about Robbie's note and then deems Lola's description of him as a "maniac" to be apt. Jackson and Pierrot, the nine-year-old twins, struggle so much in their new environment that during dinner they decide to run away, though they leave a note explaining their plans. It is during the ensuing search for them that Lola is assaulted. Briony comes upon Lola and her assailant in the dark and sees only his retreating shape, yet she makes the interpretive judgment that the shape is Robbie's. McEwan's representation of this judgment and the reasons that Briony holds fast to it are worth a longer look.

> Briony was there to help [Lola] at every stage. As far as she was concerned, everything fitted; the terrible present fulfilled the recent past. Events she herself witnessed foretold her cousin's calamity. If only she, Briony, had been less innocent, less stupid. Now she saw, the affair was too consistent, too symmetrical to be anything other than what she said it was. She blamed herself for her childish assumption that Robbie would limit his attentions to Cecilia. What was she thinking of? He was a maniac after all. (158)

Strikingly, this passage details not just the interaction of Briony's interpretive, ethical, and aesthetic judgments, but the way her interpretive judgment is overrun by her ethical and aesthetic judgments. Briony is certain that the figure she saw retreating from the scene had to be Robbie not because she has ocular proof but because that interpretation fits the narrative she is scripting on the basis of her earlier encounters with Robbie. And that narrative fit is a consequence of her ethical judgments: any one who could write that sentence in the letter to Cecilia must be a "maniac," and, hence, Lola's rapist. Indeed, the passage recalls the earlier one in which Briony thinks about the word *castle* as an example of the direct relation between signifier and signified: if Robbie is a maniac after all, then of course he is Lola's assailant. Briony, in short, now acts not according to the insights she achieved while observing Cecilia and Robbie at the fountain but rather according to the interpretive, ethical, and aesthetic vision of her youthful romances, including *The Trials of Arabella*.

McEwan, not surprisingly, clearly signals that each of these judgments is erroneous. Through several scenes dominated by the technique of internal focalization, McEwan presents Robbie as an admirable young man; what's more, as already noted, McEwan shows that his letter to Cecilia functions to break through his and Cecilia's repressions and take them to a state of passionate love.[2] Without the linchpin of Briony's ethical judgment, her interpretive and aesthetic judgments fall apart.

Although Briony's misjudgments of Robbie have the potential to be the basis of our strongly negative ethical judgment of her, McEwan carefully guides us to a more complex response, one that continues to underline her errors while also mitigating our judgment of them. On a macro level, McEwan relies on the careful tracing of the convergence of the different characters and events to show how Briony's transgression was overdetermined; on a micro level, he shows how difficult it was for Briony to change her narrative once she had articulated it.

> As early as the week that followed, the glazed surface of conviction was not without its blemishes and hairline cracks. Whenever she was conscious of them, which was not often, she was driven back, with a little swooping sensation in her stomach, to the understanding that what she knew was not literally, or not only, based on the visible. It was not simply her eyes that told her the truth. It was too dark for that. . . . Her eyes confirmed the sum of all she knew and had recently experienced. The truth was in the symmetry, which was to say, it was founded in common sense. The truth instructed her eyes. So when she said, over and over again, I saw him, she meant it, and was perfectly honest, as well as passionate. What she meant was rather more complex than what everyone else so eagerly understood, and her moments of unease came when she felt that she could not express these nuances. She did not even seriously try. There were no opportunities, no time, no permission. Within a couple of days, no, within a matter of hours, a process was moving fast and well beyond her control. (158–59)

While this passage once again emphasizes her error ("It was not simply her eyes that told her the truth. It was too dark for that"), it also emphasizes how deeply she believes in her judgments ("she . . . was perfectly honest, as well as passionate") and how, once she'd spoken, it was impossible to qualify or otherwise add nuance to her testimony: "what she meant was rather more complex than what everyone so eagerly understood," but

---

2. For an analysis of McEwan's representation of that love, see my discussion of a representative passage in *The Nature of Narrative* (Schuler, Kellogg, and Phelan, 2006), 323–33.

"there were no opportunities, no time, no permission" for her to express those complexities. Consequently, McEwan is asking us to understand and even be sympathetic toward Briony's misjudgments, even as he leaves no doubt that they are egregiously erroneous and likely to have major negative consequences for Cecilia and Robbie. Furthermore, this handling of our ethical judgments raises the aesthetic and ethical stakes of the novel at this point of intermediate configuration: how will McEwan work through the difference between Briony's intentions (and his mitigation of our negative ethical judgment) and the terrible practical consequences of her misjudgment? How will the instability about her development as a writer, now that she has failed to live up to the insight of Chapter Three in her behavior, be complicated and resolved?

## Judgments of Briony's Effort to Atone

Interestingly, this last question is not resolved either in Part Two with its focus on Robbie's experience as a soldier during the retreat to Dunkirk in 1940 or in Part Three with its focus on Briony's experience as a nurse during the war and on her pledge to Cecilia and Robbie shortly after the retreat to atone for her crime by making a full confession. Instead, McEwan opts to include "London, 1999" and its surprise disclosures as a way to resolve that instability. The surprise disclosures, as noted earlier, are that we have been reading a novel within a novel and that Briony's novel has seamlessly combined the historical events of Part One with her mixtures of fact and invention in Parts Two and Three. The first reconfiguration we have to make, then, is that all three Parts of McEwan's novel have indirectly been concerned with addressing the instability about Briony's development as a writer because they all provide evidence about the writer she has become. "London, 1999" in a sense provides Briony's preferred way of looking at her novel, especially about her choices to alter significant elements of the history she is recounting.

Thus, when Briony's 1999 diary entry reveals that Robbie and Cecilia are never reunited, that he dies during the retreat and that she dies a few months later when a German bomb blows up the Balham Underground station in London, we have to come to terms with both the ethics and aesthetics of her act of novel writing. We also have to come to terms with our recognition that McEwan himself has asked us to invest our emotions and desires in Briony's quest for an atonement that he and she both knew in their different ways was impossible. I will start with how McEwan resolves the instability about Briony's evolution as a writer by guiding our judgments of her decisions about her novel.

In her diary entry, Briony explains that, though she wrote her first draft of the novel in 1940, it is only in her final draft that she decided to alter history—to make, in effect, another judgment that is simultaneously interpretive, ethical, and aesthetic. More precisely, she explains her interpretive judgment to alter the historical record as a consequence of her aesthetic and ethical judgments. No one would want to believe the historical facts, she writes, except in "the service of the bleakest realism," and she decided it was important that her novel provide some "sense of hope or satisfaction" (350). Furthermore, "I like to think that it isn't weakness or evasion, but a final act of kindness, a stand against oblivion and despair, to let my lovers live and to unite them at the end. I gave them happiness, but I was not so self-serving as to let them forgive me" (351).

But Briony also realizes that her alteration of history for these reasons has consequences for her relation to her original purpose for writing the novel: to use the power of narrative itself as a way to atone for her crime.

> The problem these fifty-nine years has been this: how can a novelist achieve atonement when, with her absolute power of deciding outcomes, she is also God? There is no one, no entity or higher form that she can appeal to, or be reconciled with, or that can forgive her. There is nothing outside her. In her imagination she has set the limits and the terms. No atonement for God, or novelists, even if they are atheists. It was always an impossible task, and that was precisely the point. The attempt was all. (350–51)

To paraphrase, the novelist's power is also her limitation: since Briony's writing brings into being the novel's world, including both the crime and its aftermath, her decisions about the fates of her characters, whether they conform to history or not, cannot atone for what she has done to real people. There is no one external to the fiction who can serve as judge of whether her effort is sufficient to achieve atonement. Nevertheless, Briony thinks, the effort to seek the atonement is necessary, since attempting the impossible demonstrates the sincerity and depth of her desire to atone. This conclusion allows Briony, sixty-four years after the original crime, to come to terms with the impossibility of atoning for it, with the necessity of her 59-year effort, and with its result.

Before we can judge Briony's judgments here, we need to come to terms with how the knowledge that she is the author of Part One influences our prior judgments there. Our response to the beginning is not overturned but deepened. We understand the instabilities about Briony, about Robbie and Cecilia, and about the potential relation between them in the same way, but we recognize that Briony herself is the agent for our insights and for our judgments of her former self. Thus, at age seventy-seven, she has attained a view of her thirteen-year-old self that is full of insight, self-criticism, and partial sympathy. (I will shortly take up the issue of how we know that she has not invented everything we read in Parts One, Two, and Three.) And given that she has directed our judgments of her thirteen-year-old self's attraction to writing that does not judge, we can see that she has not opted for that aesthetic. Indeed, this choice of hers, enacted so brilliantly in Part One, is very much in keeping with the rejection of her submission "Two Figures by a Fountain" by Cyril Connolly at *Horizon*, which we learn about in Part Three, on the grounds that it is insufficiently narrative: "Simply put," Connolly writes in the letter reproduced in Part Three, "you need the backbone of a story" (296).

Our understanding of the beginning—and, indeed, all the segments of Part One that are given over to the representation of Robbie and Cecilia's consciousnesses via the techniques of modernist fiction—also deepens in another way. These segments of the novel demonstrate Briony's success with another part of her developing aesthetic: the writer's imperative to act upon "the simple truth that other people are as real as you" and to use narrative as a way to "enter these different minds and show how they had an equal value" (38). Since this element of her aesthetic is simultaneously a commitment to an ethical principle, Briony's successful execution of it leads us to positive aesthetic and ethical judgments of this component of her novel.

Our retrospective look at the representation of Briony's transgression adds another layer to our judgments rather than overturning them. It is one thing for us to regard McEwan's mitigation of Briony's blameworthiness as a positive feature of the narrative, quite another to make that same judgment about Briony's own representation of her behavior, since as novelist she clearly has a conflict of interest. Nevertheless, because her narrative so sympathetically enters into the consciousnesses of the other characters, and because she so clearly signals how deficient her judgments were, McEwan invites us to admire her now clear-eyed reconstruction of what she later calls her "crime" (349).

Returning to Briony's judgments in "London, 1999," however, we begin to complicate this view of Briony the novelist. A key question is whether the ethical/aesthetic credo Briony espouses and practices in her novel—entering other minds and offering nuanced judgments of them—is sufficient to warrant the liberties that she takes with history, especially since those liberties mean that she atones by allowing the fictional version of herself an atonement that she never actually achieves. The issue is complex because, as Briony notes, the readers of her novel (as opposed to the readers of her novel and her diary entry, i.e., the readers of McEwan's novel) will not know that she has altered history, will not know how much, if any, of the novel's action is actually based on the experience of historical personages. Here it is helpful to think about the judgments likely to be made by different audiences. The authorial audience of Briony's novel will simply admire the brilliant representation of the minds of her main characters, especially Briony, Cecilia, and Robbie, and her exploration of transgression and atonement. Briony's defense of her choices in relation to this audience is plausible: unable to atone for her error in her life, she tries through her art to compensate in some measure by giving such a rich mental life to Cecilia and Robbie and ending the narrative with the promise of their future happiness together. But since her authorial audience does not know the backstory of her novel the atonement is largely invisible to them: as she says, the attempt is all.

But as members of McEwan's authorial audience we are in a very different situation because we have access to Briony's diary entry which reveals the relation between fiction and history in Briony's novel and which implicitly asks us to use that revelation in our coming to terms with Briony's novel. The device of the diary entry is crucial here too, because it provides McEwan a way to stabilize the historical and the fictional in Briony's novel: since Briony is writing for herself, we have every reason to believe that she is telling the truth, not engaging in further fiction-making. If she were writing for someone else, an audience whose opinion of her she would be especially concerned with—say, a literary critic working on a biography of her—we would have more reason to suspect the reliability of what she reports in the diary entry. But this way, McEwan allows us to bank on what she tells about Robbie's death in Dunkirk and Cecilia's in Balham Station as well as on what she tells us about the historical basis for her novel. Indeed, Briony's reflections on the research she has done about the retreat to Dunkirk shows her concern for anchoring her imaginative recreation of Robbie's experience within what is actually known about the retreat.

The diary entry, with its clear separation of the historical and the invented, also helps us come to terms with the question of Briony's possible alterations within what she claims as historically accurate. This question arises from a detail in Briony's rejection letter from *Horizon*. Connolly suggests that the use of a Ming vase in "Two Figures by a Fountain" is implausible since a Ming is "rather too priceless to take outside" (295), and, sure enough, in her novel Briony has changed it to a vase by Höroldt. While this change may seem to open up the possibility that Briony's narrative of the historical events has been fictionalized through and through, the distinctions that she makes in her diary entry point to a better answer. Briony has actively shaped the historical events as she has constructed her novel. Her goal has not been to make every detail as accurate as possible but rather to highlight the disastrous consequences that follow from the historical intersection of her development as a writer with Cecilia and Robbie's discovery of their love. In other words, the diary entry does not attest to the absolute correspondence between every detail that Briony does not acknowledge having altered and the historical unfolding of events, but it does identify a line between history and invention and it shows how and why Briony crossed that line.

That Briony reveals in her diary entry that she has just been diagnosed as in the very early stages of vascular dementia is also relevant here. Since the doctor emphasizes the "slowness of the undoing" (334) and since Briony's prose is clear and consistent with what we've read in Parts One, Two, and Three, McEwan signals that neither Briony's entry nor her decisions about her novel are affected by her dementia. Instead the condition signals that we can believe Briony when she says that she has written the last draft of her novel, and it calls attention to the thematic importance of the representation of consciousness in both Briony's and McEwan's novels. That Briony will lose her memory and her own rich mental life as a novelist is affectively painful even as it carries a rough poetic justice: Briony's vivid imagination has had such terrible consequences for Robbie and Cecilia and now she will suffer its loss. At the same time, the contrast between what she has done in her novel—exploring the rich consciousness of all her central characters—and how little she will soon be able to do underlines the importance of consciousness as an issue in her novel, in McEwan's, and in the novel as a genre itself. Indeed, in representing Briony's act of writing her novel, McEwan has paid tribute to modernist fiction's achievements in its attention to representations of consciousness.

We can now move to consider the next layer of judgments generated by "London, 1999." In McEwan's authorial audience we recognize that Briony's conflict of interest powerfully affects her ethical and aesthetic achievement. To be sure, the brilliant imaginative construction of the minds of Cecilia and Robbie—and, in this regard, Part Two's representation of Robbie's experience on the retreat to Dunkirk is an extraordinary act of sympathetic imagination on Briony's part—does provide a means for Briony to assert that these people she has wronged are at least of equal value. But Briony's fulfilling her ethical/aesthetic credo is not sufficient justification for her altering history because the credo does not require such alteration. Moreover, those liberties raise the question of whether Briony has fully subscribed to the credo, because the avoidance of "bleak realism" about what happened to Cecilia and Robbie is also a way to mitigate the consequences of her transgression and, thus, suggests that she regards herself as more important than Cecilia and Robbie. Indeed, recognizing their equal value entails not giving them a happy ending that they never experienced but being true to the actual trajectory of their lives after the transgression. In other words, McEwan suggests that Briony has resolved her conflict of interest between reporting what actually happened and the temptation to soften her self-portrait in the ethically inferior way.

McEwan also includes other signals to guide our judgment of Briony's choices as a novelist. Briony's diary entry includes a description of the Tallis family's present to her on her seventy-seventh birthday: a performance of *The Trials of Arabella* by the younger generation. The entry quotes the final couplet Arabella and her prince address to the audience:

Here's the beginning of love at the end of our travail.
So farewell, kind friends, as into the sunset we sail!! (348)

More than simply rounding off the novel, this return by McEwan to thirteen-year-old Briony's romance implicitly comments on the romantic impulses governing her novel. It ends with the "continuation of love" for Robbie and Cecilia at the end of their travail and with the possibility of Briony's atonement. Indeed, if the performance of the play is not sufficient by itself to underline Briony's romanticism, the novel's farewell clinches the point. Briony writes, "but I was not so self-serving as to let them forgive me. Not quite, not yet. If I had the power to conjure them at my birthday celebration . . . Robbie and Cecilia, still alive, still in love, sitting side by side in the library, smiling at *The Trials of Arabella?* It's not impossible" (351). It's not impossible, suggests McEwan, for someone with Briony's romantic sensibility to take this next step in bending history to her own desires.

Briony's question, "who would want to believe that [Cecilia and Robbie never reunited] except in the service of the bleakest realism?" (350) reminds McEwan's audience that her romantic impulses fueled her misidentification of Robbie. Had she been more interested in realism then, she

would have required far more evidence before fingering Robbie. Had she
been more interested in realism here, she would have followed through on
revealing the grim consequences of her transgression. Her failure to do
that, in a sense, is to turn away from her quest to atone.

McEwan also signals the inadequacy of Briony's judgments through
her commentary about Lola and Paul Marshall. In Part Three, we learn that
although Marshall was, in fact, Lola's assailant, she "saved herself from
humiliation by falling in love, or persuading herself she had, and [she]
could not believe her luck when Briony insisted on doing the talking and
blaming. And what luck that was for Lola—barely more than a child, prized
open and taken—to marry her rapist" (306). In the final section, we learn
that Lola and Paul have become Lord and Lady Marshall and have enjoyed
living in the luxury made possible by the success of his candy company.
Even more important, we learn that Briony has never told anyone the truth
about how they came together, not even her parents or siblings. Briony
reflects:

> There was our crime—Lola's, Marshall's, mine—and from the sec-
> ond version [of my novel] I set out to describe it. I've regarded it
> as my duty to disguise nothing—the names, the places, the exact
> circumstances—I put it all there as a matter of historical record. But
> as a matter of legal reality, so various editors have told me over the
> years, my forensic memoir could never be published while my fel-
> low criminals were alive. You may only libel yourself and the dead.
> The Marshalls have been active in the courts since the late forties,
> defending their good names with a most expensive ferocity. . . . To
> be safe, one would have to be bland and obscure. I know I cannot
> publish until they are dead. And as of this morning, I accept that
> will not be until I am. (349)

Briony's reflections, however, actually call attention to the fact that her
long delay in finishing her novel has also been a way to avoid taking the
one concrete step toward atonement available to her: the public admission of her crime—not in a novel but in some nonfictional form, including letters to all who were present at the Tallis estate in June 1935—and
the effort to clear Robbie's name. Her reflections show how difficult and
uncertain that step would be, since the Marshalls would obviously deny
Briony's account and even sue for libel, but, in failing to take it, Briony
perpetuates her crime against Robbie. Furthermore, Briony's decision to
make her narrative a novel rather than a memoir not only allows her to

make history conform to desire, but it also allows her audience to decide that she is offering only an invented account of how Lord and Lady Marshal came together. Surely any defense in a libel suit would be on the grounds that she is writing fiction rather than nonfiction.

In sum, looked at within the frame of McEwan's novel, Briony's development as a novelist is impressive, but her aesthetic commitment to the representation of other minds and to judging those representations does not provide the ethical grounds for the liberties she takes with the story of Cecilia, Robbie, and her own transgression. These conclusions invite us to reflect on McEwan's purpose in framing Briony's judgments this way, reflections that are part and parcel of the judgments we make about his larger construction of the novel.

## Judgments of McEwan's Misidentification

McEwan's delayed disclosure pulls the rug out from under many of our judgments and emotional investments during Parts Two and Three. Many of our judgments, we suddenly learn, have been misguided because we based them on misinformation. The satisfaction we took in the reunion of Cecilia and Robbie after the horrific retreat and in Briony's promise to recant her testimony about Robbie are significantly altered because we suddenly learn that these events, as part of Briony's novel but not part of her life, exist on a different ontological level than her transgression. In this respect, McEwan's delayed disclosure is analogous to Briony's misidentification of Robbie: since we have no prior definitive signal that Parts One, Two, and Three are Briony's novel, he has implicitly misidentified the nature of his narrative up until this point. To be sure, McEwan is aware—and expects his authorial audience to be aware—of the significant difference between the consequences of the two misidentifications. Nevertheless, when Briony finally decides in her diary entry that her effort at atonement via narrative has been both impossible and necessary, we need to ask whether McEwan is speaking directly through her about his own narrative as well, since that narrative both involves its own transgression and explores the possibility of atonement.

Briony writes, "[H]ow can a novelist achieve atonement when, with her absolute power of deciding outcomes, she is also God? There is no one, no entity or higher form that she can appeal to, or be reconciled with, or that can forgive her. . . . No atonement for God, or novelists, even if they are atheists." Seen within the frame of McEwan's novel, these comments have significantly different implications than Briony could possibly be aware of. First, they invite us to add another layer to our understanding of the novel's central concerns: what is the relation between art and atonement? Second, they raise some more specific questions: (1) the delayed disclosure is an instance of McEwan's playing God, his using his novelist's absolute power not only to decide the outcome but to reveal that decision suddenly and, from the perspective of our emotional engagement in Briony's novel, violently. After playing God this way, does McEwan need to atone and, if so, how can he? (2) There is an entity to which McEwan can appeal for atonement and forgiveness: the audience that he has misled. Has McEwan also included some grounds upon which we can achieve reconciliation? Has he ultimately "set the limits and the terms" of the novel in such a way that his transgression also carries within it the seeds of his atonement? (3) Finally, what light does this dynamic between transgression and atonement in the telling shed on the similar dynamic in the represented action?

The first two questions come together in our interpretive and aesthetic judgments about the relation between the surprise disclosure and the previous three Parts of *Atonement*. As I have argued in the discussion of "Roman Fever" in the previous chapter, effective surprises are ones in which the audience begins by being taken aback and ends by nodding their heads in recognition that the surprise has been prepared for and by perceiving that the surprise enhances the narrative. Preparing the audience of *Atonement* is an especially delicate operation because the terms and limits of the novel stipulate that McEwan must write Parts One, Two, and Three as Briony's novel, and Briony of course has no conception that she is a character in McEwan's novel and thus no conception of McEwan's audience. McEwan carries out the operation in two main ways: (1) he includes in Briony's representation of the events details that, when seen retrospectively, function as clues to her introduction of fictionalizing elements; (2) he includes in Briony's novel meta-level communications about its modernist techniques, communications that function for Briony as elements in the story of her evolution as a writer but function for McEwan as a way to establish a tension about the techniques of Briony's novel—and by extension of his own.

The main clues in the representation of events occur in Parts Two and Three. At the end of Part Two, Robbie, though close to being evacuated from France to Britain, is wounded, exhausted, and only intermittently aware of his environment. Furthermore, his last utterance—and the final sentence of Part Two—is "I promise, you won't hear another word from me" (250). In short, this section of the novel ends without McEwan's audience being able to determine whether Robbie gets evacuated or dies. Part Three appears to disambiguate that ending by showing Robbie reunited with Cecilia. But in retrospect we can see that the end of Part Two is a subtle preparation for the revelation that Robbie did not survive the retreat. This conclusion is reinforced by a passage in Part Three that, in retrospect, we can understand as functioning for both Briony and McEwan as marking the seam between history and fiction.

> [Briony] left the café, and as she walked along the Common she felt the distance widen between her and another self, no less real, who was walking back toward the hospital. Perhaps the Briony who was walking in the direction of Balham was the imagined or ghostly persona. This unreal feeling was heightened when, after half an hour, she reached another High Street, more or less the same as the one she had left behind. (311)

In other words, the historical Briony returns to the hospital while her ghostly persona continues her wish-fulfilling journey to Cecilia and Robbie.

The most dramatic example of McEwan's meta-level communications is that letter of rejection from Cyril Connolly; in addition to recommending that "Two Figures by a Fountain" needs the backbone of a story, Connolly also remarks that he and the other editors "wondered whether it owed a little too much to the techniques of Mrs. Woolf" (294). Although we come to recognize that Briony's Chapter Two incorporates Connolly's advice, we also infer that McEwan's inclusion of the letter from Connolly is a way to raise questions about *Atonement*'s own extensive use of modernist techniques. The tension generated by McEwan's meta-level communication can be put this way: what does it mean for an accomplished novelist writing in 2001 to construct a novel along modernist lines and simultaneously question such a construction? The surprise ending resolves the tension even as it provides an appropriate surprise: the accomplished novelist has been writing not a straight modernist novel in Briony's (or Woolf's) mode but a more self-conscious, self-reflexive novel. In its self-reflexiveness, McEwan's surprise ending acknowledges *Atonement*'s postmodern moment, but, more important, it gives new weight to the elements of Parts One, Two, and Three that comment on Briony's evolution as a writer and new weight to the novel's theme of the relation between art and experience.

This layering of a modernist novel with its focus on the consciousness of its characters within a post-modernist, self-reflexive one and its consequences for the relation between the narrative and the authorial audiences go a long way toward explaining the division in the responses of flesh-

and-blood readers to McEwan's performance. I'll start with an analysis of the positive response to the novel, the one that I believe corresponds with McEwan's invitations to the authorial audience. Consider, first, the relation between transgression and atonement in the represented action (Briony's novel) and in the telling (McEwan's delayed disclosure about our reading a novel-within-a-novel and the corresponding delayed disclosure of the actual fates of Robbie and Cecilia). McEwan invites his authorial audience to recognize that his initial undercutting of our emotions through Briony's revelations in her diary entry allows him to engage with the problem of atonement even more deeply. This invitation depends on our responses in the narrative audience. Whatever else "London, 1999" does, it actually enhances the mimetic components of Cecilia's, Robbie's, and Briony's characters because this section demonstrates that they all have a significant existence beyond the one represented in Briony's novel. Vivid as those existences are, they are all more than they appear to be there. The effect sets up a meta-message from McEwan to his narrative and authorial audiences: our initial emotional trajectory through the problem of the crime and its atonement, however intense and difficult, has been too easy. We were too ready to believe that Robbie survived the retreat and that Briony's meeting with Robbie and Cecilia would lead to some atonement. By pulling the rug out from under our emotional satisfaction in the relatively happy conclusion to Part III, McEwan not only contrasts the hope held out by Briony's novel with "the bleakest realism," but he also makes us feel that bleakness in both the narrative and the authorial audiences.

This effect exists alongside our awareness in the authorial audience, an awareness heightened by McEwan's delayed disclosures, that he, McEwan, is the ultimate designer of the novel and, thus, of the fates of the characters. In other words, McEwan seeks to call attention to the synthetic component of his narrative without detracting from its mimetic component. This effect, in turn, underlines the difference between between Briony's project of atonement through fiction and McEwan's project of representing Briony's fascinating but flawed endeavor. This difference and the coexistence of the mimetic and the synthetic also emphasize McEwan's meditation on the power—and limits—of fiction.[3]

I have already commented on McEwan's judgments of Briony's efforts to use fiction to atone, but it bears repeating that her novel is an attempt to do in art what she failed to do in life. McEwan's transgression and atone-

---

3. For a highly intelligent and engaging account of the importance of fiction as both method and theme in the novel, see Finney.

ment remain within the boundaries of his novel. The juxtaposition conveys the message that, though art can carry out its own patterns of transgression and atonement, atonement for transgressions that occur beyond its boundaries is more difficult to achieve. Art, too, sets its standards for judgment, and Briony, in her imaginative reconstruction of other minds, meets some of those standards, but, in her return to the romanticism of her youth, falls short of others. Furthermore, the extent to which even a narrative that respected the bleak realism of Robbie's and Cecelia's fates would constitute a worthwhile atonement remains an open question. As for McEwan, he is more successful at atoning for his apparent transgressions in the novel, though it is worth noting that the nature of the atonement alters the initial judgment that the delayed disclosures were actually transgressions.

Having developed this positive account of the ethical and aesthetic dimensions of McEwan's performance, I want to complicate it by returning to his strategy of simultaneously enhancing our involvement in the mimetic component of the narrative and calling attention to its synthetic component. The strategy entails the risk that McEwan's delayed disclosures will not merely foreground the synthetic but call so much attention to his role as the ultimate designer of this narrative and of the characters' fates that we will not be able to sustain our investment in those fates. Moreover, if we lose that investment, we will also lose our trust in McEwan, since he has cultivated that investment for so much of the novel and he does not offer us anything comparably substantial in return. Instead, the novel may strike us as an elaborate display of authorial dominance over the reader, and we will therefore render negative aesthetic and ethical judgments about McEwan's achievement. I believe that flesh-and-blood readers who respond in these ways are missing some of the intricacies of McEwan's communication, but I also believe that in McEwan's strategies they have good reasons for their responses.

Strikingly, however, this conclusion does not detract from my ultimate judgment that *Atonement* is a stunning achievement formally, ethically, and aesthetically. I maintain this judgment because I believe that the divide among the readers is an inevitable consequence of McEwan's admirable effort to offer both a deeply compelling experience of the mimetic and a meta-level meditation on the powers of fiction and the relation of art and atonement.

This chapter brings to a close my exploration of judgments and progressions in fictional narratives built on strong principles of narrativity. As noted in chapter 3, my goal has not been to develop theoretical concepts that will predict what narratives must do but rather concepts that are flexible and capacious enough to help us understand what narratives have already done and what they may do in the future. The range of techniques and purposes in the four narratives we have examined, *Persuasion, Beloved,* "Roman Fever," and *Atonement,* provides some measure of assurance about the suppleness of judgment and progression as tools for understanding narrative experience. In the next chapter I will draw on the work of these analyses as I seek to refine the role of rhetorical aesthetics within rhetorical poetics. Then in Part Two, I will extend my exploration of the explanatory power of judgments and progressions by considering fictional texts built on principles not only of narrativity but also of lyricality and of portraiture.

# CHAPTER SIX

# Rhetorical Aesthetics
# within Rhetorical Poetics

Now that I have conducted these four illustrative rhetorical analyses of judgments and progressions, I would like to step back and reflect specifically on the place of aesthetic judgments in the larger theory.[1] The analyses have often shown the close connection between interpretive and ethical judgments as well as the mutual interaction of ethical and aesthetic judgments, but they have done less to show what is distinctive about aesthetic judgments in our experience of fiction. I shall proceed by returning to theses six and seven from the Introduction and further elaborating on them in light of the discussion so far.

*Thesis six: just as rhetorical ethics proceeds from the inside out, so too does rhetorical aesthetics. And just as rhetorical ethics involves a two-step process of reconstruction and evaluation so too does rhetorical aesthetics.*

*Thesis seven: individual readers' ethical and aesthetic judgments significantly influence each other, even as the two kinds of judgments remain distinct and not fully dependent on each other.*

Let me start with thesis seven. The judgments are distinct because we can ultimately separate the Beautiful from the Good, and understanding this separation helps explain their different roles in our reading experience. Although aesthetic judgments are as intrinsic to narrative experience as interpretive and ethical judgments, their precise role in narrative pro-

---

1. I want to emphasize that I am not seeking to develop a full-blown theory of aesthetics here, but instead to explain how judgments we make about the quality of fiction are related to our interpretive and ethical judgments, and, more generally, how the rhetorical theory of narrative sees the interrelations among form, ethics, and aesthetics. For that reason, the argument of this chapter draws on our experiences of fiction and on the argument of the previous chapters rather than on the vast, conflicting history of philosophical arguments about aesthetics.

gressions is different. As the analyses of the previous chapters have shown, our developing experience of narrative progressions is crucially dependent on our interpretive and ethical judgments. Experiencing Sethe's choice to kill her child is not simply a matter of becoming conscious of her action but, more importantly, a matter of interpreting and judging (or at least struggling to judge) it. More generally, each of the major aspects of progression—entrance, intermediate configuration, and completion—are syntheses of textual dynamics and readerly dynamics made possible primarily by interpretive and ethical judgments. Even in cases when our activity of configuring the narrative continues after we finish reading the text, that ongoing configuration is crucially dependent on our interpretive and ethical judgments, both local and global. In this sense, interpretive and ethical judgments are what I shall call first-order activities, ones that are co-extensive with the concept of reading narrative rhetorically.

Aesthetic judgments, like interpretive and ethical judgments, are both local and global, but, unlike interpretive and ethical judgments, they are also both first-order and second-order activities. They are first-order because we make judgments of quality that exist alongside our interpretive and ethical judgments, and they are second-order because they follow from and depend on our interpretive and ethical judgments. First-order aesthetic judgments are our ongoing assessments of the technical skills manifest in the narrative: its relative mastery of style, temporality, devices of disclosure, narrative discourse, and other elements of craft. First-order aesthetic judgments may also be thought of as threshold judgments: if our assessment of an author's technical mastery does not reach a certain threshold, we are likely to stop reading unless there are other compelling reasons to continue—and indeed, mastery of some skills can compensate for lack of mastery of others. More generally, as I will discuss below, the criteria for these first-order aesthetic judgments can to some extent shift with different narrative projects: what is skillful handling of disclosure in a narrative whose effects depend on our knowing more than the protagonist may be unskillful handling of it in a narrative with a detective narrator protagonist. But, as I will also suggest, some criteria operate across the differences in individual narratives.

Second-order aesthetic judgments are the judgments we make about the overall quality of the experience offered by the progression, both as we read and after we finish reading. Second-order aesthetic judgments are dependent on and follow from all three primary-level judgments—not just the aesthetic but also the interpretive and the ethical. Consider once again the ending of Bierce's "The Crimson Candle." "At the funeral the Woman stood at the head of the bier, holding a lighted crimson candle till it was wasted entirely away." In the first-order we make an aesthetic judgment about the effective switch to a focus on the Woman's action and the accompanying direct report that unobtrusively builds to its climactic revelation. In addition, we make several interpretive and ethical judgments about the Woman's action: what it means for her understanding of her promise, her relation to her husband, and her own sense of values. We then are in a position to make second-order aesthetic judgments about the overall efficacy of the sentence's effects. Furthermore, since the sentence is the final move in the progression, we can extend our second-order judgments to the whole narrative: now that these judgments complete our view of Bierce's performance, how do we assess its quality?

With these considerations in mind, I now turn to thesis six, and its emphases on making judgments from the inside out and on the two-step process of reconstruction and evaluation. First, in connection with reading from the inside out, the distinction between first-order and second-order aesthetic judgments underlines the importance of our post-reading (and therefore second-order) global aesthetic judgments. As we have seen with all our narratives, especially "Roman Fever" and *Atonement,* it is not until we have completed our activity of configuration and reconfiguration that we can adequately reconstruct the terms that the narrative has set for itself. This consequence and the principle that aesthetic judgments should proceed from the inside out indicate that the rhetorical approach encourages an openness to narratives with a wide range of *aesthetic goals* and an equally wide range of *aesthetic means* to those goals. (For now, let us understand aesthetic goals as part of a narrative's rhetorical purpose and aesthetic means as the elements of craft put in service of that purpose. This distinction should become clearer as the chapter proceeds.) Later in this chapter, I shall reflect on the range of aesthetic means and goals represented in my chosen narratives, but, first, it will be helpful to explore further the relation between the steps of reconstruction and evaluation. I will anchor this exploration in a discussion of Wayne C. Booth's Four Levels of Evaluation of Irony in *A Rhetoric of Irony.*[2] I will then apply my

---

2. Booth returns to the issue of evaluation in *The Company We Keep* (101–12). His discussion there is very much in keeping with the one in *A Rhetoric of Irony,* though he notes that he no longer likes the metaphor of levels because it mistakenly signals increasingly complexity as one moves from Level One to Level Four. Booth also divides his discussion differently, which reflects some new emphases resulting from the shift in focus from irony to ethics: he devotes only one section to judgments according to constants and he devotes two sections to the impossibility of finding universal constants (for arts and for wholes). I have chosen to focus on Booth's discussion in *A Rhetoric of Irony* because I find its four-part

conclusions, first, to the task of making comparative aesthetic judgments
of Raymond Chandler's *The Big Sleep* and Howard Hawks's film adapta-
tion of the novel and then to the task of making such comparative judgments among the narratives I have analyzed so far.

In *A Rhetoric of Irony,* Booth introduces his Four Levels in a chapter
entitled "Is There a Standard of Taste in Irony?" (193–229), the end of
Part Two's discussion of "Learning Where to Stop." In his Preface, Booth
remarks that in part his book "is an attempt to do with irony what Longinus did with another literary quality, the sublime" (xiv). Just as Longinus
was concerned with the sublime wherever it appeared (in epic narrative
or lyric poem or tragic drama), so too is Booth concerned with irony as a
distinctive kind of rhetorical communication wherever it appears. Furthermore, both Longinus and Booth see the experience of the chosen effect as
rooted in a meeting of minds between author and reader. But when it comes
to the task of evaluation, Booth departs from Longinus. Longinus' single-
minded focus on the sublime with its power to transport readers directly
leads to his straightforward method of evaluation: the greater the degree
of sublimity the greater the artistic achievement. For him the meeting of
minds is the means toward the end of experiencing the sublime. Although
Booth values irony highly, he values it less as an end in itself and more as
an especially powerful means to what he values even more: the meeting
of minds between authors and readers. This hierarchy of values is evident
in Booth's great comfort with (and incisive account of) stable irony, that
is, any communication in which readers reject literal meanings in favor of
a reconstructable alternative meaning that is itself not subject to further
ironic undercutting. Since irony is not an end in itself for Booth, he cannot
follow Longinus' model with the sublime and conclude that the greater the
degree of irony the greater the artistic achievement. Instead he needs to
take other factors into account, and, as a result, he develops his four-level
model. This model, while squarely focused on evaluating irony, provides
a springboard for my broader consideration of rhetorical aesthetics. Here
are the four levels:

1. Judging Parts According to their Functions
2. Judging Parts According to Critical Constants
3. Judging Wholes According to Their Implied Genres
4. Judging Wholes According to Critical Constants.

Clearly Booth generates his levels by means of a two-by-two matrix:

---

system to be a more useful framework for developing my own positions.

two objects of evaluation (parts and wholes) and two criteria of evaluation (inside out, that is, the terms set by the work itself, and outside in, that is, the terms set by critical constants or what I'll call external aesthetic criteria). As we will see, Levels One and Three are very consistent with the a posteriori principle of rhetorical poetics that I discussed in chapter 3. On each level, the critic needs to engage in the activities of reconstruction and evaluation (e.g., how does the part function within the whole, and how should we assess that function), though Levels One and Three with their inside-to-outside orientation put greater emphasis on the importance of reconstruction. The two-by-two matrix appears to give Booth's schema a commitment to symmetry, one in which each level will have the same relative weight. In his discussion of the schema, however, this symmetry breaks down because for Booth Level Two is always on the verge of collapsing back into Level One. Although my own convictions about the advantages of proceeding from the inside-out are strong, I believe that Booth ends up making too weak a case for Level Two.

It is telling that Booth begins his discussion of judging parts according to constants with a five-paragraph case against such an enterprise: the demands of individual works are so different that such constants must give way to judgments according to function. If the constant is "psychological complexity in characters is necessary for first-rate narrative," then traditional allegory cannot be first-rate narrative. But Spenser's *The Faerie Queene* among many other works suggests that the problem is not with its characterization but with the critical constant. Booth quickly goes on to note that his case goes too far, since, among other things, it would leave "us in a forest of particulars, moving without accumulated profit from unique work to unique work, unable in each new experience to make use of our past experience" (204–205). However, when he poses the question, "What makes the difference between strong and weak in an effect held to be desirable?" he replies with a strong nod to Level One: "The answers are disappointingly general, leaving all particulars to be settled by the detailed demands of each work in its special kind" (205). This statement is the general version of what he says more particularly in his discussion of Level One: "Only *Pride and Prejudice*, looked at in very close detail, can tell us where and how irony of a given kind can be effective in *Pride and Prejudice*" (200).

Moreover, there is a paradox that Booth does not explicitly register in his unsurprising identification of the most important critical constant in his system. "It is always good . . . for two minds to meet in symbolic exchange; it is always good for an irony to be grasped when intended, always good for readers and authors to achieve understanding" (205). The paradox is that this critical constant ultimately leads us back to the criteria of Level One, because the terms for the achievement of understanding between authors and readers are ultimately set not by critical constants but by individual works. In sum, at this stage of Booth's analysis, judgments based on working from the inside out are more important than those based on working from the outside in. Indeed, anyone familiar with *The Rhetoric of Fiction* will not be surprised by this result, because that book, in effect, is a brilliant execution of the principle that aesthetic judgments based on Level Two reasoning (e.g., "showing is better than telling") are inferior to aesthetic judgments based on Level One reasoning (the effects sought by some works are better achieved through telling, while the effects sought by other works are better achieved through showing).

This analysis invites us to take another look at Level Two judgments. Is the move back to Level One inevitable for a committed rhetorician? Or is there a way to avoid that move and thus avoid, as Booth recommends, the problem of radical particularism that leaves us denying that individual trees can be considered part of a larger forest? The way, I submit, runs through (a) the category of first-order aesthetic judgments and with (b) the concept of a threshold-level of quality. The experience of reading fictional narrative teaches us the difference between competence and incompetence with its materials and techniques. We recognize the difference between an elegant, pleasurable style and an awkward one, the difference between the deft and the clumsy handling of disclosures, and so on. These judgments of competence do rest on critical constants, e.g., elegance and deftness are better than clumsiness and contrivance. In this way, we can judge the degree of an author's competence with a technique independent of its function—in other words, make Level Two judgments. What we cannot do is assess the importance and effectiveness of the technique to the narrative as a whole without reference to its function.

For some works, an elegant style is crucial to its achievement of its ends (e.g., Nabokov's *Lolita*), while for others a workmanlike, and even an occasionally incompetent, style will suffice (e.g., Dreiser's *Sister Carrie*). In each case, what the novel is doing with judgments and progression—with, that is, characters and events, our responses to these things and overall purpose—puts different demands on the style. If Nabokov gave Humbert Dreiser's style, *Lolita* would be an unreadable book because that style is not able to carry the complex nuances of judgment that Nabokov builds into his relation to Humbert's artful eloquence. But Dreiser's style can adequately convey the multiple judgments he wants his audience to make about the interactions of desire, choice, and social condition in the lives of Carrie, Drouet, and Hurstwood.[3]

At the same time, even when occasional incompetence is not a fatal flaw, it still mars the overall quality of the work. Nabokov is way above the threshold of competent style, and Dreiser is about at the threshold and occasionally below it. If Dreiser were more frequently below it, our aesthetic judgment of his stylistic incompetence might be sufficient to alter our aesthetic judgment of the whole work.

To clarify my point about Level Two judgments, consider the analogy of assessing a physical skill with a clear purpose such as shooting foul shots (or free throws) in basketball. There are various means to the same end of putting the ball in the basket. One can shoot with two hands or just one. One can shoot jump shots or set shots. One can start the shot from above one's head, from off-the-ear, from in front of the chest, or even, as was common back in the day, from between the legs. One can shoot with a relatively high or a relatively low arc. One can aim for the front of the rim, the back of the rim, the middle of the rim, or even the backboard. And so on. Experience in watching free throw shooters teaches us to recognize the different levels of technical competence among them. Without looking at results as measured by percentage of shots made, experienced onlookers can tell the difference between the technical mastery of, say, Steve Nash, and the technical incompetence of, say, Shaquille O'Neal. (Just for the record, Nash makes about 90 percent of his shots and O'Neal about 50 percent.) When O'Neal makes his foul shots, he typically improves his technique—it reaches a threshold-level of competence—but it never reaches the level of Nash's technique, even when Nash misses.

Now one can argue that the best way to measure the quality of the shooter's technique is by its results. According to this argument, on those occasions when O'Neal makes his shots and Nash misses his, O'Neal should get credit for using the better technique. After all, the shooter's purpose is to make the shot, and the purpose of the game is to win by scoring more points. Consequently, regardless of the apparent skill with which the two shots are executed, the one that goes through the rim clearly has a higher quality than one that does not. Further, if both shots go in or both miss, they have the same quality. This argument raises some fascinating issues about the values and purposes of sport in general and basketball in particular, but I will resist the temptation to pursue those issues and instead restrict myself to the heuristic purpose of my analogy. As is probably

3. I elaborate on this point with these examples at considerable length in *Worlds from Words*.

evident by now, this argument rests entirely on Level One thinking: all we need to know about the quality of the shooter's technique is whether it achieves or fails to achieve its function in getting the shot made.

The trouble with this argument is that it renders irrelevant some other things that we know, namely, Nash's technical mastery and O'Neal's lack of such mastery. The relevance of this knowledge becomes apparent in a simple thought experiment. Suppose Nash and O'Neal are playing on the same team against the team that you, a knowledgeable basketball analyst, happen to be coaching and that late in a close game one of your players fouls and inadvertently injures someone on the Nash-O'Neal team. The referee awards the fouled player two free throws, but his injury prevents him from being able to take them himself. Suppose also that the rules say that you get to pick which of two other opposing players will shoot in his place and that you must choose between Nash and O'Neal. Suppose further that you know nothing about Nash and O'Neal except what you've witnessed in this game and that so far each has taken two foul shots and each has made one and missed one. Which player do you choose? If the only relevant criterion for judging their quality as foul shooters is results, you might as well flip a coin, because the results so far are equivalent and the radical particularism of this way of thinking means that one cannot make comparative judgments of their techniques. But of course you will choose O'Neal because you know from having watched both players shoot earlier that O'Neal's barely-at-threshold-level technical competence makes him far more likely to miss than Nash.

I can imagine two objections to the analysis so far. What if your choice in the thought experiment were between a player who appeared to have mastered the technique of free-throw shooting but actually made a low percentage of his attempts and one who appeared to have a poor technique but nevertheless made a high percentage? In that case, then your choice of the shooter with the poor technique would be the wrong one. The objection holds but only as the exception that proves the rule. That is, if you were to make multiple choices and used Level Two criteria in each, you would make the right choice with a Nash-like regularity. The analogy with fictional technique works the same way. Although we can think of examples of writers who do not exhibit mastery of some techniques but produce aesthetically admirable fiction (Dreiser is again a handy example), we do not generalize from these cases to the conclusion that mastery of technique is irrelevant to aesthetic success and that therefore Level Two judgments are similarly irrelevant. Instead, the exceptions remind us that Level Two judgments interact with judgments at the other Levels.

The second objection is that the analogy between art and sport limps so badly that it should be placed in a wheelchair. While most basketball fans would not care about, say, the elegant form of Nash's free throw if he missed 50 percent of his attempts, lovers of literature can imagine spending time reading a beautiful stylist regardless of the uses to which the style is put. In other words, the analogy is problematic because sports is so much more results-oriented—and indeed, the desired results are so much more widely agreed upon ("just win, baby")—than literature. This last point is well taken, but its force is not to undermine the usefulness of the analogy but to reinforce it. Literature's being less straightforwardly results-oriented makes Level Two judgments more relevant rather than less.

The analogy and the thought experiment, then, underline several points: (1) in assessing the quality of our experience in reading narrative, we want to account for both the function of technique and the degree of mastery of technique, and (2) we want to do so without having degree of mastery dominate function or having function render degree of mastery irrelevant. (3) In order to accomplish those ends, we need both Level One judgments about function and Level Two first-order judgments and the concept of threshold competence. These conclusions significantly disrupt the neat symmetry of Booth's model, but by sacrificing elegance we gain explanatory power.

With this way of thinking about Level Two in mind, we can now take a closer look at aesthetic judgments on Level One. My major claims here are that (1) these judgments of function within the whole are second-order aesthetic judgments and that (2) they are crucially dependent on interpretive and ethical judgments. My discussion of the last sentence of Bierce's "The Crimson Candle" illustrates the point. It is not just that the whole narrative sets the basic terms for our judgments of the quality of that sentence, but also that those judgments of quality follow so strongly from the interpretive and ethical judgments it generates. A more elaborate example is my discussion of the efficacy of "London, 1999" in *Atonement*. Before I could offer any definitive aesthetic judgments, I needed to work through the complex set of interpretive and ethical judgments McEwan builds into his presentation of Briony's diary entry. Had I decided that the delayed disclosure was ethically flawed I'd have reached a more negative aesthetic evaluation, though not a completely negative one given my Level Two assessment of McEwan's mastery of so many fictional techniques.

Moving to Level Three (judging wholes according to their implied genres), and Level Four (judging wholes according to critical constants), we

can, first, carry over the general conclusions from our discussion of Levels
One and Two. We need both Levels and do not want one to dominate the
other. In addition, with Level Three we are again talking about second-
order aesthetic judgments. For Booth, understanding a work's implied
genre is the first step toward understanding its implied standards of quality. "We experience every work under the aspect of its implied general
kind, or genre" (208). I propose to revise this element of Booth's system by
replacing "genre" with "purpose(s)" as the source of our standard of quality. "Purpose(s)" is of course more in keeping with the overriding conception of narrative I have been working with (somebody telling somebody
else on some occasion and for some purpose[s] that something happened),
but it also is much less likely to lead to violations of the a posteriori
principle. Thus, our question is whether the work under consideration is
a high-quality example of how to achieve such a purpose whatever that
purpose happens to be. And the same logic that applies to our qualitative assessment of parts applies to our qualitative assessment of wholes.
In order to make that assessment we need, first, to determine the precise
nature of that whole and its purpose(s). Such a determination is crucially
dependent on our interpretive and ethical judgments throughout the narrative and in our post-reading final configuration. Once we have made
that determination, we can then proceed to judge the quality of the work
within the terms appropriate to that kind. Thus, for example, we judge
*Persuasion* not as a comedy of fulfillment with a defective beginning and
early middle because such a judgment mischaracterizes the nature of the
novel's specific purpose Instead, we judge it as a highly successful variation of Austen's previous narratives with comic purposes because those
variations enhance our affective and ethical engagements with it even as
they help her achieve her purpose of constructing a more muted, somewhat darker narrative comedy.

In order to understand how aesthetic judgments work on Level Four,
we need to think through the implications of our conclusions about Level
Two and Level Three. On the one hand, we can carry over from Level Two
the idea of threshold level of competence and apply it to the task of constructing a whole work. Once again our experience as readers allows us to
be able to discriminate between a work that achieves a threshold level of
competence on a global scale and one that does not. On the other hand,
Level Three's grounding in the a posteriori principle and the ensuing lessons about the need to judge works according to the standards implicit in
their purpose(s) combine with our recognition of the great variety of those
standards to make us abandon the idea of a set of universal constants (and,

indeed, some hierarchy among them) for judging whole works. Putting the two implications together generates the main principle of judgment on Level Four: rejecting universals does not mean that we can never make *comparative aesthetic judgments* of whole works, but it does mean that in many cases such comparative judgments will be either virtually impossible or ultimately subjective. Thus, I propose to re-label Level Four as Judging Wholes according to Nonuniversal But Transpurpose Criteria.

In order to show these principles of rhetorical aesthetics in practice, I turn to cases, starting with Raymond Chandler's and Howard Hawks's versions of *The Big Sleep*. In the interest of efficiency, let us stipulate that both Chandler and Hawks are above the threshold level of technical competence (Level Two) for their respective art forms.[4] And let us focus on the ending of each narrative as a way to bring in Level One and Level Three considerations on our way to those of Level Four.[5]

As Peter J. Rabinowitz and David Richter have noted, Chandler's novel deviates from the conventions of the standard detective story because the detective protagonist, Philip Marlowe, does not have a final confrontation with the chief villain, Eddie Mars. In addition, although Marlowe figures out who killed Rusty Regan, solving the crime does not restore order to his world. In the terms of this chapter, our Level Three judgments depend on our recognition of Chandler's generic innovation, including the problem that this innovation poses. How can he provide an effective arrival and completion (a Level One issue) when the generic innovation rejects the standard signs of these elements? Here is Chandler's solution in the final passage of the novel:

> What did it matter where you lay once you were dead? In a dirty sump or on a marble tower on top of a high hill? You were dead, you were sleeping the big sleep, you were not bothered by things like that. Oil and water were the same as wind and air to you. You

4. I realize that my discussion overlooks the important complex issue of the relative difficulty of achieving competence in the different media. I do not take up the issue because I want to keep moving efficiently toward my main goal of considering comparative aesthetic judgments on Level Four.

5. This more efficient consideration and my concern with *comparative* aesthetic judgments means that I will bracket the undeniable misogyny and sexism of both narratives (seen especially in their representations of Carmen Sternwood), but I do want to note that these elements mar the underlying ethical structure of both narratives and thus our second-order aesthetic judgments. In other words, our judgments of the terms of both narratives include negative judgments of this dimension of their ethical bases, and these judgments would have consequences for our comparative aesthetic judgments of each of them in relation to other narratives.

just slept the big sleep, not caring about the nastiness of how you died or where you fell. Me, I was part of the nastiness now. Far more a part of it than Rusty Regan was. But the old man didn't have to be. He could lie quiet on his canopied bed with his bloodless hands folded on the sheet waiting. His heart was a brief uncertain murmur. His thoughts were as gray as ashes. And in a little while, he too, like Rusty Regan would be sleeping the big sleep.

On the way downtown I stopped at a bar and had a couple of double Scotches. They didn't do me any good. All they did was make me think of Silver-Wig and I never saw her again. (230–31)

Chandler here seeks to provide arrival and completion through Marlowe's reflections on the case, reflections that reveal how it has permanently changed him. Marlowe conducts his life as a quest for justice and according to a code of integrity, but he now realizes that his integrity has been compromised by this particular quest. He has been compromised because the evil he has been fighting is so pervasive that it has left him with an unsatisfactory ethical choice. By protecting his client General Sternwood ("the old man" of the passage) from the knowledge that his daughter Carmen murdered Rusty Regan, Marlowe becomes complicit in Vivian and Mars's cover-up of the murder, and that complicity makes him "part of the nastiness." On the other hand, not protecting General Sternwood would be an even greater violation of Marlowe's code. Furthermore, Marlowe recognizes that there is no way out of his predicament—and no solace to be found for it (not even in Scotch or thoughts of Silver-Wig)—and thus Chandler uses the farewell to underline the force and lasting power of Marlowe's new self-understanding.

Chandler's ending provides an aesthetically effective completion because (a) Marlowe's reflections convey his difficult, unsatisfying, but nevertheless admirable ethical choices in a world that has little use for such choices and (b) those choices are the appropriate culmination of the clear and less difficult ethical choices he has made throughout the narrative (the chief of which is continuing to investigate what happened to Rusty Regan after he has completed the assignment for which General Sternwood hired him, investigating Arthur Geiger's blackmail of Carmen). Because Chandler guides us to endorse both Marlowe's interpretive judgments about his being part of the nastiness and the ethical judgments that lead him to that position, we find the ending and the narrative as a whole to be affectively powerful. In short, our Level Three reconstruction leads to a very positive set of second-order aesthetic judgments of the novel on its own terms.

The ending of Hawks's film is very different, and that difference highlights the different terms the film narrative sets for itself. Instead of following Chandler's generic innovation, Hawks synthesizes the standard hard-boiled detective narrative with some elements of the romance. In his ending, Marlowe (played by Humphrey Bogart) and Mars have a final confrontation in which Marlowe outmaneuvers Mars so that Mars ends up getting shot by his own men. In addition, Marlowe is given an assist by Vivian Sternwood (played by Lauren Bacall) and, after Mars's death, the flirtation that they have engaged in throughout the film appears to blossom into a romance. The final camera shot is a close-up of the two of them looking into each other's eyes. In sum, the chief criminal is identified and eliminated, order is restored, and love is on the wing.

Hawks's ending provides a very satisfying arrival and completion because it effectively resolves the narrative's two central instabilities: that of the conflict between Marlowe and Mars and that of the relationship between Marlowe and Vivian. Hawks raises the ethical and affective stakes of his narrative in three ways: (a) making the relationship between Marlowe and Vivian a central instability in the film, a choice that necessitates that Vivian not be married to Rusty Regan; (b) calling attention to the potential for that instability to interfere with Marlowe's investigation; and (c) showing that that potential will be realized or not according to ethical choices by each character. Vivian does not want Marlowe to discover Mars's hold over her, and so she tries to make Marlowe focus on the good time they could have together and thus distract him from pursuing the question of who killed Rusty Regan. Since General Sternwood has not hired Marlowe to investigate what happened to Rusty, she has a reasonable hope she can succeed. But Hawks's Marlowe, like Chandler's, remains committed to his quest and to his sense that Sternwood really wants to know what happened to Rusty. By having Vivian ultimately help Marlowe against Mars, Hawks shows Vivian yielding to Marlowe's values, a choice that ultimately frees her from Mars and makes the two of them freer to act on their mutual attraction. In this way, Hawks's ending not only shows Marlowe restoring order by eliminating Mars but also offers both of them a reward for their ultimately appropriate ethical choices. The farewell close-up underlines this reward and invites the audience to take pleasure in it. As with Chandler's novel, the ending is fit, efficient, and satisfying within the terms that the narrative sets for itself. And again as with Chandler's novel, our Level Three reconstruction of the film leads to a positive set of second-order aesthetic judgments.

To this point, then, we do not have grounds for judging Chandler's overall achievement as better or worse than Hawks's. As I move to Level Four, however, I have no hesitation in judging Chandler's achievement as greater than Hawks's for two main reasons: Chandler successfully executes a more difficult and more ambitious narrative project, and, in the course of that execution he offers his audience a more significant ethical experience. These reasons in turn rest on two nonuniversal but transpurpose criteria: (1) Successfully executing a formally innovative, difficult, and worthwhile purpose is a greater aesthetic achievement than successfully following the grooves of a conventional structure toward a worthwhile but conventional purpose. (2) Engaging an audience in complex ethical judgments that are integrally related to the narrative's working out of its formal problems is a greater achievement than working with a simple binary between good and evil.

These are nonuniversal criteria because they would not be the ones I would appeal to for every situation of comparative judgments. Successful formal innovation will not always trump successful implementation of the tried-and-true (see the comments below about magnitude), and ethical complexity is not always a better route to aesthetic achievement than ethical simplicity. Fielding's *Tom Jones* requires much simpler ethical judgments than the ones Chandler invites us to make in his ending, yet no one would be surprised to hear me say that Fielding's aesthetic achievement is superior. But I believe that these two criteria are appropriate for this case because they apply to significant elements of the terms that the two narratives set for themselves. In other words, the a posteriori principle and the emphasis on doing aesthetics from the inside out does not mean that we have to eschew Level Four judgments, but it does mean that the choice of the nonuniversal criteria for the judgments should arise out of Level One and Level Three judgments.

Although I do not expect every reader to agree with my comparative judgment in favor of Chandler here, I also do not expect it to be terribly controversial. Indeed, I have chosen the example because I think that most readers would be inclined to make a similar judgment, even if they did not articulate their reasons in the same way. But let us see what happens if we expand our field and try to make comparative aesthetic judgments of the narratives I have analyzed so far, including these two versions of *The Big Sleep*. I have no trouble saying that "The Crimson Candle" is the slightest achievement for reasons I have articulated in the Introduction, especially its relatively minor ambition. Bierce simply sets his bar lower than all the other narrative artists we have considered here do. One sign of his setting the bar lower is the brevity of the story. While Bierce makes that brevity work to his advantage in the swiftness of the story's reversal and in the pleasure associated with the numerous inferences he invites us to make over such a short span, it also points to the story's relative lack of magnitude. It does not offer—indeed, is not interested in offering—a sustained engagement over time. This difference in magnitude between "The Crimson Candle" and all the other narratives we have considered provides sufficient grounds for regarding it as the least significant aesthetic achievement.

Magnitude is also a relevant criterion in thinking about the comparative achievement of "Roman Fever" relative to *Persuasion, Beloved,* or *Atonement.* In comparison with each of the novels, Wharton's short story aims for less and achieves less. But the lesser magnitude intrinsic to the short story form does not mean that all short stories will be lesser achievements than all novels. In other words, there is no simple equation between magnitude and aesthetic achievement. To take an easy example, any novel that does not meet the threshold level of competence on Levels Two or Four will be a lesser achievement than "Roman Fever." To take another, more challenging example, I believe that Wharton's short story is a greater aesthetic achievement than Hawks's *Big Sleep.* Like Chandler's story, Wharton's offers a more significant ethical experience. But more than that, her decision to work on the smaller canvas of the short story actually raises the aesthetic stakes. To put the point in hyperbolic terms, part of her purpose is to pack as many interpretive and ethical judgments about the past, present, and future relation between Grace and Alida into as short a space as possible and to sequence those judgments for maximum effect. Had she tried to turn the story into a medium-length novel by spelling out things that are implicit, she would have greatly attenuated its effect. Her success within her chosen frame seems more difficult and, thus, more significant than Hawks's within his.

But is Wharton's story a more significant achievement than Chandler's novel? Is *Beloved* a more significant achievement than *Persuasion?* Is *Atonement* more significant than *Beloved?* I could offer a list of my preferences here, but I do not think I could offer substantial reasons for you to agree with me, precisely because at Level Four we are dealing with nonuniversal criteria, and I cannot find grounds why you should opt for my nonuniversals, or better, my hierarchy of nonuniversals, rather than your own. It is in this sense that, after a certain point, we enter the realm of what for convenience sake we can call subjective judgments—subjective because we cannot find grounds for a hierarchy of possible criteria of judgment, but not thoroughly subjective because we do apply criteria in

addition to personal taste. The nonuniversal character of Level Four judgments is also why making or debating such things as the list of the Top
100 Novels of All-Time (or even of the Twenty-First Century) is not much
more than an interesting diversion.

The analogy with free-throw shooting is again helpful here. Imagine
the same thought experiment except that your choice is between Steve
Nash and Dirk Nowitzki, another excellent shooter, and that you have
seen each of them make nine out of ten shots. You have noticed that much
about their technique is different—Nash, for example, shoots from shoulder
level, while Nowitzki shoots from above his head; Nash's legs are straight,
while Nowitzki's are bowed—but you have found much to admire in each.
You may decide on Nash because you are suspicious of Nowitzki's bowed
legs, but if, say, your assistant coach argued that you should pick Nowitzki
because his greater size and strength make the shot more effortless for him,
you couldn't legitimately argue that your criterion should trump his.

Another analogy is also illuminating because it will become more than
an analogy. Is it possible to make a rank-ordered list of ethical values? Is
justice more important than unselfishness, responsibility more important
than generosity? Again, even if one could make such a ranking for some
values in line with Level Two thinking (e.g., unselfishness is greater value
than reliability), one could not insist on its universality across all situations (Level Four). Furthermore, since our aesthetic judgments at Level
Three are second-order judgments that are partially dependent on our ethical judgments, we would need to be able to do a Level Four rank-order of
ethical values in order to be able to make comparative aesthetic judgments
that would be more than subjective. We can legitimately say that in some
situations some ethical values are more relevant than others and in that
sense more important (Level One thinking) and that some exemplifications
of a given value are stronger than others (Level Three thinking), but I see
no grounds for establishing a universal hierarchy among ethical values.
Similarly, I see no grounds for the establishment of a hierarchy of aesthetic
values.

— PART TWO —

Judgments and Progressions
in Lyric Narratives
and Portrait Narratives

# CHAPTER SEVEN

# Interlacings of Narrative and Lyric

Ernest Hemingway's "A Clean Well-Lighted Place"
and Sandra Cisneros's "Woman Hollering Creek"

The work of Part Two follows from—and is designed to substantiate—the claim that some of the most innovative and effective short stories and dialogue poems of the past century are hybrid forms of narrative, lyric, and/or portraiture that narrative theory has not yet done justice to. A partial list of such stories indicates that a diverse group of writers have experimented with these hybrid forms and that the hybrids themselves are of multiple kinds: Robert Frost's "Home Burial," Virginia Woolf's, "Slater's Pins Have No Points," Ernest Hemingway's "Now I Lay Me," and "A Clean, Well-Lighted Place," Tillie Olsen's "I Stand Here Ironing," J.D. Salinger's "Uncle Wiggly in Connecticut," Eudora Welty's "Powerhouse," Sandra Cisneros's "Woman Hollering Creek," and "Barbie-Q," Alice Munro's "Prue," John Edgar Wideman's "Doc's Story," and Ann Beattie's "Janus." Even some brief observations about a selection of these stories will show the diversity of relations between lyric, portraiture, and narrative among the group. Cisneros's "Woman Hollering Creek," as I will argue at greater length shortly, introduces a major instability, then switches primarily to a lyric revelation of that unstable situation throughout its middle, and then switches back to a narrative mode in the final sections of the story. Hemingway's "Now I Lay Me" uses Nick Adams's metamemory—his recall of nights he spent remembering his past—as a way not to recount any change in Nick but rather to reveal both his desire for and repulsion from intimacy. Wideman's "Doc's Story," to take just one more example, uses an embedded narrative about a character other than the protagonist as a key to the revelation of the protagonist's desire for his lost love. Munro's "Prue," as I'll discuss in the next chapter, employs two mini-narratives as key means in its unfolding portrait of the protagonist's character and situation.

In order to develop an adequate understanding of these hybrid forms, we need (1) to develop a more extensive list of such works; and (2) to conduct detailed examinations of the individual stories and poems with an eye both to their particular dynamics and to the general principles underlying them. In *Living to Tell about It,* I have offered a small contribution to this second task through close analyses of "Now I Lay Me" and "Doc's Story" as part of my larger investigation into the rhetoric and ethics of character narration. In this part of *Experiencing Fiction,* I attempt a more substantial contribution by focusing on five works—in this chapter, "Woman Hollering Creek" and "A Clean, Well-Lighted Place"; in the next "Prue" and "Janus"; and in the final chapter "Home Burial"—and by bringing the hybridity of portrait narratives into the conversation. One consequence of this addition is to prompt some further reflection on the concept of narrativity from the perspective of rhetorical theory. I will offer those reflections at the end of chapter 9, and I start here by reviewing what the Introduction had to say about narrativity, lyricality, and portraiture.

That discussion identifies the fundamental elements of narrativity on the textual side as character, event, and change, and on the readerly side as judgment, affect, and ethics. With lyricality, each of these fundamentals is different in some important way. On the textual side, character is better described as speaker. Event gets displaced by thought, attitude, belief, or emotion; while event may be present, it is subordinated to the expression of one or more of these elements. Change, too, becomes optional; it may occur—as in meditative lyrics where speakers reach decisions—but it is not necessary. On the readerly side, ethical judgment drops out and is replaced by participation, an entering into the speaker's situation and perspective without judging it. That participation in turn influences the affective side of the experience—we share the speaker's feelings or take on the speaker's thoughts, beliefs, or attitudes. Finally, as a result of the replacement of judgment by participation our ethical evaluation is of that participation—and thus it is simultaneously an evaluation that applies to the whole work.

The contrast with narrative will help clarify this point. An implied author of a narrative may guide us to judge a character as ethically deficient in his or her actions, and we may regard that negative ethical judgment as a positive feature of our reading experience. To take just one example, much of the pleasure in reading *Persuasion* involves our sharing the implied Austen's negative ethical judgments of Sir Walter Elliot and many of her characters. The implied author of a lyric, by contrast, by inviting our participation in the speaker's perspective, tacitly asks us to approve of that perspective, to regard it as ethically legitimate. Thus, our ethical evaluation of that participation is an ethical evaluation of the central experience offered by the poem. (Here we see a dramatic example of the way Level Three aesthetic judgments follow from ethical judgments. Although we may make positive first-order aesthetic judgments of, say, the poet's handling of such formal matters as rhythm, rhyme, and word choice, if we do not judge our participation in the speaker's perspective as ethically desirable, we will ultimately judge the poem as aesthetically flawed.)

The space between narrativity and lyricality is occupied by portraiture, a rhetorical *design inviting the authorial audience* to apprehend the revelation of character. If narrativity can be reduced to somebody telling that something happened, and lyricality can be reduced to somebody telling that something is, portraiture can be reduced to somebody telling that someone is. In portraiture, events typically are present, but not because they are essential to the progression of a story of change but because they are an effective means to reveal character. Change is not present, because portraiture is focused on depicting a character at a particular moment or a particular phase of life that we understand as ongoing. On the readerly side, ethical judgment is present, and our affective experience is rooted in our coming to apprehend and judge the character, and so, too, is our second-order aesthetic experience. As with narrative, both positive and negative ethical judgments of the portrayed character can be the basis for satisfactory aesthetic experiences. Indeed, as in Browning's "My Last Duchess," the skillful revelation of a brilliant but despicable character can provide an especially satisfying reading experience.

I want to underline the point that these conceptions of narrativity, lyricality, and portraiture are heuristic accounts of pure forms, not recipes for writing or for analyzing individual works. Authors are of course free to combine the fundamental elements of the pure forms in any way they wish, and rhetorical critics set themselves the task of reasoning back from the multilayered effects of those individual works to their causes in those combinations of elements.

I have chosen to analyze "Woman Hollering Creek" and "A Clean, Well-Lighted Place" in this chapter in part because these two lyric narratives are themselves quite different from each other and from both "Now I Lay Me" and "Doc's Story." In "A Clean Well-Lighted Place," the lyric dimension only gradually emerges but then becomes central to its effect. In "Woman Hollering Creek," as I noted above, we start with signals of narrative, but then switch to a lyric progression for most of the story, and then switch back to a strongly narrative progression in its final sections. Thus, the juxtaposition of the two stories should help illuminate what is distinctive about each even as it indicates something of the variety of progression in lyric narratives. Furthermore, while "A Clean, Well-Lighted Place" relies on a fairly specialized ethical system, one closely associated with Hemingway himself and that many flesh-and-blood readers are not likely to bring to the story themselves, "Woman Hollering Creek" relies on a more conventional underlying ethical system that most flesh-and-blood readers will bring to the story. As a result, the relations between ethics and aesthetics in the two stories also provide an opportunity for productive comparisons.

I connect my analysis of "A Clean, Well-Lighted Place" to the long-standing debate about the attribution of dialogue in the story and about Scribners' decision to alter the text after Hemingway's death. In this way, Hemingway's story can function as a kind of New York for me: if my attention to judgment and progression can make it here, with a problem that seems largely to be the province of manuscript and biographical study, then such attention can presumably make it anywhere. To put this point another way, if rhetorical poetics can help adjudicate this controversy about the decision to alter Hemingway's text, then it can claim to be worthy of the attention of readers who are not themselves rhetorical critics. I shall argue that attending to progression and judgment and their relation to the lyric narrative hybridity of the story indicates that Scribners made the right call.

Even as "Woman Hollering Creek" relies on a set of widely accepted ethical positions, it is an aesthetically innovative work, an experiment in voice and temporality melded with an experiment in progression. Cisneros uses many voices and fourteen discrete sections to tell the story of Cleófilas Hernandez's unhappy marriage to a husband who abuses her and of her escape home to her father and brothers. No one voice displays an explicit awareness of the interrelation among the sections; there are no transitional devices and no explicit cross-references between them. The fourteen narrative sections are like different pieces of a mosaic whose overall shape and design the authorial audience needs to deduce. Furthermore, the most salient features of that design are the introduction of the global instability at the end of section one—Cleófilas's unhappiness; the frequent shifts in voice and temporality within and between sections; the lyric exploration of the global instability in sections 2 through 11; and the shift to a narrative resolution in sections 12 through 14. I shall argue that Cisneros's management of these elements of the story makes "Woman

Hollering Creek" not only a distinctive lyric narrative hybrid but also an aesthetic achievement on a par with "A Clean, Well-Lighted Place."

## A New Approach to the Textual Controversy about "A Clean, Well-Lighted Place"

Any analysis of Hemingway's story needs to address the long and ongoing critical debate over the attribution of the dialogue between his two waiters, and, in particular, needs to take a stand on whether the textual emendation by Scribners' in 1965 is appropriate. The debate is about whether the older waiter or the younger waiter speaks the line, "You said she cut him down" (289), referring to the old deaf customer, and thus, which waiter has prior knowledge of the customer's suicide attempt. The attribution matters because it affects our understanding of the attribution of nineteen lines of dialogue (among other things, it affects our answer to the question of which waiter introduces the concept of "nothing" into their first conversation about the customer). Not surprisingly, our decisions about that attribution have larger consequences for our interpretive judgments about the relations between the speakers and about the overall trajectory of the progression. Here is the disputed line in its immediate context, as it appeared in all editions of the story until 1965. The younger waiter is clearly marked as the speaker of the first line:

> "A wife would be no good to him [the old deaf customer] now."
> "You can't tell. He might be better with a wife."
> "His niece looks after him."
> "I know. You said she cut him down."
> "I wouldn't want to be that old. An old man is a nasty thing."
> (20)

The manuscript of the story in the John F. Kennedy Library in Boston indicates that Hemingway inserted the sentences "I know. You said she cut him down" rather than composed them as part of single, smooth sequence. [item 337, of the Ernest Hemingway Collection, Kennedy Library, p. 4]. Since the younger waiter is clearly marked as the speaker of "A wife would be no good to him now," the older waiter seems to be the speaker of "I know. You said she cut him down." Consequently, Hemingway's insertion indicates that the younger waiter is the one with prior knowledge of the customer's suicide attempt. That attribution, in turn, means that the younger waiter introduces the concept of "nothing" into the story, though it is the older waiter who reflects on "nothing" at the end of the story.

The problem with the pre-1965 text is that other evidence points to the older waiter as the one with the prior knowledge, including knowledge that the customer's niece interrupted the suicide attempt. Hemingway clearly identifies the younger waiter as the one who serves the customer his brandy, and who then returns to his fellow worker and begins this conversation.

> "He's drunk now," he said.
> "He's drunk every night."
> "What did he want to kill himself for?"
> "How should I know."
> "How did he do it?"
> "He hung himself with a rope."
> "Who cut him down?"
> "His niece." (289)

Since this conversation continues on to the inserted lines, those lines seem to introduce an inconsistency about which waiter knows what. In addition, the older waiter is more sympathetic to the customer's desire to linger at the café and this alignment fits with (though of course it doesn't definitively prove) the reading that he is the one who knows something about the customer's life. In order to eliminate the inconsistency, Charles Scribner, Jr., with permission from Mary Hemingway, authorized the change in the text. Here is the revision in its immediate context, where once again the first line belongs to the younger waiter.

> "A wife would be no good to him now."
> "You can't tell. He might be better with a wife."
> "His niece looks after him. You said she cut him down."
> "I know. "
> "I wouldn't want to be that old. An old man is a nasty thing."
> (289)

Besides eliminating the inconsistency in which waiter knows about the customer's suicide attempt, the change retrospectively marks the older waiter as the one to introduce the concept of "nothing" into the story (the concept that becomes the thematic center of the story ["It was all a nothing and a man was nothing too," as the older waiter puts it later]), and, thus, establishes strong continuity between his mentioning the concept at the beginning and his meditating upon it at the end.

Scribners' decision delighted one group of Hemingway critics, including John Hagopian, who recommended the change, even as it distressed another group, who have continued to justify the originally published text. These critics appeal not only to the manuscript evidence but also to Hemingway's practice in other stories of using line breaks in quoted dialogue to signal pauses rather than shifts of speakers. Thus, for example, one can apply this logic to both "He's drunk now" and "He's drunk every night" and read each line as spoken by the younger waiter, with the line break signaling a pause.

Because the debate has focused so closely on the early conversations between the waiters and considered them from multiple angles, and because good arguments have been made for multiple ways of attributing the lines, I do not believe that we can resolve the issue by more close reading of the dialogue, or even of the manuscript in the Kennedy Library.[1] Instead, I suggest that we approach the controversy from the perspective provided by attention to judgments, progression, and the relation between lyricality and narrativity in the story, especially as these issues apply to the second half of the story, about which there is no textual dispute.

## Lyric Participation and Narrative Judgment in "A Clean Well-Lighted Place"

Charles May's case against the 1965 emendation provides an excellent starting point. May very astutely observes that, if the older waiter learns of the suicide attempt from the younger waiter, then is "forced to confront his affinity with the old man's despair, he arrives at his *nada* prayer at the end as a *result* of the story" (328). May's larger point is that what's at stake in the attribution debate is a view of the story "as a static or a dynamic action": if the older waiter already knows of the suicide attempt, nothing substantial happens to him during the waiters' conversations. Strikingly, May assumes rather than argues for the superiority of the dynamic to the static view, and that assumption authorizes his preference for the pre-1965 version of the story.

---

1. Among the key contributors to the debate, those on the side of the emendation include Hagopian, Bennett, and Lodge, while those on the side of the pre-1965 text include May (1971), Kerner (1975, 1985, 1992), Reinert, and Ryan Smith ("A Note"), Kerner ("Foundation") and Kann offer useful discussions of the manuscript evidence. Smith's 1989 *Reader's Guide* provides an excellent summary of the debate to that point.

From my perspective, May's assumption rests upon another one: short stories should be driven by the principles of narrativity. If, however, we adopt a more expansive view of the short story (and indeed, of the novella and the novel) and acknowledge that highly effective stories can also be— and, in fact, have also been—built on other principles, including those of lyricality and portraiture, and of hybrid combinations of all three modes, then May's initial assumption no longer seems warranted.[2] Furthermore, and equally important, the evidence of the second half of the story does not support the conclusion that the older waiter's purported new knowledge of the customer's suicide attempt brings about the *nada* prayer. He speaks and thinks of himself not as a man with new insight or a deeper sense of despair but rather as a man who has been in the same condition for a long time: "I am one of those who like to stay late at the café" (290). "What did he fear? It was not fear or dread. It was a nothing that he knew too well" (291). The man who prays the *nada* prayer is one who has known that nothing for a long time, not one suddenly driven to the prayer in the face of new knowledge. To put this case another way, if Hemingway wants his audience to see the waiter's prayer as a result of new knowledge about the old customer, Hemingway includes some textual details that work against that interpretive judgment. These same details, however, fit very well with the interpretive judgment that the older waiter does not learn anything new in the present time of the story. That hypothesis in turn raises the question of how Hemingway generates the textual and readerly dynamics of the progression, and that question invites us to consider his use of some elements of lyricality.

Testing May's assumption and conclusion, in other words, leads us to remain open to the idea that the 1965 emendation was appropriate because it fits with Hemingway's choice of a hybrid lyric narrative form to create the effects he sought. The story has obvious elements of narrativity: a retrospective narrator reports a clear sequence of events, involving a protagonist whom we observe and judge, as it follows the older waiter from his initial conversations with the younger waiter to their closing the café and then on to the older waiter's *nada* prayer, his visit to another bar, and his final ironic remark about insomnia. Nevertheless, Hemingway constructs this sequence of events and audience response so that it lacks strong narrativity, as we can see, even if we bracket the debate about the attribution of dialogue.

The first paragraph introduces a mild instability, but it is never complicated and easily resolved: "while he [the old customer] was a good client

2. May's own further work on the short story form itself indicates that he has a much more capacious view of the form; see, for example, his 2004 essay.

they knew that if he became too drunk he would leave without paying, so they kept watch on him" (288). The first conversation between the waiters introduces a mild tension about which waiter speaks which lines, but this tension does not give the story much forward movement. The subsequent conversations between the waiters introduce the potential for a progression by instability, since these conversations indicate differences in their attitudes toward the old customer with the younger waiter expressing disrespect and impatience and the older waiter showing sympathy and consideration. Indeed, as David Lodge points out, these differences between the waiters become greater as the conversations continue, but this potential for these differences to be the global instability of a narrative never gets realized. Similarly, the younger waiter's disrespectful treatment of the old customer provides another potential for a progression by instability between two characters that does not get realized. Rather than launching the narrative movement of the story, these mild instabilities function primarily as a means by which Hemingway reveals, either directly or indirectly, the older waiter's character and especially his attitudes. Indeed, once we recognize that what would be false starts in a progression by narrative are positive moves in the revelation of the older waiter's attitudes, we can also recognize that revelation as part of a progression with a different underlying logic from that of a straight narrative.

The unusual logic of the progression is also evident when we consider the location of launch and entrance in this story and their consequences for arrival and completion. The launch and entrance do not occur until its last page (there are 4 pages in the Finca Vigia edition), when the older waiter "continue[s] the conversation with himself" (291). It is not until then that the authorial audience can confidently recognize that the story's central instability is not one between any of the characters but rather one involving the older waiter's relation to the nothingness of existence. Furthermore, this location of the launch and entrance and the reference to the "nothing that he knew too well" underlines the disclosure of this instability as one that is ongoing—something that long pre-exists the narrated event. The location, the reference, and the lack of development of the earlier instabilities also mean that we do not develop any strong expectation that the story will resolve the instability. We expect, instead, that the rest of the story will explore that instability. This expectation raises questions about what would constitute effective arrival and completion to this unusual progression, an issue I will return to below.

These points enable us to gloss Hemingway's own hyperbolic claim in "The Art of the Short Story" about what he left out of the story: "Another time I was leaving out good was in 'A Clean, Well-Lighted Place.' There I really had luck. I left out everything. That is about as far as you can go so I stood on that one and haven't drawn to that since" (140). What he leaves out is the origin, the complication, and the resolution of the instability. But what he leaves in is the gradual revelation of the ongoing instability and the older waiter's response to it as well as some clear signals for our response to these revelations.

One consequence of Hemingway's delayed location of the entrance is that its retrospective light helps us better configure what we've read before. Looking at the movement from middle to end with the benefit of this retrospective light, we can recognize that Hemingway (a) increasingly emphasizes the older waiter as a superior ethical character to the younger waiter; (b) more fully reveals the older waiter's attitudes and invites the audience to stop judging him and simply participate in his expression of them; and, finally, (c) again separates the audience from the character for a final ethical judgment. It is the movement from ethical judgment to participation and back to judgment that I am most interested in because it further illuminates the nature of the story's progression and because it sheds light on the debate about the attribution of dialogue.

Through the conversations between the waiters as they are closing up, Hemingway represents the older waiter consistently challenging the younger waiter's ways of thinking while also always treating him with respect. In other words, the older waiter invites the younger waiter to rethink the ethical judgments he makes about the relation between his own wishes and those of the customer.

"Why didn't you let him stay and drink? . . . It is not half-past two."
  "I want to go home to bed."
  "What is an hour?"
  "More to me than to him."
  "An hour is the same." (290)

The younger waiter, as we have previously seen in his interactions with the customer, is self-absorbed, while the older waiter is other-directed. He does not take the conversation down a road that would encourage the young man's self-absorption (no "I know what you mean" or even "how is your wife?") but always brings things back to what would be better for the customer. The older waiter implicitly asks the younger waiter to adjust his attitudes, but he also manages to do it in a way that never causes a breach in his relation with the younger waiter. This conversation, in short, establishes the older waiter as the superior ethical character.

Later in the conversation, Hemingway has the older waiter himself articulate the differences between him and his coworker.

> "I am of those who like to stay late at the café. . . . With all those who do not want to go to bed. With all those who need a light for the night."
>
> "I want to go home and into bed."
>
> "We are of two different kinds. . . . Each night I am reluctant to close up because there may be some one who needs the café."

In part, this conversation simply reveals a difference in personal preference, and, as such, there is no negative ethical judgment tied to the younger waiter's preference. But the older waiter's mention of his affinity with and interest in staying open for those "who need a light for the night" further aligns him with the old deaf customer. Because he is interested in doing something, however simple, for such people, the conversation also aligns him with the implied Hemingway's beliefs and values: the night is a time when one can be overwhelmed by the nothingness of existence, but there are temporary refuges available, and the act of providing them can itself be a stay against that nothingness.

Furthermore, this conversation and the attitudes that the older waiter expresses in the story's last paragraphs reveal that his ethical judgment about the value of keeping the café open late is tightly linked to his aesthetic judgment about the kind of café that is valuable: a clean, well-lighted one. The last paragraphs reveal that these ethical/aesthetic judgments are themselves a consequence of the older waiter's prior, underlying interpretive and ethical judgment: "it was all a nothing and a man was nothing too" (291). As noted above, this judgment is fully endorsed by Hemingway, but its nihilism will be resisted by many flesh-and-blood readers. Indeed, I am among those who cannot endorse it. I will have more to say about this difference between the implied Hemingway's ethical values and my own, but first I need to look more closely at the story's final paragraphs.

Once the older waiter turns off the light and leaves the café, Hemingway shifts the narrative technique from the report of conversation to an extensive use of internal focalization, a shift that greatly facilitates the audience's gradual participation in the older waiter's perspective. Hemingway carefully guides the audience into that perspective by the way he handles voice and focalization; his method is to move us gradually to a point of full participation in the *nada* prayer. "What did he fear? It was not fear or dread. It was a nothing that he knew too well. It was all a nothing and a man was nothing too. It was only that and light was all it needed and a certain cleanness and order" (291). Here we have both the vision and the voice of the older waiter but we are still observing him, seeing him from the outside. That angle of vision changes in the *nada* prayer.

In that prayer, Hemingway uses the Spanish word rather than the English word for nothing, in order to emphasize its every appearance in the prayer and to reinforce the juxtaposition between the language of faith and that of utter disbelief. Furthermore, by employing both the vision and voice of the waiter, by adapting the Our Father, the most familiar prayer in Christianity, and by quickly establishing the pattern of substitution of "nada" for the important nouns of the prayer, Hemingway, in effect, invites us to anticipate his substitutions: "Our *nada* who art in *nada, nada* be thy name, thy kingdom _____ thy will be _____ in _____ as it is in _____." With "The Hail Mary" he switches from "*nada*" back to "nothing," a sign that he is ending his prayer, but the switch does not interfere with our anticipation of his substitutions. "Hail nothing full of nothing, _____ is with thee" (291). In short, in the prayer Hemingway completes the authorial audience's movement from outside the waiter observing and judging him to inside his perspective participating in it. In this respect the prayer is not only the thematic but also the lyrical climax of the story.

Hemingway, however, does not end with this climax but returns to principles of narrativity by once again showing the waiter interacting with another character and, most importantly, by moving us back into the observer role and asking us to judge him once again. Strikingly, the story does not record but leaves us to infer the older waiter's physical motion between his turning off the light in his café and his arrival at the bar where he stops for his nightcap. His interaction with the barman shows the waiter still in the grip of his awareness of nothingness but also able to deal with that awareness with irony:

"What's yours?" asked the barman.
"*Nada.*"
"*Otro loca mas,*" said the barman and turned away. (291)

Having had his ironic joke, the waiter drops the game and asks for "A little cup" of coffee, though his next comment indicates that he continues

to be preoccupied by his previous thoughts. He renders an aesthetic judgment that also has an ethical dimension. "The light is very bright and
pleasant but the bar is unpolished" (291). The bar is ultimately not a satisfactory refuge, and so he does not stay. After he leaves, he anticipates what
will happen next: "Now, without thinking further, he would go home to his
room. He would lie in the bed and finally, with daylight, he would go to
sleep. After all, he said to himself. It is probably only insomnia. Many must
have it" (291). The irony of the final two lines stems from the waiter's self-
deflating interpretive judgment—I don't have existential angst but simple
insomnia. His ironic adoption of the attitude of one who "lived in it but
did not feel it" indicates that he will neither take himself too seriously nor
deny what he knows. What Hemingway gives us between the late entrance
and this farewell are both an inside look at the older waiter's contemplation of the nothing that he knew too well and an external look at how he
responds to his intimate acquaintance with that nothing. Hemingway asks
us to endorse both the contemplation and the response, the waiter's ability to face the fundamental truth about the pervasiveness of *nada* and his
ability to poke ironic fun at his own awareness.

Our endorsement of the older waiter's response, in turn, intensifies
the effect of the *nada* prayer. The lyrical nature of the prayer means that
Hemingway is adopting the technique of what I call "mask narration,"
that is, using the waiter as an effective and almost direct means to convey
his own views.[3] In the *nada* prayer, the older waiter becomes, in effect, a
character narrator, and the lyricality of the prayer effectively merges him
with both the implied Hemingway and the authorial audience. The power
of that merger is heightened because of our ethical judgments of the older
waiter before—and after—that moment. Consequently, Hemingway's invitation to share in the older waiter's perspective, to take on these interpretive and ethical judgments about the nature of existence is very strong.

If my analysis of the role of judgment in this latter part of the story
is close to being on target, then Scribners' revision of the text is the cor-
rect call. If the story is built primarily on principles of narrativity and the
younger waiter introduces the idea of nothing into the story, which in
turn sets the older waiter on this path to thinking about nothing, we can
still regard it as having genuine ethical and aesthetic merit. It is a story
in which Hemingway uses his ethical system as the basis for a story of
significant change. But even laying aside the recalcitrant evidence of the
second half of the story, this hypothesis leaves us with an older waiter
whose interpretive and ethical judgments both during the prayer and in

3. For a fuller discussion see the Epilogue to *Living to Tell about It*.

his response to his newly acquired knowledge are less impressive precisely because they are first-time judgments. A story which treats this night in the older waiter's life not as a night of discovery but rather as one in a long series of nights in which the same despair-inducing knowledge is faced yet value is affirmed is a greater story for at least two related reasons. (1) It essentially encompasses the story of change as part of its backstory. That story of change had to occur in some form or another for this story to exist, but (2) this story focuses on the more difficult ethical problem of how to live with the knowledge acquired during the change.

At the same time, to return to the discussion of rhetorical aesthetics in the previous chapter, this argument for the superiority of the revised version of the story is only an argument about a comparative aesthetic judgment in these two cases. With these materials of character, event, attitude/belief, judgment and participation—indeed with these two almost identical versions of the text of the story—we can use the principles of rhetorical poetics to judge one as an aesthetically greater achievement, but we cannot extract aesthetic universals from this example. Hemingway himself, in *A Farewell to Arms,* develops a very powerful narrative of change which shows Frederick Henry's gradual acquisition of the knowledge that the older waiter has well before "A Clean, Well-Lighted Place" begins. But because so many of the other materials of the two stories are different, I believe it is much more difficult to make a comparative aesthetic judgment of them.

Let me return to the details of the progression. The movement of the final paragraphs also sheds light on the readerly dynamics connected with Hemingway's building the story on an ethical system whose key principle is that "It was all a nothing and a man was nothing too." First, the lyric participation allows us to take on the belief in those ethics temporarily. Second, the movement back to judgment shows that the consequences of the ethical beliefs are not themselves nihilistic and that there are other important principles of the system: self-deprecating irony is a superior response to the knowledge of nothingness than the more logical despair; to the extent that response enables one to go on and provide comfort for others who recognize what Carlos Baker has aptly called the Something That is Nothing it is even more valuable. Indeed, when we think about the ethics of the telling here, the way in which Hemingway crafts his innovative communication about the older waiter's attitudes, we can see that Hemingway's story itself stands as a clean, well-lighted place for his audience. What all this means is that the story does not wholly rise or fall on whether we can endorse the ethical principle that "it was all a nothing and a man was nothing too." In my own case, I can endorse this premise only in my blackest bleakest moments—or on some occasions when I'm in the midst of reading the story—but my more common disagreement with that premise does not destroy my satisfaction in and admiration for the story. I remain moved by the innovative nature of its lyric-narrative hybridity and by the ethics of its telling, its effort not just to promulgate a nihilistic world view but also to provide some counterbalance to such a view. In other words, recognizing the story as itself a version of the older waiter's clean, well-lighted place enhances my understanding of Hemingway's aesthetic achievement in this story, and it also helps me understand why I can value the story so highly without fully accepting its most fundamental interpretive and ethical positions. Again this overall aesthetic judgment is a second-order one, since it follows from both the interpretive and ethical judgments in the story. But because the story itself foregrounds both the older waiter's aesthetic judgments ("The light is very bright and pleasant but the bar is unpolished") and their interrelation with his sound ethical judgments, the connection between our ethical and our aesthetic judgments is arguably tighter than in any of the other narratives we've looked at.

## The Beginning and Middle of "Woman Hollering Creek"

In contrast to "A Clean, Well-Lighted Place," "Woman Hollering Creek" is built on a set of ethical positions that most of its flesh-and-blood readers are likely to endorse: to name just a few, women are as valuable as men; spousal abuse is a horrible crime; women who have a sense of their own value should be cherished; women who move toward a recognition of their own value should also be cherished. The story's effectiveness, then, depends not on its ability to have its audience try on challenging ethical positions, but rather on the way it deploys these widely accepted positions while making the specific situation represented fresh rather than clichéd and moving rather than flat. The progression is crucial to these effects, and it is quite different from the progression of Hemingway's story. As noted above, the beginning introduces a global instability, the middle is given over to the lyric exploration of that instability, and then the ending shifts to the narrative mode as it brings about the resolution of the instability. I begin with a description of the main narrative line so that we can better appreciate the way Cisneros builds principles of lyricality into her treatment of this narrative material.

In Mexico Cleófilas Enriqueta DeLeón Hernández marries Juan Pedro Martínez Sánchez and crosses the border with him to Seguín, Texas. Isolated in the new culture, Cleófilas soon has to endure beatings from her husband and the likelihood of his infidelity. She has few cultural resources to draw on other than her memory of her father's love and his promise that he would never abandon her. Unexpectedly aided by Graciela and Felice, two sympathetic Chicanas, the pregnant Cleófilas begins her journey back across the border. Cleófilas is initially amazed by everything about Felice, especially by Felice's "hollering like Tarzan" as they cross the creek called "La Gritona." The amazement leads to the climactic moment described in the story's concluding sentences: "Then Felice began laughing again, but it wasn't Felice laughing. It was gurgling out of her own throat, a long ribbon of laughter, like water" (56).

It's also important to identify at the outset the cultural narratives in relation to which "Woman Hollering Creek" is situating itself. It's clearly a story of border crossing, and in 1991 such a story by a Chicana writer will have Gloria Anzaldúa's *Borderlands/La Frontera* as an intertext. While "Woman Hollering Creek" is not Anzaldúa's book rendered as allegory, Anzaldúa's discussion of the borders of identity and of mestiza consciousness is relevant to the story. As Cleófilas crosses the border from Mexico to Texas and then back again to Mexico, her primary identity changes from daughter to wife and back again to daughter, but the ending suggests that her return to daughter is a return with a difference.

More specifically, "Woman Hollering Creek" sets up Cleófilas's story against the backdrop of the *telenovelas* in Mexico, commercialized tales of romance and passion used to sell cosmetics and clothes. These *telenovelas* shape Cleófilas's ideas—and those of the other Mexican women in the story—about love, marriage, and consumerism. The grim reality of Cleófilas's story functions as an anti-*telenovela,* an exposure of their dangerous ideological messages about the value of suffering for love and their association of romance with certain clothes, cosmetics, and other fashions.

"Woman Hollering Creek" is also in part a feminist coming-to-consciousness narrative. Graciela, Felice, La Gritona, and of course Cleófilas herself all contribute to Cleófilas's sudden recognition that there is a life for women beyond the roles of daughter, wife, and mother. While this recognition of course does not alter the material conditions of her life, it does alter her understanding of what is possible for women. Finally, the story works with the myth of "La Llorona," the maternal figure who is weeping for her lost children, and my analysis will address how Cisneros rewrites the myth.

Let us now turn to consider the story's beginning, the first of its four-teen sections. I start with the temporal exposition and the initiation in the opening paragraphs.

> The day Don Serafín gave Juan Pedro Martínez Sánchez permission to take his daughter Cleófilas Enriqueta DeLeón Hernández as his bride, across her father's threshold, over several miles of dirt road and several miles of paved, over one border and beyond to a town *en el otro lado*—on the other side—already did he divine the morning his daughter would raise her hand over her eyes, look south, and dream of returning to chores that never ended, six good-for-nothing brothers, and one old man's complaints.
>
> He had said, after all, in the hubbub of parting: I am your father, I will never abandon you. He had said that, hadn't he, when he hugged and then let her go. But at the moment Cleófilas was busy looking for Chela, her maid of honor, to fulfill their bouquet conspiracy. She would not remember her father's words until later: I am your father, I will never abandon you.
>
> Only now as a mother did she remember. Now, when she and Juan Pedrito sat by the creek's edge. How when a man and a woman love each other, sometimes that love sours. But a parent's love for a child, a child's for its parents, is another thing entirely.
>
> This is what Cleófilas thought evenings when Juan Pedro did not come home, and she lay on her side of the bed listening to the hollow roar of the interstate, a distant dog barking, the pecan trees rustling like ladies in stiff petticoats—*shh-shh-shh, shh-shh-shh*—soothing her to sleep. (43–44)

These paragraphs move across three different temporal moments:

*Time 1 and Time 2:* Cisneros begins with what appears to be a narrative summary, in past tense, of the thoughts of Cleófilas's father, focalized first through the narrator, then through him, and finally through Cleófilas: "The day Don Serafín gave Juan Pedro Martínez Sánchez permission to take his daughter Cleófilas Enriqueta DeLeón Hernández as his bride, across her father's threshold . . . already did he divine the morning his daughter would raise her hand over her eyes, look south, and dream of returning . . ." (43). The first half of the sentence suggests that the Narrative Now, that is, the temporal moment from which we can identify past and future, is Cleófilas's wedding day, but, the second half establishes the Narrative Now as the morning Cleófilas would look to return home.

As the narration continues, we learn that Don Serafín did not literally "divine the morning" his daughter would dream of returning but rather that Cleófilas makes an interpretive judgment that his parting words (or her summary translation of them), "I am your father, I will never abandon you," implied such a divination ("He had said that, hadn't he"). This inference in turn suggests that the shift in the focalization is not from the narrator to Cleófilas's father but right to Cleófilas herself. She is thinking of his words and their meaning on this morning, this "now" of the present time, when she looks to return home: "Only now as a mother did she remember. Now, when she and Juan Pedrito sat by the creek's edge"(43). This last sentence actually wavers a bit between singulative and iterative narration—it could be either—but the previous reference to "the morning" tips the scales in favor of the singulative.

*Time 3:* As the narration continues into the summary statement of the last paragraph of the section, the Narrative Now shifts again. "This is what Cleófilas thought *evenings* when Juan Pedro did not come home" (44; my emphasis). The Now is not the morning when Cleófilas is by the creek but evenings when she is in her bed. Furthermore, *evenings* marks the clear shift from singulative to iterative narration: Cleófilas's memory of her father's promise is not a singular event occurring on a particular morning or during a particular outing to the creek but something that she experiences over and over again.

This unusual movement of the temporal exposition has multiple effects. First, it is part of an initiation in which Cisneros immerses us in the perspective of her protagonist in order to give us some sense of how she experiences time. For Cleófilas, time does not move in straight linear fashion but rather jumps from one moment to another, past and present intermingle, and any one moment is layered with other similar or contrasting moments. Second, the exposition emphasizes the global instability, Cleófilas's unhappiness in her marriage and her longing to return home. The first section gradually unfolds this instability, culminating in the shift to the iterative description at the end of the section. That shift in turn reduces the degree of narrativity in the launch. Although the global instability is introduced, the shift from singulative to iterative emphasizes this instability as something that is ongoing and something that may well continue. Of course the instability may be complicated in the very next section, but this launch does not propel us toward any such complication. Consider the difference between this launch and the one that occurs at the end of Chapter 3 of *Persuasion,* where the narrative suddenly kicks into a higher gear. If there is any changing of gears at the end of this section, it is a downshift.

Third, both of these effects contribute to the authorial audience's ethical judgments of Cleófilas as wronged by her husband and, thus, deserving of our sympathy. To be sure, other elements of the treatment also support that judgment: her willingness to return to "chores that never ended, six good-for-nothing brothers, and one old man's complaints" (44); her loneliness on the "evenings when Juan Pedro did not come home." This combination of effects means that, at the end of the first section, we enter a world where we observe and judge, but also one in which there is already the beginning of lyric revelation.

Moving on to the middle of the narrative, we discover that throughout the voyage Cisneros continues to show that Cleófilas's experience of time is both layered and full of gaps and that our initial judgments get reinforced as more of her situation gets revealed. It is impossible to place sections one to eleven on a clear time-line (although we can place some individual sections in relation to each other) or to determine how much time passes between many of the juxtaposed sections. Indeed, we cannot determine with any confidence whether the Narrative Now of the action in sections two to eleven ever advances past the point we reach at the end of section one. In addition, more than once, Cisneros presents what initially appears to be a singular event and reveals it to be part of a repetitive pattern. The last two sentences of section five, a section that begins as a description of the "first time" Juan Pedro beats Cleófilas, provide a telling example of this technique: "She could think of nothing to say, said nothing. Just stroked the dark curls of the man who wept and would weep like a child, his tears of repentance and shame, *this time and each*" (48; my emphasis). With the four monosyllabic words I have stressed, Cisneros transforms what appears to be a singular, distinct event into one that is indefinitely repeated—and experienced essentially the same way every time. Again, the effect is to emphasize the lyric exploration of her static, emotionally and physically painful situation, but our interpretive and ethical judgments of that situation reinforce our desire for some narrative movement that will allow her to escape it—even as the middle sections do not contain any clear means for such movement.

To put this point another way, after introducing the central instability in section one, Cleófilas's unhappy marriage, and the possible, though imperfect, resolution, her return home, Cisneros neither complicates nor begins to resolve this instability until section twelve. Just as there is no sense of launch toward new complications at the end of section one, there is no sense of a voyage toward a destination in the middle sections. Instead the voyage explores the depth and texture of the instability, giving us a greater awareness of its layers. It's not just that her love has soured but that she is in a situation where she gets beaten, something that raises the stakes for any attempt to escape. If she should try and fail, she would face even more abuse. Furthermore, although we continue to observe and judge Cleófilas and that situation rather than participate in it as we do in the *nada* prayer, Cisneros's technique of focalizing the narrative through Cleófilas deepens our sympathy for her.

Although the middle does not complicate the global instability, it does introduce and complicate a significant tension: what is the meaning behind the name of the creek La Gritona? In section four, we learn that Cleófilas wants to know that meaning, but "no one could say whether the woman hollered from anger or pain" and, indeed, "Woman Hollering" was "a name no one from these parts questioned, little less understood" (46). At the end of section four, we learn that upon first hearing the name, Cleófilas "had laughed" because she thought it "such a funny name for a creek so pretty and full of happily ever after" (47). In section nine, we see that Cleófilas, now a mother, no longer thinks that the creek's name is funny or that its sound is full of happily ever after. Instead, she wonders whether the creek, with "its high, silver voice," is "La Llorona, the weeping woman. La Llorona, who drowned her own children" (51). She becomes "sure" that La Llorona is calling to her. The link between "La Gritona," "La Llorona," and Cleófilas's situation suggests that Cleófilas is right to be sure, and so, this tension appears to be resolved in a way that again deepens our sense of Cleófilas's sorrow and grief.

A third significant feature of the middle is that Cisneros gives us two pairs of sections that are each repetitions with a difference. Section nine is a variation of section one, as Cisneros gives us Cleófilas's thoughts as she plays with her child beside the creek; section eleven is a variation of section five, as Cisneros recounts Juan Pedro's abuse of Cleófilas. In section one, we acquire only a general knowledge of Cleófilas's situation; by section nine, with its apparent resolution of the tension, we know all that is entailed by her thoughts of how her love has "soured." Returning home to her father's house is attractive only by comparison with staying in Seguín with Juan Pedro. Indeed, by section nine, most of the lyric revelation is complete; all that is needed is the fuller revelation of the circle of male hostility that Cisneros provides in the description of Maximiliano at the ice house in section ten.

Section eleven, the other scene of repetition, represents Juan Pedro hitting Cleófilas with a book, but it does not explicitly contain any new revelations about Cleófilas's situation. The difference in the repetition here is that the book Juan Pedro throws at Cleófilas is a love story that she is reading as a substitute for the *telenovelas* she is now unable to watch because she has no television. The incident becomes the occasion for Cleófilas to make a significant interpretive judgment about the difference between the romantic narratives of the *telenovelas* and her own life, and this judgment provides the basis for the shift to the narrative movement of section twelve:

> Cleófilas thought her life would have to be like that, like a *telenovela*, only now the episodes got sadder and sadder. And there were no commercials in between for comic relief. And no happy ending in sight. . . . Everything happened to women with names like jewels. But what happened to a Cleófilas? Nothing. But a crack in the face. (52–53)

I will return to the significance of Cleófilas's interpretive judgment after considering how Cisneros uses the interplay of voices as part of the interaction that further contributes to the lyric revelation of the beginning and the middle.

Cisneros marks a significant difference between the voice of Cleófilas's father, on the one side, and those of her husband and the men at the ice house in Seguín on the other. Her father speaks only once, but, as we've seen, he speaks with a voice of parental love that Cleófilas can later recall despite her failure to pay attention on her wedding day. "I am your father, I will never abandon you" (43).

Juan Pedro's voice is also not prominent in the story; indeed, his longest unmediated speech occurs about halfway through in a passage that moves from indirect to direct discourse. Like the voice of Cleófilas's father, the voice of Juan Pedro is heard within one of her meditations. The indirect discourse works to allow Cisneros both to represent the different qualities of the two men's voices and to show how Cleófilas has, if not internalized both voices, at least kept them playing inside her head. Cleófilas has to wonder why she loves her husband, the narrator tells us, when he

> says he hates this shitty house and is going out where he won't be bothered with the baby's howling and her suspicious questions, and her requests to fix this and this because if she had any brains in her head she'd realize he's been up before the rooster earning his living to pay for the food in her belly and the roof over her head and would have to wake up again early the next day, so why can't you just leave me in peace, woman? (49)

We easily infer both the contrast between Juan Pedro's harsh, complaining voice and Don Serafín's loving one and Cisneros's privileging of the father's voice. Again the ethical judgments are clear and straightforward: while Cleófilas "has to . . . wonder a little" (49 ) why she loves her husband, we recognize that he does not deserve her love.

Cisneros gives other evidence of the values associated with Juan Pedro's voice by associating him with the men at the ice house, whose voices are weakened by drink, whose words are often replaced by belches. Yet before the alcohol takes over, they are the leading gossips of the town: "the whispering begins at sunset at the ice house" (50). When Cisneros shows the direct speech of Maximiliano, she reveals a voice of crude misogyny: "Maximiliano who was said to have killed his wife in an ice-house brawl when she came at him with a mop. I had to shoot, he had said—she was armed" (51). All the others laugh. Again, the interpretive and ethical judgments are clear: the physical abuse Cleófilas endures is part of a larger atmosphere of male hostility in which she lives. The effect is to add another layer to our sense of the misery of her situation.

The women's voices Cisneros presents in the middle of the story also represent a limited range, though they express far different concerns from the men's voices. The women in Cleófilas's hometown who watch the *telenovelas* speak the language of romantic fantasy, a language whose values Cleófilas adopts. By not identifying the speaker of the following passage from section two, Cisneros invites us to read it as the voice of any young woman in Cleófilas's home town:

> Because you didn't watch last night's episode when Lucia confessed she loved him more than anyone in her life. In her life! And she sings the song "You or No One" in the beginning and end of the show. *Tú o Nadie.* Somehow one ought to live one's life like that, don't you think? You or no one. Because to suffer for love is good. (45)

Other, older women in her hometown also come under the sway of the *telenovelas*, though they give voice to more conventional gossip:

> She's always been so clever, that girl. Poor thing. And without even a mama to advise her on things like her wedding night. Well, may God help her. What with a father with a head like a burro, and those six clumsy brothers. Well, what do you think! Yes, I'm going to the wedding. Of course! The dress I want to wear just needs to be altered a teensy bit to bring it up to date. See, I saw a new style last night [on the *telenovela*] that I thought would suit me. (45–46)

Again our interpretive and ethical judgments of these voices are clear: they show a startling ignorance, one linked to their attachment to the *telenovelas,* about the reality that Cleófilas will face once married. The first voice articulates the fantasy that suffering for love makes pain sweet, when—as Cleófilas comes to discover—suffering at the hands of a lover makes the pain cut more deeply. The second voice comes closer to real problems in Cleófilas's situation but can only talk about them in conventional terms before moving on to the more serious business of discussing her *telenovela*-inspired dress.

Trini, the Laundromat attendant in Seguín, has a different kind of female voice but it, too, is no model for Cleófilas. "What do you want to know for?" is Trini's reply to Cleófilas's question about the name for the creek. Trini's reply is delivered in "the same gruff Spanish she always used whenever she gave Cleófilas change or yelled at her for something" (46). While Trini's voice offers a useful counter to the *telenovela*-inspired voices, it is too full of impatient imperatives, and Cisneros wants us to recognize that her yelling has its roots in different sources than the ones Cleófilas imagines for the hollering of the woman for whom the creek was named: "anger or pain" (46). Trini's hollering is motivated by her concern for the practical business of fitting in in Seguín, as she yells at Cleófilas for "putting too much soap in the machines" or "sitting on the washer," or "for not understanding that in this country you cannot let your baby walk around with no diaper and his pee-pee hanging out" (46). We endorse Cleófilas's interpretive judgment that she could not explain to Trini "why the name 'Woman Hollering' fascinated her" (46).

In sum, Cisneros uses the interactions by means of voice in the beginning and the middle as a way to contextualize Cleófilas's situation, to locate her among belief systems that have either led her into her plight or that emphasize its difficulty. But as the story moves, in section twelve, from its lyric revelation to a narrative resolution, Cisneros does something new with voice as well.

## The Ending:
## Sections Twelve, Thirteen, and Fourteen

Cleófilas's interpretive judgment at the end of section eleven spurs her to action in section twelve, as she persuades Juan Pedro to take her to the doctor. The interaction is significant here: Cisneros presents Cleófilas speaking aloud in her own voice for the first time, and that voice assumes an equality with her husband's. She has stopped imagining herself the heroine of a *telenovela,* has stopped waiting for things to happen to her, and begins to take some responsibility for her own unromantically painful life. She explains to Juan Pedro that she wants to see the doctor "Because she is going to make sure the baby is not turned around backward this time to split her down the center" (53). It is this same desire to take responsibility for her life that allows her to go along with Graciela's plan for escape that we learn about in section thirteen and that gives her the courage to stand by the Cash N Carry and wait for Felice, despite her fear that she will be discovered by Juan Pedro.

Section twelve is just the second time we hear Juan Pedro's voice directly, and he has just two lines in his own voice: "Please don't anymore. Please don't [write to your father and ask for money]" and one in indirect discourse, "Why is she so anxious?" about her pregnancy that she must ask her father for money to pay for her visit to the doctor (53). Cisneros here marks Juan Pedro's speech as having shifted from complaining to requesting, from dominating to wondering. The shift in his voice and the shift back to indirect discourse signal a shift in the balance of power between them, a shift that makes possible not only Cleófilas's visit to the doctor but also her eventual escape.

Section thirteen is given over entirely to Graciela's voice as Cisneros presents her side of the telephone conversation with Felice in which they arrange for Felice to drive Cleófilas to the bus station in San Antonio. Graciela has a voice comfortable with both American English and Spanish; American idioms flow off her tongue and her voice combines pragmatism with compassion and with irony. "She needs a ride. . . . If we don't help her, who will? I'd drive her myself but she needs to be on that bus before her husband gets home from work. . . . Yeah, you got it, a regular soap opera sometimes" (54–55). Graciela's voice is something new for both Cleófilas and the authorial audience, a woman's voice that is independent of men's values and power and opposed to the values of the *telenovelas.* But Graciela cannot herself realize the depth of the irony in her remark about soap operas, which Cisneros uses to call attention once again to the contrast between the *telenovelas* and "Woman Hollering Creek."

Section fourteen not only represents Cleófilas's escape and thus the lyric narrative's arrival but it also continues Cleófilas's exposure to a new kind of woman's voice, indeed, a new kind of woman: "Felice was like no woman she'd ever met" (56). She drives her own pickup truck; she doesn't have a husband; she uses men's phrases such as "pussy car" (to refer to the Pontiac Sunbird she drove before the pickup); and, when they drive across the creek, she "open[s] her mouth and let[s] out a yell as loud as any mariachi"

(55). Felice explains, "Every time I cross that bridge I do that. Because of the name, you know. Woman Hollering. *Pues,* I holler. . . . Did you ever notice . . . how nothing around here is named after a woman? Really. Unless she's the Virgin. I guess you're only famous if you're a virgin. She was laughing again" (55). This is the independence of Graciela's voice combined with a deeper irreverence and sense of humor. Cisneros leaves open the possibility that Felice's voice marks her as a Chicana lesbian, perhaps the partner of Graciela, perhaps not. In any case, she is certainly a woman who is comfortable with her identity and her independence. That Cleófilas responds so positively to her and her hollering is, thus, all the more telling.

After listening to Felice, Cleófilas recognizes for the first time that her categories for thinking about the source of the creek's name—pain or rage—are inadequate and that thought provides the opening to the arrival, farewell, and completion. "Then Felice was laughing again, but it wasn't Felice laughing, it was gurgling out of her own throat, a long ribbon of laughter, like water" (56).

This arrival and farewell constitute a brilliant completion, one whose various components lead us to a very positive second-order aesthetic judgment of the story as a whole. First, Cleófilas's spontaneous overflow of powerful feeling has been well-prepared for by both the lyric revelation and the play and progression of voices, culminating in those of Graciela and Felice. Second, the final metaphors comparing Cleófilas's "ribbon of laughter" to "water" unites Cleófilas's voice not only with Felice's but also with the sound of the creek itself. Third, the arrival presents a direct contrast with section five's representation of the relation among the voice, the body, and oppression. Overpowered not only physically but emotionally and psychologically by Juan Pedro's violence inflicted on her body, Cleófilas can neither act nor speak:

> She had always said she would strike back if a man, any man, were to strike her.
> But when the moment came, and he slapped her once, and then again, and again; until the lip split and bled an orchid of blood, she didn't fight back, didn't break into tears, she didn't run away as she imagined she might when she saw such things in the *telenovelas*. . . .
> She could think of nothing to say, said nothing. (47)

The story's final sentences invert the situation of section five, as Cleófilas's body responds almost involuntarily to the psychological and emotional release she feels in exchanging the presence of her abusive husband for the company of Felice and the new possibility for female responsibility—and perhaps female sexuality—she represents in Cleófilas's eyes. The involuntary quality of Cleófilas's response is beautifully captured in the narrator's sentences, even as the onomatopoeic "gurgling" and the metaphorical "long ribbon of laughter" convey something of the sound of Cleófilas's voice. In a sense, Cisneros uses Cleófilas's own moment of lyric intensity, her instinctive participation in Felice's hollering, as the moment of the story's arrival, farewell, and completion.

Fourth, this ending allows Cisneros to re-write or at least add to the narrative surrounding the figure of "La Llorona" in Chicano/a culture. There is a long tradition in Chicano storytelling of the mythical figures being reinterpreted to fit new cultural situations. The myth of "La Malinche," the Aztec woman who became the interpreter for and sexual partner of Hernando Cortéz, is perhaps the most notable example. Originally thought to be a traitor to her people, La Malinche has been reinterpreted as a figure of resistance, one who managed to maintain her identity as an Aztec and used her influence to preserve the lives of many native Americans. In one version of the story, she drowned a son rather than have Cortéz take him back to Spain. In this version, she and "La Llorona" get conflated, as La Malinche weeps continually about what she has done to her son (see Novas's *Everything You Need to Know about Latino History* 60–62). When Cisneros introduces the question of whether "La Gritona" is weeping from pain or rage, the myths of both La Malinche and La Llorona become relevant to the story. The ending then suggests that "La Malinche" and "La Llorona" need not be hollering only from pain or from rage, because there are other more appealing possibilities to consider: women can holler like Tarzan, they can give a hoot as Felice does, they can yell "as loud as any mariachi band" (55), they can laugh in a way that their voices sound just "like water," just like the high, silvery voice of the creek itself. Thus, in crossing the physical border marked by the creek, Cleófilas also crosses a psychic border and Cisneros crosses a mythic border, adding the story of "La Felice" to the narratives surrounding "La Malinche" and "La Llorona."

The fifth important effect of the ending involves Cisneros's use of a break in the temporal progression. Just before the final sentences, the narrator flashes forward in time to Cleófilas's report of Felice's hollering to her father and brothers: "Can you imagine, when we crossed the arroyo she just started yelling like crazy, she would say later to her father and brothers. Just like that? Who would have thought?" (56). This proleptic move not only signals that Cleófilas did succeed in her escape but also reminds us that the escape is to "chores that never ended, six good-for-nothing brothers and one old man's complaints" (43)—and in that way tempers the euphoria of the final sentences. One moment of laughter will not change the material conditions of Cleófilas's life. Cisneros is not offering us a *telenovela* plot but something much more realistic. Nevertheless, by ending not with the return itself but with Cleófilas's hollering, Cisneros underlines the point that Cleófilas is returning home as a very different woman, one with a new sense of herself. Indeed, Cleófilas's telling the story about Felice to her audience of seven men is itself a sign of that change, one that shows her using her voice among them to celebrate the extraordinary woman.

# CHAPTER EIGHT

# Narrative in the Service
# of Portraiture

## Alice Munro's "Prue" and Ann Beattie's "Janus"

In this chapter, I turn to another kind of hybrid form, what I call portrait narratives, works constructed on principles of narrativity and of portraiture in which the narrative principles ultimately serve those of portraiture. My specific examples are short stories of the 1980s by women writers about women protagonists: Alice Munro's "Prue" (1982) and Ann Beattie's "Janus" (1986), both of which are reprinted in the Appendix. Munro's story attempts to capture and convey what it means to be Prue, a woman in her late forties whom everyone likes but no one takes seriously. Beattie's story attempts to capture and convey what it means to be Andrea, a married, childless real estate agent obsessed with a cream-colored bowl. Although this description of the stories emphasizes what they have in common, the stories themselves represent two very different ways of using narrative in the service of portraiture: in "Prue" Munro uses two distinct mini-narratives within her overarching frame that reveal essential features of her protagonist's character, whereas in "Janus" Beattie uses a global tension to drive the progression of the narrative and then uses the resolution of that tension via backstory not to signal a change in her protagonist but rather to complete the portrait. The two stories also work with different kinds of initiation and interaction, and these elements of the progression have consequences for our ethical judgments both of the protagonist and of the implied author.

Before I turn to a detailed look at the roles of judgment and progression in each story, I want to offer four more general points about the dynamics of portrait narratives.

1. Just as lyric narratives typically involve some degree of portraiture, portrait narratives typically involve some degree of

lyricality. (Indeed, standard narratives can have degrees of lyricality and portraiture but their subordination to principles of narrativity is typically clear.) Since portrait narratives are primarily concerned with the revelation of character, they, like many lyrics, focus not on change but on stability, on character in a fixed situation. But unlike those lyric narratives that may ask the audience to participate, at least for a time, in the protagonist's emotions and situation, portrait narratives ask the authorial audience to remain in the twin roles of observer and judge. As a result, the readerly dynamics of portrait narratives are markedly different from those of lyric narratives.

2.  The emphasis on portraiture naturally gives special prominence to the mimetic component of the protagonist's character and of the narrative as a whole. But the emphasis on portraiture also invites careful attention to the thematic component of character and its role in what we might call the particular shading of the portrait. In analyzing portrait narratives, we need to attend, first, to ways in which the author invites us to thematize the character, and, second, the consequences of that thematizing for our ethical and aesthetic judgments.

3.  Progressions in portrait narratives often depend upon the introduction of a global tension that must be resolved before completeness can be achieved. Instabilities may be introduced but they are more commonly local, connected with the movement of subordinate mini-narratives rather than with the larger trajectory of the hybrid work. In "Prue," the global tension arises primarily from the narrator's initial descriptions of Prue's character. In "Janus" the global tension involves the mystery of Andrea's strong attachment to the bowl.

4.  Just as lyric narratives can synthesize principles of narrativity and lyricality in different ways so too can portrait narratives. I have already noted some large differences between the progressions of "Prue" and "Janus," so here I will mention four specific strategies that are frequently but not necessarily employed in portraiture along with brief comments on their use by Munro and Beattie:

    a.  Straightforward descriptions of the protagonist by the narrator. Munro uses these, but Beattie does not, choosing instead to represent Andrea through her thoughts or her actions.

b.  The use of the present tense for the present-time of the story. Munro uses the present both for her straightforward descriptions in the beginning, shifts to the past for the mini-narrative in the middle, and then shifts first to historical and then to genuine present in the conclusion. Beattie, however, never uses the present tense, shifting instead from past to past perfect when she tells the backstory that resolves the tension about Andrea's attachment to the bowl.

c.  Iterative accounts of the protagonist's behavior. Both authors use this device.

d.  Mini-narratives that illustrate key traits or other information crucial to our understanding of the relation between character and situation. Again both authors use this device.

The descriptions and iterative accounts may also invite ethical judgments, and the narratives inevitably do. These judgments are crucial to the completion of the portraiture because they are integral to our comprehension of the character.

To illustrate this last general point, I will offer some brief comments here on the ethical judgments accompanying the mini-narratives of "Prue" and "Janus," holding off more extended commentary until the detailed analysis of the progression. "Prue" concludes with a mini-narrative about Prue's theft of a cufflink from her lover's house, and "Janus" concludes with a mini-narrative that, among other things, reveals that Andrea has been guilty of adultery. In the authorial audience we're invited to judge both characters, though the precise nature and function of our judgments are different in each case. In "Prue" we are not invited to make the kind of strongly negative ethical judgment that we are in "Janus," but in each case the judgment is connected with the way the revelation serves to resolve tensions in the portrait, and, in that way, connected to the unfolding sequence of judgments. In other words, in each case our judgments are not simply based on our recognition that the protagonist is guilty of an ethical transgression. Instead, we recognize that both the story of the theft and the story of the adultery serve to resolve some tensions in the portrait, and we then make rather complex ethical judgments about the character as now revealed. In that way, the theft and adultery play crucial roles in the completion of the portraits both because they resolve the tensions and move us toward our overall judgments of the characters.

## Progression and Judgment in "Prue"

The progression of "Prue" divides very neatly into beginning, middle, and ending. The beginning goes from the title to the end of the fifth paragraph, and it both introduces an instability and gives us extensive exposition about Prue's character. The middle consists of a mini-narrative that I'll call "Dinner at Gordon's," and while this mini-narrative gets its own movement from a pattern of instability-complication-partial resolution, its function is to expand upon the instability and the exposition of the beginning. The ending consists of another mini-narrative, which I'll call "Prue's Taking Ways." This mini-narrative gets its movement from a pattern of instability-tension-partial resolution, but it also stands in for similar narratives that are suggested but not fully told, and its function is to complete the portrait of Prue. This description of the progression is overly schematic on the textual side, and it is incomplete because it does not attend to readerly dynamics, so I turn now to a more thorough analysis of that progression.

The first paragraph introduces the global instability about Prue's relationship with the other significant character, Gordon, even as it offers exposition:

> Prue used to live with Gordon. This was after Gordon left his wife and before he went back to her—a year and four months in all. Some time later, he and his wife were divorced. After that came a period of indecision, of living together off and on; then the wife went away to New Zealand, most likely for good. (227)

The move from the title to this paragraph calls attention to the facts that Prue herself plays a very minor role in this opening and that she has almost no agency. Instead, the agency belongs to Gordon and his wife: he left her, then went back; they divorced; she went away. Though the narrator is focused on Gordon's agency, both the title and the initial narrative discourse make it clear that the protagonist of the story is Prue. Although Prue is not the focalizer, the narrator is aligned with her rather than with Gordon or his wife, who never gets a name and who is just "the wife" in the final sentence. The gap between the title and the focus on Gordon's agency invites us to infer something about him: though Prue "used to live with Gordon," his decisions about his life are relatively unaffected by her presence. Consequently, even as the paragraph opens up the possibility that Prue can resume her relationship with Gordon, it invites us to make an initially negative ethical judgment about him, and, thus, about that possibility. It also invites us to make an interpretive judgment that, for Prue, resuming a relationship in which her presence matters so little cannot be a good thing. At this stage, however, Munro does not invite us to make any specific ethical judgment about Prue herself.

Rather than complicating this initial instability, as she would do if "Prue" were governed by principles of narrativity, Munro takes the progression in a different direction. First, she presents several paragraphs of what look like straight exposition, as they describe Prue and her situation: "Prue did not go back to Vancouver . . . She got a job in Toronto, working in a plant shop" (227). But these paragraphs also introduce significant tensions about the portrait the exposition is beginning to sketch, and they also invite our initial ethical judgments of Prue. In moving from the initial instability to the expository descriptions of Prue, Munro also shifts from the past tense to the present: "She is very likable. She has what eastern Canadians call an English accent. . . ." (227). This shift in tense signals Munro's interest in portraiture: rather than recounting that something happened, the narrator is telling us that someone is.

The present-tense description of Prue's way of telling stories is one of the first significant strokes in the portrait:

> [Her] accent helps her to say the most cynical things in a winning and light-hearted way. She presents her life in anecdotes, and though it is the point of most of her anecdotes that hopes are dashed, dreams ridiculed, things never turn out as expected, everything is altered in a bizarre way and there is no explanation ever, people always feel cheered up after listening to her; they say of her that it is a relief to meet somebody who doesn't take herself too seriously, who is so unintense, and civilized, and never makes any real demands or complaints. (227)

Though the passage does not introduce any narrative movement, it does reinforce the inferences invited by the initial instability. If the point of Prue's storytelling is that "hopes are dashed," the point of Munro's description of that storytelling is that Prue is likable because she is so nondemanding and nonassertive—qualities that make it easy for Gordon not to take her into account as he makes decisions about his life. At the same time, the paradox in the description—the way Prue's cheerful manner of telling her anecdotes belies their pessimistic substance—establishes a tension in the developing portrait. We read on, in part, to find out whether the paradox will be resolved, or at least explained. Though we have no doubt about the dominant qualities of Prue's character, we also need to find out how the pessimistic substance of her narratives fits with those dominant qualities.

Munro reinforces and rounds out these initial strokes of Prue's portrait in four different ways before turning to the mini-narrative of the middle. First, Munro uses Prue's reflections on her name to introduce another tension: "The only thing she complains about readily is her name. Prue is a schoolgirl, she says, and Prudence is an old virgin; the parents who gave her that name must have been too shortsighted even to take account of puberty" (227). Munro's authorial audience would know that "Prudence" comes from "plaisance" which means "pleasant." That pleasant Prue is dissatisfied with her name raises the possibility that she is also in some way dissatisfied with herself. That she identifies the dissatisfaction as having a name that is not appropriate for a sexually mature woman once again highlights the instability of her relationship with Gordon.

Second, Munro uses her narrator's comment on Prue's reflections to show that others do not take her seriously, the way they take other adults seriously: "In her late forties now, slight and fair, attending to customers with a dutiful vivacity, giving pleasure to dinner guests, she might not be far from what those parents had in mind: bright and thoughtful, a cheerful spectator. It is hard to grant her maturity, maternity, real troubles" (227–28). Once again the narrative discourse here invites us to look not only at the strong colors of the portrait but also at the more subtle shadings. The strong colors also underline another meaning of her name: a spectator is out of the game or the play, and in that respect, more cautious and prudent than those who are directly involved. And of course being always a spectator and never a player or an actor is to live an overly cautious, overly prudent life. The more subtle shadings of Munro's portraiture suggest that we do not yet have all the signs needed to finalize our portrait. Prue "might be" what her parents had in mind; "it is hard to grant her . . . real troubles" (228), but she might also be something other than a "cheerful spectator," and she might very well have "maternity, maturity, and real troubles."

Munro's third move to fill out the initial portrait adds to the tension because the narrator reveals that Prue does, in fact, have maternity: she has grown children from an early, long-dissolved marriage that she calls a "cosmic disaster" (228). Although Munro does not say more about the marriage, this description in Prue's voice is a nice example of her storytelling: the hyperbole puts a light tone on the situation, but for Munro's audience it does not hide the fact that at one time at least she had "real troubles." Nevertheless, the rest of the information about Prue in her maternal role builds on the initial, dominant strokes of the portrait, as it reveals that the parent-child roles are, for all practical purposes, reversed. The children do not ask her for money or other things but instead give her gifts and see that her life is in order. Prue, for her part, "is delighted with their presents, listens to their advice, and, like a flighty daughter, neglects to answer their letters" (228).

Munro's fourth move to elaborate the initial portrait is the narrator's report on Prue's active social life. Prue "would laugh at the idea" (228) that she stays in Toronto because of Gordon, since she goes to and gives parties, and she goes out with other men. In addition, "her attitude toward sex is very comforting to those of her friends who get into terrible states of passion and jealousy, and feel cut loose from their moorings. She seems to regard sex as a wholesome, slightly silly indulgence, like dancing and nice dinners—something that shouldn't interfere with people's being kind and cheerful to each other" (228). Again Munro reinforces the dominant strokes of the portrait: Prue's attitude toward sex, however comforting to others, is possible because she does not take its connections, physical or emotional, seriously—and thus does not ask the men she sleeps with to take its connections seriously. And again Munro keeps some tension alive through subtle shading, since the narrator never unequivocally confirms that Prue's staying on in Toronto is independent of Gordon's separation from his wife.

With this description of Prue's attitudes toward sex, the beginning of the story is complete, and we can recognize that we are entering a world built on principles of both narrativity and portraiture. We interpret Prue as a likable woman in her forties, someone whom others find amusing and easy to be with precisely because she lacks the gravity, the self-confidence, and self-assertiveness to be taken seriously. Furthermore, her attitude toward her name and the gap between her cynicism and her manner of expressing it suggests that she is more uneasy about who she is and what she is doing with her life than she shows. At the same time, we are aware that we do not yet have the full portrait of her character and expect the progression to return to both the global instability of her relation with Gordon and to the global tensions in the portrait. The initial narrative discourse has taught us to look for both the broad strokes and the shadings in the narrator's reports about Prue.

At this stage, our sympathy for Prue exists alongside a partially negative ethical judgment of her, as Munro invites us to register a problem with

Prue's putting the approval of other people so high on her own scale of values that she does not ask them to take her seriously. But Munro's attention to how Prue is perceived by others—and how Prue herself likes to be likeable—also invites us to thematize her character in ways that complicate this ethical judgment. Prue represents a certain type of woman, one who obeys many of the demands of 1980s North American culture on women, demands that can be seen as a response to the feminist movement of the 1970s: to be likable by being self-effacing—above all, to avoid seeming to be pushy or otherwise susceptible to being labeled a "bitch"—to be tolerant and understanding of others, especially of men. The thematizing also includes a recognition that this type of woman is likely to pay a price for obeying these cultural demands. The price Prue pays is her role as "cheerful spectator" rather than "effective agent" in her own life, and this price in turn is the source of her uneasiness with herself. At the same time, Munro invites us to infer that the "cosmic disaster" of Prue's first marriage plays some role in how and who she now is. Though we do not get any mini-narrative about the marriage or other revelations of how Prue was at that period in her life, it seems reasonable to conclude that her painful experience in the marriage influences her willingness to pay the price of her cheerful spectatorship.

Recognizing these thematic and mimetic components of the portrait mitigates our ethical judgment of Prue by deflecting some of the responsibility for her condition to a culture that sets up these expectations for women and by suggesting why she would be especially responsive to these expectations. Recognizing these components also enhances our sympathy for her. But again, our judgment here is provisional, since the tensions Munro has introduced have not yet been resolved.

Munro's next move in the progression is to set up the mini-narrative of the middle by means of an iterative report that picks up from the end of the first paragraph's statement that Gordon's wife had gone to New Zealand, "most likely for good." "Now that his wife is gone for good, Gordon comes to see Prue occasionally and sometimes asks her out for dinner" (228). By framing the mini-narrative with this iterative report in the present tense, Munro indicates that the ensuing past tense narrative is not going to recount significant change in the present but rather one that is going to illustrate the kinds of interactions that Prue and Gordon now have.

Part of the mini-narrative entails some exposition about Gordon that underlines some significant differences between them, differences connected in part to their gender. She works in a plant shop, a low-prestige, low-paying job that does not require specialized knowledge or skill (she had previously been a hostess at a resort hotel), though it does involve the nurture of living things that in turn typically enhance the environments of other people. Gordon works as a neurologist—a high-prestige, high-paying job (the narrator tells us that he is rich "by Prue's—and most people's—standards" [228]) that involves specialized knowledge and expertise and that focuses less on nurturing than on correcting aberrations. Gordon himself, rather than being accommodating to the feelings of others, takes charge and speaks his mind. Once he lives by himself he "put his mind" to learning how to cook and now "says truthfully" that he is a better cook than either Prue or his wife. This exposition about Gordon in combination with what we have already seen of Prue helps explain why he has the power to dictate their relationship.

A little later in the mini-narrative we get additional exposition about Gordon's character: the narrator tells us that the expression in his often bloodshot blue eyes "indicates that there is a helpless, baffled soul squirming around inside" (228) his large body. This information, besides showing another layer to his character, helps explain some of his behavior, especially his lack of decisiveness about his relationship with Prue. In addition, it also suggests that Prue may be staying with Gordon because she senses this side of his character and wants to help him—even though every other aspect of his character and hers makes that impossible. More generally, Munro uses this portrait of Gordon as a way to heighten our understanding of Prue and her situation.

During dinner, Prue and Gordon are twice interrupted by an unnamed woman (first instability and its complication). The first time, Prue hears her angry voice at the door but not her words, and Gordon sends her away. The second time the woman rings the doorbell until Gordon opens the door, at which point she flings her overnight bag at him, slams the door shut, and leaves. In the interval between the two interruptions, Prue, in an effort to take his mind off the first one, asks him questions about his plants. Munro then reports the following conversation:

> "I don't know a thing about them," he said. "You know that."
>> "I thought you might have picked it up. Like the cooking."
>> "She takes care of them."
>> "Mrs. Carr?" said Prue, naming his housekeeper.
>> "Who did you think?"
>> Prue blushed. She hated to be thought suspicious. (229)

The conversation effectively dramatizes the relationship. Prue tries to help,

Gordon rebuffs her, Prue keeps trying, and when she asks her question of clarification (which also indicates some reasonable anxiety in light of Gordon's caller), he treats her roughly and she feels bad.

Then, however, the mini-narrative takes a turn as Gordon tells Prue that he has a problem (second instability): "The problem is that I think I would like to marry you" (229). Prue responds with characteristic lightness—"What a problem," though the narrator's additional comment shows that she takes it seriously: "she knew Gordon well enough to know that it was" (229). Before the conversation can continue, the second interruption occurs.

After that interruption, Gordon and Prue have the following conversation, which brings the two instabilities together and leads to an odd, partial resolution:

> "I think I'm in love with this person," he [Gordon] said.
> "Who is she?"
> "You don't know her. She's quite young."
> "Oh."
> "But I do think I want to marry you, in a few years' time."
> "After you get over being in love?"
> "Yes."
> "Well. I guess nobody knows what can happen in a few years time." (229–30)

What stands out most in this mini-narrative, so much so that Munro does not need her narrator to comment on it, is the apparent equanimity of both characters: on Gordon's part when he tells Prue, first, that his problem is that he would like to marry her and, second, that he has to get over being in love with the younger woman, and, on Prue's part, as she seems to take these statements in stride. Gordon's equanimity dramatically reveals that Gordon sees her as someone "who never makes any real demands or complaints." Prue's equanimity reveals that he is right to see her this way. Indeed, this mini-narrative recapitulates in miniature the previous history between Gordon and Prue that we learn about in the story's first paragraph: after living together for sixteen months, he left her to go back to his wife, only to return to the relationship when his wife went off to New Zealand.

We judge Gordon here as ethically deficient for treating Prue so cavalierly, but we also judge her as deficient for accepting the treatment so readily. Munro reinforces this judgment in a coda to the mini-narrative that completes the middle. The narrator reports that when Prue tells the story, she makes excuses for Gordon: "And it's quite reasonable to think of marrying me [and] telling me to sort of put my mind at rest" (230). In sum, "Dinner at Gordon's" does not move us any closer to a resolution of the initial instability but rather reveals more about its nature and, in so doing, reinforces the dominant strokes of the portrait of Prue. However, because the tensions in the portrait have not yet been resolved, the narrative cannot properly end with this coda to the mini-narrative.

Munro, in fact, brilliantly resolves the tensions and, in so doing, alters our judgments of Prue by completing the story with her second mini-narrative, "Prue's Taking Ways." Again, it is easily summarized: the morning after the dinner, Prue, alone in Gordon's house, steals an expensive cufflink he had purchased in Russia while on a trip with his wife (instability). Upon returning home, she puts the cufflink in an old tobacco tin, a gift from her children, where it takes its place alongside a set of other mildly expensive keepsakes she has pilfered from Gordon's house (no complication but further revelation). Munro concludes both the mini-narrative and the story as a whole with the indirect discourse commenting on Prue's thefts:

> These are not sentimental keepsakes. She never looks at them, and often forgets what she has there. They are not booty, they don't have ritualistic significance. She does not take something every time she goes to Gordon's house, or every time she stays over, or to mark what she might call memorable visits. She doesn't do it in a daze and she doesn't seem to be under a compulsion. She just takes something, every now and then, and puts it away in the dark of the old tobacco tin, and more or less forgets about it. (230–31)

(No further complication and no resolution, just further revelation.)

"Prue's Taking Ways" neither complicates nor resolves the instability between Prue and Gordon, and it does not signal the likelihood that some change will occur. Indeed, Munro's return to the true present tense and the iterative mode for the final passage, after using the historical present to recount the singulative events of "Prue's Taking Ways," reinforces this point. But the mini-narrative does alter the portrait of Prue because it gives us new information that alters both our interpretive and ethical judgments of her character. "Prue's Taking Ways" resolves the tensions in the earlier portrayal by showing that Prue is a woman with "real troubles," who has stayed in Toronto because of Gordon, and who, at some level of

consciousness, very much feels the pessimism she hides behind the cheerful manner of her storytelling. Above all, the mini-narrative strongly confirms her uneasy relationship to herself and her position in life as it reveals
her to be an adult woman with deep, unsatisfied desires, albeit ones that
she is not fully capable of expressing or acting on. Despite her apparent
equanimity and what she says both to Gordon and to others, she is deeply
hurt by Gordon's cavalier treatment of her, his taking advantage of her
good nature. Her thefts are not really a way of striking back: they are ultimately inconsequential for both of them, and Prue herself is too invested
in wanting to be liked to retaliate or in any way confront Gordon and his
refusal to commit to her. Instead, the thefts are a way for Prue to express
her hurt feelings, to have some outlet for them. What she takes does
have some symbolic value for her: on this occasion, after the accelerated
replay of waiting for Gordon to resolve his relationship with his wife, she
takes something closely linked to her. But this theft, like all the others, in
remaining invisible from Gordon, will do nothing to alter her situation.
She will go on being likable, being dissatisfied with herself, getting hurt
by Gordon, and making petty thefts: that is just Prue being Prue.

This point helps us identify the distinctive function of "Prue's Taking
Ways" for Munro's audience. It does nothing for the progression of Prue's
unstable situation, but it does everything for the authorial audience's
understanding of Prue's situation and her character. In other words, the
resolution here is experienced not by Prue and Gordon but by Munro's
readers, and, because that resolution eliminates the tensions and rounds
out the portrait, it produces a sense of completion.

As part of that completion, our ethical judgments of Prue become more
complex. First, we do not condemn Prue for her thefts but place them in
the larger context in which they occur. Though we continue to be aware
of Prue's deficiencies, our sympathy for her deepens because we see more
clearly now the price she pays for being such a thoroughly agreeable and
likeable woman and her ineffectual response to that price: stealing things
from Gordon that she has no use for. Indeed, as we attend to the price Prue
pays and return to the thematic component of her character, we direct our
judgments about ethical deficiencies less to her and more to the culture
that imposes the standards of likeability for women and to Gordon and the
men he represents who assume that it is not just acceptable but perfectly
fine to treat women as he treats Prue. (And who knows how he treated the
woman who throws her overnight bag at him.)

Having judged Prue and her situation in this way, we are now in
a position to assess the ethics of Munro's storytelling, particularly her

relation to her protagonist and to her audience. Given the gap between Munro's authority and agency as a female writer, on the one hand, and Prue's passive spectatorship on the other, Munro could very easily have developed a condescending attitude toward her protagonist, despite her genuine sympathy. But such condescension never appears because of the way she constructs the progression as a whole. First, Munro's adroit introduction of the tensions in the beginning and her skillful resolution of them in "Prue's Taking Ways" emphasizes throughout that Prue is more than she initially appears to be. Second, "Prue's Taking Ways" not only adds significant depth but also considerable sympathy to that portrait. As a result, Munro treats her character with both respect and a clear-eyed lack of sentimentality.

Munro's handling of the progression indicates that she treats her own audience with a similar respect. She confidently relies on her audience to recognize the unusual movement from beginning to end, to pick up on the tensions in the initial descriptions of Prue, and to make the appropriate interpretive and ethical judgments of the characters during "Dinner at Gordon's" and "Prue's Taking Ways." Indeed, it is striking that after using the narrator to offer the explicit interpretive commentary in the beginning of the story, Munro limits the narrator for the rest of the story largely to the reporting function: the narrator describes Gordon's behavior, Prue's behavior, and many of her thoughts, but the narrator does not evaluate these descriptions. Indeed, there is no direct farewell to the audience but rather only a final report in the indirect discourse that characterizes the whole last paragraph: "She just takes something, every now and then, and puts it away in the dark of the old tobacco tin, and more or less forgets about it" (231). In other words, after providing the frame of the beginning, Munro invites the audience to follow her unobtrusive guidance toward her implicit evaluations of Gordon and Prue and toward a recognition of their importance in the overall portrait of Prue.

Our interpretive and ethical judgments throughout the progression lead to our very positive second-order aesthetic judgment. Munro has fashioned her materials—which, abstracted from the story itself, may seem extremely unpromising (overly accommodating fortysomething woman in an unhappy relationship with man who doesn't get it; no change possible)—into an emotionally compelling and ethically rewarding reading experience. Furthermore, Munro demonstrates the potential for such effective experiences that lies within the hybrid form of portrait narrative. When we add that the story participates in a broader effort by short story writers of the 1970s and 1980s to break away from the dominant modernist mode of the short story, a movement toward epiphany, we deepen our appreciation of Munro's aesthetic achievement in "Prue."

## Progression and Judgment in "Janus"

Beattie's story focuses on Andrea, a married real estate agent who becomes inordinately attached to a cream-colored bowl that she uses to decorate homes she is trying to sell. Beattie generates the progression largely through the tension of unequal knowledge surrounding Andrea's relationship with the bowl, but she also traces some small developments in Andrea's relation to the bowl—she becomes more attached to it over time. Rather than building to any substantial change in Andrea's situation, however, these developments contribute to the progression by tension: the more attached she becomes the more we want to know the how and why of that attachment. Consequently, when Beattie resolves the tension by recounting the story of how Andrea acquired the bowl, she all but completes "Janus" because that story all but completes her portrait of Andrea. In other words, although there is a slight difference from "Prue" in that over the course of the progression the protagonist's situation does change a little—Andrea is more deeply attached to the bowl than she was at the beginning—"Janus" too is a short story in which narrativity is subordinate to portraiture. Andrea's deeper attachment functions not as a sign of a significant change in her situation but rather as part and parcel of Beattie's gradual unfolding of her character.

The beginning of the story runs from the title to the report that "in time," Andrea "dreamed of the bowl" (234). Although Beattie focuses on the bowl from the very first sentence ("The bowl was perfect" [232]), she only gradually reveals the instability of Andrea's relationship to it. At first she emphasizes the bowl's role in Andrea's real estate sales; she strategically places it in houses that she is showing. Like letting her dog play in a house that she wanted to sell to dog lovers, placing the bowl in the right light is one of "the tricks used to convince a buyer that the house is special" (232). Beattie slowly moves the bowl from real estate agent's helper to object of obsession by depicting Andrea's detailed thoughts about it, beginning with her contemplation of its aesthetics:

the wonderful thing about the bowl . . . was that it was both subtle and noticeable—a paradox of a bowl. Its glaze was the color of cream and seemed to glow no matter what light it was placed in.

There were a few bits of color in it—tiny geometric flashes—and
some of these were tinged with flecks of silver. They were as mysterious as cells seen under a microscope; it was difficult not to study
them, because they shimmered, flashing for a split second, and then
resumed their shape. (232–33)

By this point, if not before, the authorial audience recognizes that
Beattie is setting up an intertextual relation between her story and Henry
James's *The Golden Bowl,* and the chief effect of that intertextuality as
we read is to add another dimension to the global tension. As we wonder
about the reasons for Andrea's attachment to the bowl, we also wonder
whether it, too, despite its appearance of perfection, will turn out to be
flawed. Beattie's ending resolves this tension, but before looking at how it
does so, we should follow the other moves of the progression.

The effect of the gradual revelation of Andrea's obsession is to establish
Andrea as a competent professional before solidifying and then slightly
complicating the instability of her relationship with the bowl. Indeed, at
first blush, the instability itself seems only minor, as if Andrea is simply
too taken with one of the tricks of her trade, and, indeed, the description
of the bowl's aesthetics makes that response understandable. But as the
beginning continues, Andrea's behavior toward the bowl becomes increasingly weird—she lies to a customer interested in purchasing one like it;
she displays it in her own home; she becomes convinced that the "bowl
brought her luck" (233); once when she leaves it behind, she races back to
get it; finally, she dreams of it. At this point, we are not only aware of the
instability of her excessive attachment but hooked on the tension about
its cause.

Beattie also uses the gradual revelation of Andrea's attachment as a
way to introduce a second instability, this one about Andrea's relation to
her husband, without making that instability central to the progression.

When her husband first noticed the bowl, he had peered into it
and smiled briefly. He always urged her to buy things she liked. In
recent years, both of them had acquired many things to make up
for all the lean years when they were graduate students, but now
that they had been comfortable for quite a while, the pleasure of
new possessions dwindled. Her husband had pronounced the bowl
"pretty," and he had turned away without picking it up to examine
it. He had no more interest in the bowl than she had in his new
Leica. (233)

This paragraph shows a significant communication gap between Andrea and her husband, one that indicates some emotional distance as well. He has no idea of the bowl's importance to her, and she doesn't try to inform him about it. She, for her part, has no interest in his new possessions. But like Munro in her depiction of Prue's relationship with Gordon, Beattie does not take this initial unstable situation and complicate it, and, like Munro, as we shall see, she never resolves it. Furthermore, while the passage invites us to judge the communication gap and the emotional distance as a problem in their relationship, our interpretive judgments about what is missing are firmer than our ethical judgments, because we have only limited knowledge of each one's behavior in the marriage. Similarly, at this point in the story, Andrea's mimetic portrait is slowly beginning to take shape, but we do not yet have clear signals about the thematic component of her character.

As this commentary suggests, Beattie initiates us into the story by using the narrator to report and occasionally interpret but almost never to pass an explicit ethical judgment—even as the reporting and the interpreting guide us to several judgments about Andrea and her situation. The narration fluctuates between the narrator's vision and voice and Andrea's, but when we have the narrator's perspective, it is always a cool, detached one. Andrea is out there, someone whom the narrator dutifully reports on but not someone she views with sympathy. Consequently, the authorial audience finds Andrea more of an interesting case study than a character to whom we develop a strong emotional attachment.

Beattie frames the story's middle with a statement about the temporal progression and Andrea's business success: "She had a very profitable year selling real estate. Word spread, and she had more clients than she felt comfortable with" (234). But soon the narrative returns its focus to the instability and tension involving the bowl: "She had the foolish thought that if only the bowl were an animate object she could thank it" (234). Throughout the rest of the middle, Beattie increases the tension about the bowl's significance for Andrea in two ways. First, as noted above, she complicates the instability about Andrea's relation to the bowl by showing that over time Andrea's attachment increases at the expense of her relationship with her husband. It is as if the bowl is a rival lover. The narrator notes that Andrea "was often tempted to come right out and say [to her husband] that she thought that the bowl in the living room, the cream-colored bowl, was responsible for her success. But she didn't say it. She couldn't begin to explain it. Sometimes in the morning, she would look at him and feel guilty that she had such a constant secret" (234). Again, however, the story does not progress by complicating the instability about the marriage to the point that the marriage seems in jeopardy. Beattie's concerns are different; rather than giving us a voyage that traces the progress of this marriage, she explores Andrea's character and situation within it. Thus, Andrea's guilt is important not because of how it moves the action forward but because of what it contributes to Beattie's unfolding portrait of her.

Beattie's second strategy in the middle is to show that Andrea herself is confused about the reasons for her increasing attachment to the bowl. In a sense, Beattie matches the tension the authorial audience experiences with Andrea's own tension.

> Could it be that she had some deeper connection with the bowl—a relationship of some kind? She corrected her thinking: how could she imagine such a thing, when she was a human being and it was a bowl? It was ridiculous. Just think of how people lived together and loved each other. . . . But was that always so clear, always a relationship? She was confused by these thoughts, but they remained within her mind. (235)

Nevertheless, the interaction also leads us to see the situation more clearly than Andrea herself does and to move us toward further interpretive and ethical judgments. Andrea's inability to distinguish between her relationship to the bowl and relationships between people who lived together and loved each other is a clear sign of her severely limited understanding as well as an important marker of her unhealthy emotional attachment to the bowl. Nevertheless, because we remain in the dark about the reasons for her attachment, our negative ethical judgments continue to remain tentative.

Beattie continues tracing Andrea's thoughts along these lines until she herself articulates her understanding of her feelings toward the bowl. "The bowl was just a bowl. She did not believe that for one second. What she believed was that it was something she loved" (235). And she acts toward it—and toward her husband—as if the bowl is in fact her lover, ceasing to talk to her husband about her real estate sales "for all her strategies involved the bowl," and becoming "more deliberate with the bowl and more possessive" (235).

Having reached this point in the development of the instability and the tension, Beattie nevertheless delays the resolution still further—and she does so in a way that re-emphasizes the story's indifference to standard narrative progression by instability. "She wondered how the situation would end. As with a lover, there was no exact scenario of how matters would come to a close. Anxiety became the operative force" (235). What's striking is that Andrea's anxiety is not something that leads to a change in her character or condition, and it is not something that gets altered by the end of the story. Instead, it is part of who she is—and of course another sign of her very unhealthy attachment.

The interaction in the middle continues the pattern of the initiation with some modification. The narrator retains the cool and distant attitude, but a greater proportion of the narration is through Andrea's focalization and her voice mixes with the narrator's more frequently. As a result, we become more knowledgeable about Andrea without becoming sympathetic to her the way we are with Prue. The most significant consequence of this effect comes in the ending.

Beattie completes the story in the last three paragraphs. The first two of these finally resolve the tension through an analepsis telling the story of how Andrea acquired the bowl. The key revelation of this mini-narrative is that Andrea received the bowl "several years earlier" (236) as a gift from her then lover, who bought it for her at a crafts fair they'd attended several years earlier. Almost as important is the specific sequence of events that led to the purchase because it provides several key strokes in Beattie's portrait of Andrea. Initially, she'd admired it but passed on buying it; her lover went back to the booth and bought it for her, and over time it became the gift from him she liked best. This revelation that, left to her own devices, she'd have admired the bowl but not taken action to possess it becomes especially salient in the conclusion to the mini-narrative, narrated in Beattie's penultimate paragraph.

> Her lover said that she was always too slow to know what she really loved. Why continue with her life the way it was? Why be two-faced, he asked her. He had made the first move toward her. When she would not decide in his favor, would not change her life and come to him, he asked her what made her think she could have it both ways. And then he made the last move and left. It was a decision meant to break her will, to shatter her intransigent ideas about honoring previous commitments. (236)

This paragraph resolves the tension because it enables us to recognize that her attachment to the bowl is a kind of substitution by metonymy. She has replaced her lover with the bowl, the gift of his that she liked best. In effect, her relationship with the bowl is the one she has entered into on the rebound after her lover left her. This relationship is of course much safer than any relationship with a man would be—the bowl can't leave her as the lover did—but it also keeps Andrea distant from her husband. And the fact that it can't leave does not prevent her from feeling anxiety about the future, because it can easily break. Just as her lover left her, so might his replacement.

Beattie loads considerable irony into the ethical language rendered in indirect discourse about Andrea's "intransigent ideas about honoring previous commitments." The first layer of irony is that the affair itself suggests that her idea of what it means to honor "previous commitments" is not at all intransigent but extremely flexible. The second layer of irony is that the lover's decision to leave has not resulted in her acting, on an emotional and psychological level, to honor those commitments any better. The third layer is that in practical terms this otherwise ill-fitting language does capture something about Andrea's position. Just as she was unable to decide to purchase the bowl she is unable to decide to choose between her lover or her husband. And now she has replicated the situation via the substitution by metonymy.

With the resolution of the tension about the origin of Andrea's attachment to the bowl, we also understand the meaning of the story's title, and we have some firmer grounds upon which to thematize Andrea's character. Andrea is Janus, looking in two directions but moving toward neither. She looks at her husband and at another object of desire—indeed, she has been looking in these two directions for "several years"; the only change has been her substituting the bowl for her lover. Furthermore, although the evidence suggests that she more strongly desires the extramarital object, she is unable to choose it. To be Andrea is to decide by not deciding, to be stuck—and filled with anxiety at being stuck—between two possible directions.

Beattie completes the revelation of Andrea's character and condition, both mimetically and thematically, in the iterative description of the final paragraph:

> Time passed. Alone in the living room at night, she often looked at the bowl sitting on the table, still and safe, unilluminated. In its way, it was perfect: the world cut in half, deep and smoothly empty. Near the rim, even in dim light, the eye moved toward one small flash of blue, a vanishing point on the horizon. (236)

The iterative mode underlines the point that Andrea has occupied this position for some time, even as it reinforces the audience's arrival at the completion of her portrait. The farewell brilliantly moves between the narrator's and Andrea's vision and voice as Beattie subtly guides our inferences. She starts with the narrator's vision and voice, moves at "looked at" to Andrea's vision and voice and then moves back out to the narrator's vision and voice as she gives an external description of how "the eye moved." Beattie communicates her judgments to us largely through her choice of adjectives, several of which cluster together because of their semantic family resemblance: "alone," "still," "safe," "empty," and "vanishing." This cluster of adjectives then puts pressure on Andrea's aesthetic judgment of the bowl, repeated from the first line of the story, as "perfect." Those adjectives illuminate the aesthetic judgment as a sign of her ethical deficiency, because they apply so well to Andrea herself. To be Andrea is to be alone, still, safe, and empty; it is to spend one's nights staring at an empty bowl that constitutes half of her world. The eye may move toward the flash of blue, but Andrea herself is incapable of movement.

At this point, we can also see how Beattie uses the intertextual connection to James's *The Golden Bowl*. James uses his gilded crystal bowl whose beautiful surface hides fundamental flaws as a way to comment on Maggie Verver's flawed perception of her marriage to Prince Amerigo and the marriage between her father and Charlotte Stant that she had been so eager to promote. Beattie, on the other hand, never reveals any flaw in Andrea's bowl itself; the flaw rather is in Andrea's relation to it. Furthermore, where James's commitment to narrative allows him to trace Maggie's impressive progress after she learns of the flaws both in the bowl and in the two marriages, Beattie's commitment to portraiture leads her to place Andrea in an essentially static position.

Beattie's final paragraph indicates that she, unlike Munro, does not ask us to sympathize with her protagonist as we observe and judge her. Instead, Beattie presents and analyzes Andrea with a kind of clinical detachment as she guides us to our negative ethical judgments. If both portrait narratives represent dangerous possibilities for women and both outcomes are chilling and poignant, Munro's presentation of that danger puts greater emphasis on the poignant side of the scale, while Beattie's puts greater emphasis on what's chilling.

Consequently, individual readers are more likely to diverge in their estimations of Beattie's ethical relation to them than they are in their estimations of Munro's. Some readers will find Beattie's clinical analysis of Andrea and her condition to be a sign of coldness, of a lack of compassion on Beattie's part. They may even find her to be arrogant in her presentation.

Needless to say, such decisions about Beattie's ethics will negatively influence their second-order aesthetic judgments of the story as a whole. However technically skillful these readers will find the story to be, they will find that her attitudes (that is, what they interpret those attitudes to be) mar her overall achievement. Other readers, however—and I put myself in this camp—will be more impressed by Beattie's careful construction of the narrative, a care that extends to her audience and the subtle guidance she provides us in our efforts to comprehend Andrea. In other words, the clinical detachment that Beattie exhibits in her presentation of Andrea is not at all evident in her relation to her audience. Consequently, in this view the ethics of the telling are markedly different from the ethics of the told, and these ethics create a bond of trust between implied author and authorial audiences. Readers who feel that bond will also make positive second-order aesthetic judgments of Beattie's achievement.

# CHAPTER NINE

# Dramatic Dialogue as Lyric Narrative

## Robert Frost's "Home Burial"

In this last chapter of Part Two, I return to lyric narrative but consider a considerably different experiment with the hybrid form in Robert Frost's "Home Burial." The difference is evident in the verse form itself as well as in Frost's choice of technique. Although Frost employs a narrator early in the poem, he primarily communicates to his audience through the dialogue between husband and wife. But, as I shall argue, Frost also uses the lyric narrative form to construct a different kind of ethical dimension in the authorial audience's reading experience than we have seen in any of the texts we have examined, and that ethical dimension naturally has significant consequences for our aesthetic judgments. Finally, Frost's experiment provides additional grounds for a re-examination of narrativity within rhetorical poetics that I will take up at the end of this chapter.

In "Home Burial" Frost packs into his dramatic presentation of a husband's and a wife's very different responses to the death of their child an extremely powerful mixture of emotions: grief, fear, love, and anger. The poem's dramatic mode is crucial to its affective power because it allows Frost to confront the audience with the very rawness of those emotions. As Seamus Heaney says, "the entrapment of the couple, their feral involvement with each other as each other's quarry and companion is not held at a safe narrative distance but erupts into the space between the reader and the text. . . . The top of the reader's head is lifted like the latch of the protagonist's tormented home" (76). More specifically, the dialogue highlights the conflict between the unnamed husband and his wife, Amy, as it represents their miscommunication, their recriminations, Amy's desire to flee, and the husband's threats of violence, themselves borne out of his now desperate love. At the same time, the poem indicates that their

dialogue is suffused with their pain over their beloved child's death and
that their interaction (or lack of interaction) between his burial and this
dialogue has only compounded their pain.

## Judgments and Progression in "Home Burial"

HOME BURIAL[1]

He saw her from the bottom of the stairs
Before she saw him. She was starting down,
Looking back over her shoulder at some fear.
She took a doubtful step and then undid it
To raise herself and look again. He spoke                          5
Advancing toward her: "What is it you see
From up there always?—for I want to know."
She turned and sank upon her skirts at that,
And her face changed from terrified to dull.
He said to gain time: "What is it you see?"                       10
Mounting until she cowered under him.
"I will find out now—you must tell me, dear."
She, in her place, refused him any help,
With the least stiffening of her neck and silence.
She let him look, sure that he wouldn't see,                      15
Blind creature; and awhile he didn't see.
But at last he murmured, "Oh," and again, "Oh."
"What is it—what?" she said.

        "Just that I see."

"You don't," she challenged. "Tell me what it is."

"The wonder is I didn't see at once.                              20
I never noticed it from here before.
I must be wonted to it—that's the reason.
The little graveyard where my people are!
So small the window frames the whole of it.
Not so much larger than a bedroom, is it?                         25

1. From *The Poetry of Robert Frost,* edited by Edward Connery Lathem (Henry Holt and
Co., New York, 1916, 1969).

There are three stones of slate and one of marble,
Broad-shouldered little slabs there in the sunlight
On the sidehill. We haven't to mind *those*.
But I understand: it is not the stones,
But the child's mound—"
        "Don't, don't, don't,             30
don't," she cried.

She withdrew, shrinking from beneath his arm
That rested on the banister, and slid downstairs;
And turned on him with such a daunting look,
He said twice over before he knew himself:
"Can't a man speak of his own child he's lost?"      35

"Not you!—Oh, where's my hat? Oh, I don't need it!
I must get out of here. I must get air.—
I don't know rightly whether any man can."

"Amy! Don't go to someone else this time.
Listen to me. I won't come down the stairs."      40
He sat and fixed his chin between his fists.
"There's something I should like to ask you, dear."

"You don't know how to ask it."

      "Help me, then."

Her fingers moved the latch for all reply.

"My words are nearly always an offense.       45
I don't know how to speak of anything
So as to please you. But I might be taught,
I should suppose. I can't say I see how.
A man must partly give up being a man
With womenfolk. We could have some arrangement    50
By which I'd bind myself to keep hands off
Anything special you're a-mind to name.
Though I don't like such things 'twixt those that love.
Two that don't love can't live together without them.
But two that do can't live together with them."      55

She moved the latch a little. "Don't—don't go.
Don't carry it to someone else this time.
Tell me about it if it's something human.
Let me into your grief. I'm not so much
Unlike other folks as your standing there                          60
Apart would make me out. Give me my chance.
I do think, though, you overdo it a little.
What was it brought you up to think it the thing
To take your mother-loss of a first child
So inconsolably—in the face of love.                               65
You'd think his memory might be satisfied—"

"There you go sneering now!"

"I'm not, I'm not!
You make me angry. I'll come down to you.
God, what a woman! And it's come to this,
A man can't speak of his own child that's dead."                   70

"You can't because you don't know how to speak.
If you had any feelings, you that dug
With your own hand—how could you?—his little grave;
I saw you from that very window there,
Making the gravel leap and leap in air,                            75
Leap up, like that, like that, and land so lightly
And roll back down the mound beside the hole.
I thought, Who is that man? I didn't know you.
And I crept down the stairs and up the stairs
To look again, and still your spade kept lifting.                  80
Then you came in. I heard your rumbling voice
Out in the kitchen, and I don't know why,
But I went near to see with my own eyes.
You could sit there with the stains on your shoes
Of the fresh earth from your own baby's grave                      85
And talk about your everyday concerns.
You had stood the spade up against the wall
Outside there in the entry, for I saw it."

"I shall laugh the worst laugh I ever laughed.
I'm cursed. God, if I don't believe I'm cursed."                   90

"I can repeat the very words you were saying:
'Three foggy mornings and one rainy day
Will rot the best birch fence a man can build.'
Think of it, talk like that at such a time!
What had how long it takes a birch to rot                                  95
To do with what was in the darkened parlor?
You *couldn't* care! The nearest friends can go
With anyone to death, comes so far short
They might as well not try to go at all.
No, from the time when one is sick to death,                               100
One is alone, and he dies more alone.
Friends make pretense of following to the grave,
But before one is in it, their minds are turned
And making the best of their way back to life
And living people, and things they understand.                            105
But the world's evil. I won't have grief so
If I can change it. Oh, I won't, I won't!"

"There, you have said it all and you feel better.
You won't go now. You're crying. Close the door.
The heart's gone out of it: why keep it up?                                110
Amy! There's someone coming down the road!"

"*You*—oh, you think the talk is all. I must go—
Somewhere out of this house. How can I make you—"

"If—you—do!" She was opening the door wider.
"Where do you mean to go? First tell me that.                             115
I'll follow and bring you back by force. I *will!*—"

Frost's poem has received excellent commentary from some first-rate poet-critics, including Randall Jarrell, Joseph Brodsky, and Seamus Heaney, and from highly accomplished Frost scholars and critics, including Frank Lentricchia, Richard Poirier, Katherine Kearns, and Walter Jost, and their analyses have deepened my own understanding of the poem. In my view, Brodsky's analysis is the most trenchant,[2] and I shall draw upon it here both because of its insight and because I have one significant disagreement

2. Jost is also very insightful as he analyses the way Frost explores and exposes the powers and the limits of talk in this dramatic dialogue.

with it that also underlines how attention to progression yields different results from Brodsky's widely practiced method of analysis. Brodsky's method, like that of most other commentators on the poem, analyzes its developing drama through careful attention to Frost's linguistic choices. The approach through progression, while also attending to Frost's language and the developing drama, seeks to identify the underlying logic of the poem's sequence of interpretive and ethical judgments from beginning through middle to ending and the relationship among its elements of narrativity, portraiture, and lyricality. This analysis then provides the basis for our second-order aesthetic judgments.

"Home Burial" has some significant markers of narrativity: a narrator telling us that something happened, specifically a narrator telling us about the linked sequence of actions and speeches of Amy and her husband; the sequence begins with the husband's vision of Amy at the top of the stairs and ends with her leaving the house while he shouts after her. "Home Burial" progresses, in part, through a dynamics of instability as the husband seeks unsuccessfully to connect with Amy, and she, in reaction to him, moves from resisting his efforts, to granting him a chance, to criticizing him and, finally, leaving the scene. The poem also progresses through a dynamics of tension: the poem in its first half only hints at Amy's response to her child's death and then in its second half gives a full revelation of her attitude. Amy's leaving the house as the poem ends does provide closure (this conversation is over), but her act complicates rather than resolves the instabilities between the couple. Indeed, Frost heightens that lack of resolution by ending the poem with a dash after the husband's threat: "I'll follow you and bring you back by force. I *will!—*" (120).

If the poem were constructed only on the principle of achieving a high degree of narrativity, this lack of resolution of the instabilities would be a flaw because the poem would take us in the direction of a clear change but would stop short of disclosing that change. But the widely acknowledged effectiveness of the ending suggests that narrativity is not the only principle behind Frost's construction of the poem. And, indeed, the marks of narrativity co-exist with marks of portraiture and especially of lyricality. (I will come back to these points in my discussion of narrativity later in this chapter.)

The marks of portraiture arise from the link between the characters' speeches and the revelation of each character's identity: Amy with her fierce allegiance to fixed ideas about death and grief is sharply distinct from her husband, who sees death more as part of life and whose fierceness is directed at Amy's withdrawal from him. Furthermore, the poem progresses not only according to the logic of instability and tension but also through the double logic typical of the dramatic dialogue: as each character's speech is motivated by the specific situation, Frost uses that speech to sketch a larger picture. In other words, as Frost shows Amy and her husband responding to each other in their moments of painful conflict, he also uses those responses to reveal something beyond the particulars of the drama: their different attitudes toward grief and the consequences of those attitudes. As these descriptions suggest, the signs of portraiture are subordinated to the poem's narrativity and lyricality. More important than the revelation of the characters of Amy and her husband are the revelation of their attitudes and the representation of the ongoing, unresolved conflict between them. The ending of the poem is effective, despite its failure to resolve the instabilities, because it does complete Frost's representation of the way the couple's opposed attitudes have brought them to their situation of perilous stalemate.

There are other features of the poem that point to its lyric narrative hybridity. First is Frost's use of the interior of the house as the setting, a lyric space in which the characters' differences get articulated but not resolved. As these differences are revealed, Frost shows the characters' movement: Amy is initially upstairs and her husband down, and in the course of their dialogue they change places. However, once Amy leaves that house, the lyric frame is broken; any answer to the question of "and then what?" would almost inevitably make the narrative component of the hybrid dominant.

Second, Frost gives his audience various signals to lead us to the interpretive judgment that the present conflict is part of an ongoing unstable situation, an impasse that began when the child died. These signals include not only Amy's report of her offense at her husband's seemingly matter-of-fact speech the day he dug the child's grave but also the husband's references to the recent past: "don't go to someone else this time" (41); "Let me into your grief" (62). To be sure, Frost does not represent this current conversation as a repetition of previous ones, but rather highlights its potential to be different: the husband for the first time sees what Amy "see[s]/ From up there always" (6–7)—the child's grave; Amy for the first time explains how he has offended her and how she views what she owes to the dead child. But the failure of the new conversation to bring about any break in their impasse only serves to highlight its intractability. Something happens, but nothing substantial changes: that's the nature of the lyric narrative hybridity of "Home Burial."

Third, as the progression develops, the narrator intervenes less, with the result that the past tense narrative comes to resemble a present-tense dialogue. Fourth, Frost typically restricts the narrator's function primarily to reporting the characters' actions (e.g., "He saw her from the bottom of the stairs / Before she saw him" [1–2]; "She was opening the door wider" [118]), though he occasionally uses the narrator to interpret some of the actions: ("She took a *doubtful* step and then undid it" [4; my emphasis]). But Frost never uses the narrator to evaluate either character, leaving those ethical judgments to his own communications to the audience through the characters' speech.

At the same time, Frost shows that the characters frequently judge each other, something that often invites our ethical judgments of them. And in fact, the history of criticism on the poem shows that many readers have made such judgments. But that history also shows that there is no consensus about which character should be judged negatively and which positively.[3] Indeed, a closer look at the attitudes and techniques in the poem indicates that, though Frost does judge the characters' behavior toward each other during this interaction, he does not ultimately take sides on the question of whose response to the child's death is more adequate. Frost's treatment creates an unusual but very powerful relation among the ethical positions in the poem, including his position in relation to his audience, a point that I will return to after further analysis of the poem's progression.

Perhaps the most striking feature of the progression—one that certainly deserves to be accounted for—is that Frost saves the main revelation of both characters' attitudes for Amy's two long speeches in the second half of the poem. In the first half, he does give us some signals about each one's attitudes—clearer ones about the husband's than Amy's—but he focuses primarily on the unstable situation between the two characters. The husband directs his efforts—uncertain and sometimes clumsy—to connecting with Amy ("let me into your grief" [59]), and Amy is torn between responding to those efforts and escaping from the scene altogether. Consequently, she fluctuates among three responses: resisting and rebuking him, remaining open to his next effort, and walking out. Her own emotions, we recognize, are themselves conflicted: she still has enough residual feeling for her husband to stay and listen as long as she does, but she feels very distant from and distrustful of him because he is grieving so differently—indeed, from her perspective, not really grieving. For the same reason, she is well on her way to despairing that he will ever understand what she is going through.

3. Amy, as the character who takes the more extreme position, often becomes the focal point of judgment. For negative views, see especially Poirier (1977) and Lentricchia (1975). For positive ones, see especially Oehlschlager (1981) and Carroll (1990). Brodsky is among those who contend, as I do, that Frost does not side with one character over the other.

Amy's conflict and her varied responses cause our emotions to fluctuate as we see the two characters, in this atmosphere suffused with their separate pain and mutual suspicion, teeter on the brink of either moving back toward each other or breaking further apart. Frost shades his treatment of the two characters in the first half so that we are more sympathetic to the husband, though he introduces tensions about Amy's attitudes and invites us to make only mild negative judgments of each.

Because Frost starts with the husband as the focalizing character ("He saw her from the bottom of the stairs" [1]), we enter the poem oriented toward his perspective. In addition, because Frost soon uses a shift to Amy's perspective to reveal that her view of her husband's perceptions is both harsh ("blind creature") and erroneous, our initial alignment with the husband increases:

> She let him look, sure that he wouldn't see,
> Blind creature; and awhile he didn't see.
> But at last he murmured, "Oh," and again, "Oh." (15–17)

His "Oh," we learn, signifies that he does "see" that Amy has been looking out the window at the child's grave. We should also note, however, that Amy's misjudgment (both interpretive and ethical) is not egregious—he sees only "at last"—a sign that Amy's harshness, though primarily a product of her grief and estrangement, is not entirely without foundation and that, consequently, mitigates our ethical judgment of her.

Frost continues to align us more closely with the husband throughout the first part of the poem even as Frost gives us signals not to rush to judgment about Amy. After Amy cuts off the husband's description of the child's grave by saying "Don't, don't, don't, don't" (30), as if his words themselves will hurt her physically, he twice asks, "Can't a man speak of his own child he's lost?" (35). Although this utterance has the surface form of a rhetorical question, it is, in effect, a complaint about her being unreasonable, and it appears to deserve at least a "Yes, but" answer. Such, however, is the painful distance between them that Amy's initial response is a harsh rebuke: "Not you!—Oh, where's my hat?" (36). Her quick softening of this response, "I don't know that any man can" (38), points to her torn feelings in the situation and again kindles some hope in us that they will move back toward each other, even as the line itself does not express any real hope that he can understand her grief. This softening indicates that she cares enough for her husband to take some of the sting out of her answer and to stay and talk for now—or at least listen further. In addition, the content of the line complicates the tension about just what her attitudes are.

Frost's focus on the husband's efforts to connect with Amy reveals not only that the husband genuinely cares about her and their marriage but also that he is far less overcome with grief than she. He acts, she reacts, and as the poem progresses we recognize that both his actions and her reactions are tied as much to their different attitudes toward their loss as to what either of them says on this occasion. This dimension of the poem's dynamics begins to move into the foreground at the end of the husband's appeal to "Give me my chance" (62) to be let into Amy's grief. Rather than stopping with that appeal, the husband moves on to judge her:

> I do think, though, that you overdo it a little.
> What was it brought you up to think it the thing
> To take your mother-loss of a first child
> So inconsolably—in the face of love. (63–66)

The poem pivots because, prior to this point, the husband has seemed willing to do whatever was necessary to re-connect, even offering to agree to

>           some arrangement
> By which I'd bind myself to keep hands off
> Anything special you're a-mind to name. (50–52)

In lines 63–66, the husband's negative judgment is so obviously premature and so counterproductive to what he claims to want that it complicates our understanding of him and, thus, of the whole interaction—and, indeed, of Frost's purposes. We recognize that underneath this judgment are several complex emotions. These lines have the quality of a preemptive strike, a warning about what he is able to sympathize with. He is clearly fearful that she will tell him something that he will not be able to handle. Furthermore, line 66 suggests that there's a tinge of jealousy in his judgment, a worry that her being inconsolable means that she loves the child more than she loves him, even as it registers his concern that she has found no solace for her grief in their love. The suggestion of jealousy is reinforced when the next line reveals for the first time that the baby was a boy: "You'd think *his* memory might be satisfied—" (66; my emphasis).

At this juncture, we see that it is not just Amy who is torn about how to respond; her husband, even as he is trying his best to connect, fluctuates among loving kindness, fearful defensiveness, and threats. Frost has chosen to present the characters at the moment when their emotions are most conflicted, and their interaction most charged; consequently, each of them is very ready to give and to take offense. If the couple's relationship were still dominated by love, they could progress back toward each other, and if they had already moved further apart, they could not hurt each other so much. As it is, Frost challenges his audience to attend to the gut-wrenching dynamics of their current interaction.

The husband's reference to Amy's being satisfied, with its presumption to know how she should feel, brings out Amy's fierce defensiveness: "There you go sneering now!" (67). His immediate and not unreasonable denial soon leads to her articulation of their respective attitudes toward their son's death. Brodsky says that in this conflict of attitudes the husband stands for "reason" (49), a designation that is fair enough, if we add that reason recognizes that death entails loss and pain even as it sees death as part of life. Amy's first speech castigates the husband for being unfeeling, for digging the child's grave and being able to talk of how a birch fence rots, for bringing the spade that dug the grave into the house. Frost captures the husband's pain—rooted in his comprehension not of her pain but of her incomprehension of him—by quoting his brief interruption: "I shall laugh the worst laugh I ever laughed. / I'm cursed. God, if I don't believe I'm cursed" (89–90).

At the end of her second speech Amy herself comes close to capturing the gap between her husband's attitude and her own in lines that link up with her earlier "I don't know rightly whether any man can" (38):

Friends make pretense of following to the grave,
But before one is in it, their minds are turned
And making the best of their way back to life
And living people and things they understand.
But the world's evil. I won't have grief so
If I can change it. Oh, I won't, I won't! (102–108)

Amy's husband, in her view, is among this company of "friends," and Frost has given us considerable evidence that her view is only slightly overstated. The husband's previous failure to recognize the grave from the upstairs window; his comments on the day that he dug the grave—"Three foggy mornings and one rainy day / Will rot the best birch fence a man can build" (92–93)—that she objects to so strenuously; his belief that Amy's giving expression to her thoughts will make her feel better; and especially his general effort throughout the poem to make his "way back to" the living person who is the mother of his child: all this behavior indicates that his focus is less on his son than on his ongoing life.

Amy, for her part, finds this view not just intolerable but a sign that the world is "evil" and that this view of grief must not only be resisted but changed. Brodsky describes Amy as now "rambling on in an increasingly incoherent fashion about death, the world being evil, uncaring friends, and being alone," and he describes the speech as "a hysterical monologue, whose only function, in terms of the story line, is to struggle toward a release for what has been pent up in her mind" (46). If Brodsky is right, then Frost, in effect, has chosen to end Amy's second long speech with a distinct anticlimax, one in which the exact details of what she says matter little. I see the content of Amy's speech as much more significant than that, and this disagreement highlights the difference between Brodsky's approach and the rhetorical one.

As noted above, Brodsky, like most commentators, is primarily concerned with the developing drama between Amy and her husband, and focuses on the language of the poem as the key to that drama. Brodsky sees Amy's speech about grief as anticlimactic because he (quite rightly) sees her expression of outrage over her husband's behavior on the day he dug the grave as the point in the dialogue that most dramatically shows the distance between them. By contrast, the rhetorical perspective focuses on what I have called the double logic of the poem's progression: as the drama plays out, Frost also reveals the underlying attitudes of both Amy and her husband, attitudes that are essential to the lyric side of "Home Burial"'s lyric narrative hybridity. Before Amy's speech about grief, Frost has essentially completed his revelation of the husband's attitudes but has not yet fully revealed Amy's. The revelation of this attitude, because it is more unconventional, needs to be direct and it needs to be in Amy's own words. Those words indicate that Amy is neither rambling nor hysterical; instead she uses them to offer a clear, coherent, and fiercely passionate expression of the difference between her view of grief and that of her husband—indeed, of almost everyone else. For her, the death of her child is not just part of life but the end of *his* life, and so it changes everything about *her* life. Those who, like her husband, act as if life goes on must be ignorant and insensitive, because life can't go on in the same way now that this life no longer goes on. Her view is stark, implacable—and absolutely incompatible with her husband's.

Strikingly, Frost does nothing to undercut Amy's view just as he did nothing to undercut the husband's view—except to juxtapose them and to show that, in each case, the view leads to some interpretive and ethical misjudgment or some mistreatment of the other. But those misjudgments are the product not of the views themselves but of the difference between them.

Alas, her husband does not understand Amy's view—indeed, cannot allow himself to understand it because it is too threatening to his own attitudes. Consequently, he responds by focusing not on the content of her speech but on her having spoken from the heart: "There, you have said it all and you feel better" (108). Having explained herself and been so misunderstood, Amy reaches her breaking point: "*You*—Oh, you think the talk is all. I must go—/ Somewhere out of this house" (112–13). Her resolve arouses his fear, and so he resorts to threats: "If—you—do!" (114), and, when she leaves anyway, "I'll follow you and bring you back by force. I *will!*—" (116). In reading these concluding lines, we watch with horror as they now seem about to fall from the precipice upon which they have been so precariously swaying into a very uncertain future. Our understanding of their ways of dealing with their child's death now makes that fall appear inevitable, but that sense of inevitability does not make it any less painful to witness.

## Ethical Purpose and Second-Order Aesthetic Judgments

From the ethical perspective, the most significant choice Frost makes is not to judge either response to the child's death as interpretively or ethically superior: more discerning, more appropriate, more human, or otherwise of greater insight or value. This choice is simultaneously crucial to our second-order aesthetic judgment of the poem. I believe that the analysis of the progression already shows that Frost's skill in managing the technical aspects of his dramatic dialogue is well above the threshold of competence. Thus, if we find that the choice of not privileging Amy's view or husband's leads to a valuable ethical dimension of our experience, then we will judge the aesthetic quality of that experience as similarly valuable. If, on the other hand, we find that the choice leads to a muddled or otherwise unsatisfying ethical experience, then we will judge the overall aesthetic quality of the experience as disappointing despite Frost's technical skill.

Frost's choice not to take sides matters for the ethical relation between the two characters because, as I noted above, we make the interpretive judgment that, although they do mistreat and misjudge each other, those actions are a result not of their fundamental ethical deficiencies but of the sharp differences in their response. To put this point another way, there is no necessary connection between either attitude and the mistreatments and misjudgments represented in the poem. Instead, the mistreatments are a consequence of the gap between the two views and each character's deep conviction that his or her view is right. Frost's choice not to privilege one attitude over the other also matters for the narrator's ethical position in relation to the characters because it leads to the narrator's even-handed treatment of them.

Above all, the choice matters for Frost's ethical purpose and his rela-tion to us, though it is of course not the only thing that matters. Because the progression requires us to see the situation from each character's per-spective and because that progression also underlines the merit of each view, Frost, in effect, asks us to dwell inside each character's perspective. The result is an ethical and aesthetic challenge: to participate in each char-acter's attitude while recognizing the fundamental incompatibility of those attitudes and the way in which that incompatibility, now more powerful than the prior bond between the characters, is driving them apart. Frost's intertwined ethical and aesthetic purpose, in other words, is to make us feel validity, incompatibility, and consequence without seeking to resolve the conflict among these responses. He takes us deep inside the complexity of the relation between death and mourning, on the one hand, and life and love, on the other, without providing us with any clear way out, any par-ticular answer to the question of what are the true and the good here. His ethical challenge to us is to see whether—and perhaps how long—we can stay inside that complexity.

In this respect, "Home Burial" invites us to consider the ethical conse-quences of a reading experience that I have elsewhere (Phelan 1996) called "the stubborn," by which I mean an experience that proves ultimately recalcitrant to our efforts to develop a single, coherent understanding of it even as that recalcitrance adds to rather than detracts from the power of the experience. In Morrison's *Beloved,* for example, we cannot offer a single, coherent account of Beloved's character but Beloved's fundamental incoherence contributes significantly to the range and force of Morrison's historical fiction. In "Home Burial," the stubbornness resides in Frost's insistence on the equal validity of the fundamentally incompatible atti-tudes—and his decision not to provide a third alternative from which these two could be judged.

The first ethical consequence of the stubbornness is that it challenges us not only as authorial readers to stay inside Frost's vision of the simultaneous validity and incompatibility of the two attitudes but also as flesh-and-blood readers to re-examine our own attitudes toward death and grief. The stubbornness challenges us to re-examine those attitudes precisely because it insists that there is no one superior attitude. Furthermore, because the poem also shows how their incompatible beliefs lead Amy and her husband ineluctably to torment rather than comfort each other, we must question both our individual beliefs and the depth of commitment to any belief.

The second ethical consequence of the stubbornness involves the relation between Frost and both the authorial and flesh-and-blood audiences. In challenging his audiences this way, Frost is also complimenting us through the respect implicit in that challenge and implicitly requesting a similar respect from us. Frost's construction of the poem indicates not only his belief in the efficacy of the dramatic dialogue for accomplishing his multiple purposes but also his confidence that we can unpack that dialogue and its implications. By demanding that we be worthy of the poem, he shows that he has a high regard for our cognitive, emotive, and ethical capacities. That demand also includes his implicit request that we do what we need to in order to be worthy of the poem. As a result of our efforts, then, we are likely to find that Frost's window on death, grief, mourning, love, and life, changes us, that we cannot simply get on with life as we knew it before we dwelt within the poem because we no longer know life in the same way. That is, we now have a new and deeper awareness of the significance of death and the need to come to terms with it, even as we may be less confident of any one way of coming to terms. Individual readers, then, will come to terms in their own ways, even as the poem will resist any easy coming to terms.

As these last few paragraphs indicate, I see Frost's choice not to take sides as leading to a rich, if difficult, ethical experience and consequently to a significant aesthetic achievement. But the specifics of the argument also underline a more general point about the rhetorical poetics of narrative, namely, the importance of the connection between reading within the authorial audience and reading as flesh-and-blood readers. If we had opted, for example, to bypass the authorial audience and say that flesh-and-blood readers inevitably resolve the stubbornness of the poem by giving greater weight to the attitude that most closely resembles their own, we would have effectively set aside Frost's careful management of his ethical purpose and thereby diminished his aesthetic achievement. Similarly, if we had opted to leave the flesh-and-blood reader out of the analysis of the rhetorical communication, ending it with the recognition of the poem's stubbornness, we would have short-circuited our consideration of the ethical and aesthetic consequences of Frost's communication. By insisting on the connection between the two kinds of reading, rhetorical poetics provides a space for productive exchange between authorial communication and readerly response, and, indeed, among different readers.

## Narrativity Redux

After the extended analyses of the four narratives of Part One and the five hybrid forms of Part Two, we are ready to return to the issue of degrees of narrativity that I touched on early in the Introduction. At that juncture, I argued that the degree of narrativity is a function both of the textual dynamics (the introduction of a substantial or insubstantial instability and whether the complications and resolution increase or decrease what's at stake in it) and of readerly dynamics (our multiple and layered judgments of the characters and events as well as their telling and the consequences of those judgments for our experience of the progression). In the discussions of the hybrid forms I have referred to several more specific features of textual dynamics that lead to a weaker degree of narrativity in these works:

1. in "A Clean, Well-Lighted Place" the false starts (initial instabilities that never get complicated) and the very late launch of a pre-existing and unresolvable instability;
2. in "Woman Hollering Creek" the substitution during the story's middle of further revelation about the global instability for complication of that instability;
3. in "Prue" and "Janus" the subordination of mini-narratives to the revelation of character;
4. in "Home Burial" cutting off the dialogue at a point that highlights the unresolved nature of the global instability without producing an effect of incompletion.

As far as readerly dynamics go, the shift to participation rather than judgment in "A Clean, Well-Lighted Place" and in "Home Burial" also contributes to the weaker degree of narrativity. The issue, then, is how the findings about degree of narrativity in the hybrid forms intersect with the two general points about it I offered in the Introduction. More particularly, given the findings about "A Clean, Well-Lighted Place" and "Home Burial," is the degree of narrativity also tied to the degree of resolution or what we might call satisfactory arrival?

The short answer is no. Narrativity is the independent variable and resolution the dependent variable. In other words, the degree of narrativity influences the kind of resolution that is satisfactory but not vice versa. One can have works with botched or no arrivals—think of unfinished narratives—that nevertheless have strong narrativity. And of course works can have strong resolutions and weak narrativity. The longer answer requires (a) a reminder that, as the two general points indicate, within the rhetorical approach narrativity is a concept with multiple variables; and more importantly (b) a distinction between completion in general and narrative completion in particular. Because narrativity is a double-layered phenomenon, the degree of narrativity within any one work is a consequence of both the extent to which its movement is generated by the instability-complication-resolution pattern and the extent to which it engages our interpretive and ethical judgments of the characters and the tellers involved in that sequence. Very strong narrativity depends on the work's commitment to both sets of variables (textual and readerly). Weak narrativity arises from the work's lack of interest in one or both sets of variables. Works that follow the instability-complication-resolution pattern but invite participation rather than judgment on the readerly side (e.g., Frost's "Stopping by Woods on a Snowy Evening") have relatively weak narrativity. Works that focus on characters and invite judgment but do not follow the instability-complication-resolution pattern also have relatively weak narrativity.

Again within the rhetorical framework, completion in general refers to the way in which a text rounds out both the patterns generating its movement and the developing responses of its audience, while narrative completion refers to the rounding off of narrative patterns both textual (instability-complication-resolution) and readerly (the sequence of judgments and their affective, ethical, and aesthetic consequences). In "A Clean, Well-Lighted Place" and "Home Burial," Hemingway and Frost each face the challenge of finding the most effective ending for his specific experiment in lyric narrative hybridity. I have tried to show why and how each one succeeds so well.

# *Experiencing Fiction* and Its Corpus

## Extensions to Nonfictional Narrative
## and Synthetic Fiction

Although *Experiencing Fiction* has focused primarily on five fictional narratives and five narrative hybrids, I doubt anyone will be surprised by the observation that the corpus on which it is based is actually much larger. While each of the ten texts raises its distinctive challenges, my analyses of each tacitly draws on my knowledge of other literary fictions, and the principles I develop across the ten analyses are designed to be relevant to our understanding of numerous other narratives and hybrid forms, including ones that I (and you) have not yet read. These assumptions operate right from the beginning of the Introduction, where I set out and develop the seven theses about judgments in connection with the six sentences of Bierce's "Crimson Candle." Indeed, the grand ambition of *Experiencing Fiction* is to have the reading practice it models be relevant to as wide a range of literary fiction as possible. At the same time, as I noted in chapter 3, the project of rhetorical poetics is always under construction precisely because it is committed to an a posteriori method, the idea that its concepts and principles follow from rather than dictate the dynamics of individual works. A corollary to this thesis is that rhetorical poetics, like any theory designed to account for a range of data, is significantly influenced by the corpus from which it develops its principles. Consequently, as I move toward the end of this study, I would like to reflect on the relation between the corpus I have worked with and the principles about progressions and judgments I have developed by considering two kinds of narrative not represented so far: (a) nonfictional narratives and (b) fictional narratives that foreground their synthetic component at the expense of the mimetic. Although nonfictional narrative is beyond the boundaries I have set for this study, it is not beyond the boundary of rhetorical poetics more generally. Therefore, it is worth at least glancing at the main issues a rhetorical poetics of nonfictional narrative would need to contend with. Synthetic fictions, on the other hand, represent a possible lacuna within the boundaries of this study, and, therefore, I would like to take steps to close up that space before I end.

The project of extending the principles and concepts of rhetorical poetics to nonfictional narrative entails accounting for a significant new variable in the rhetorical communication: referentiality. The project is a formidable one, requiring as it does an engagement with such issues as (a) whether the border between fiction and nonfiction is rigid, permeable, or, for all practical purposes, nonexistent, and (b) how what we might call local referentiality in fiction, that is, the presence of historical figures or events, compares with the global referentiality implicitly claimed by non-fiction, that is, the claim that the entire narrative refers to actual people and events. In addition, the task of accounting for referentiality also involves identifying the relevant differences in referential claims among the various genres of nonfictional narrative, including history, biography, autobiography, memoir, and such hybrid forms as historical essay and memoiristic essay. In short, the project of developing a full-fledged rhetorical poetics of nonfictional narrative is well beyond the scope of this epilogue.[1] Nevertheless, sketching the key principles of such a poetics will identify the starting points for such a poetics, including some of its continuities with and departures from the rhetorical poetics of fiction.

1.  The presence of global referentiality provides the basis for a qualitatively different reading experience from that offered by fictional narrative. Global referentiality not only ties both implied author and authorial audience more closely to people and events external to the narrative itself but it alters rhetorical purposes. A text that purports to tell it like it was is different from one that purports to tell it like its author imagines it to be, even if the texts are otherwise identical. If *Great Expectations* is not a novel but Dickens's autobiography (with Pip becoming Chuck?), then its claim to be the account of the novelist's life changes both our engagement with it and our understanding

---

1. There is of course a substantial body of work on nonfiction narrative relevant to the project of developing a rhetorical poetics of nonfiction, including the large body of theory and interpretation that addresses autobiography. For a sample of this work, see Cohn, Smith and Watson, Lehtimaki, Heyne (1987), Lehman (1998), and the dialogue between Heyne and Lehman in *Narrative* (2001).

of its purpose. Rather than being a narrative that offers us a strong affective experience of Pip's trajectory to maturity even as Dickens explores so many issues in Victorian culture, it becomes an account of how Dickens got to be Dickens. Conversely, if *Angela's Ashes* is not a memoir but a novel, then the implied McCourt's persistent good humor about the grim realities his narrative depicts takes on a wholly different character. Rather than being a reassuring sign of his own successful overcoming of those grim realities, it is likely to be a sign of his lack of empathy for his own creations.

2. Although this way of talking suggests that rhetorical poetics favors a rigid border between fiction and nonfiction, the a posteriori principle trumps any such hard and fast conclusion. There is no restriction on language or on narrative that necessitates a rigid border. While some narratives do clearly reside on one side of the border or the other, another group may move back and forth across the border or even straddle it altogether. Texts such as Tim O'Brien's "The Things They Carried" operate on the premise that the events and experiences they represent cannot be firmly classified as fictional or nonfictional and that making the border between them permeable or blurry offers their audiences richer ethical and aesthetic engagements.

3. Referentiality means that nonfictional narratives can be contested in ways that fictional ones cannot, whenever the nonfictional narrative refers to public figures and events. If you read my account of the 2004 U.S. Presidential election in Ohio and then do your own research and find that the public record contradicts key points of my narrative, you can not only write a new narrative that is more in line with the public record but that is also very likely to displace mine. When Jean Rhys writes *Wide Sargasso Sea* and gives a new history for the wife of Charlotte Brontë's Rochester, she does not displace *Jane Eyre*— indeed, the shelf life of Rhys's novel is crucially dependent on the continued vitality of Brontë's.

4. Referentiality has a significant ethical dimension. To continue with the previous example, in writing my account of the 2004 election in Ohio, I claim to offer not an objective view of the events and people I refer to (narrative's necessary processes of selection and emphasis render objectivity an irrelevant concept even for historical narrative) but one that is responsible to the

historical record. If I am not responsible to that record, I not only run the risk of having my narrative dislodged by one that is more responsible but I also violate the ethics of referentiality, the tacit understanding between author and audience in historical narrative that the historian's narrative is rooted in the events and facts that have an existence independent of that narrative.

Similarly, if I write a memoir, I claim to offer not an objective view of my life and its events but one that corresponds to my experience of that life. I may find that I can serve that purpose better by employing some techniques usually associated with fiction such as the verbatim presentation of dialogues or even internal focalization of characters other than my former self. But again my narrative as a whole needs to be responsible to my actual experience. If, like James Frey in *A Million Little Pieces,* an example I will return to below, I invent major events in my memoir, then I have violated the ethics of referentiality.

5. Positive judgments about the ethics of referentiality are a necessary but not sufficient condition for positive second-order aesthetic judgments of nonfictional narrative. In *A Million Little Pieces* Frey tells a story about his recovery from addictions to drugs and alcohol, and he tells it well enough for Oprah Winfrey to have made it a selection of her book club. (To be sure some readers offered negative Level Two aesthetic judgments of it, but these readers were in the minority.) When, however, the website thesmokingun.com revealed that Frey had not experienced but invented some of the more spectacular events in the book, *A Million Little Pieces* lost both its reputation for being an honest confrontation of the difficulties of addiction and recovery and its status as a worthy aesthetic achievement. The irony of course is that Frey included the inventions in order to make the memoir more compelling. But once the ethical judgments about Frey's inventions came into play, these inventions made the book more embarrassing than compelling. At the same time, being responsible to the demands of the ethics of referentiality is not a sufficient condition for aesthetic success. Such success also requires skill with the craft of narrative, and an ability to exercise that skill in the service of a significant set of rhetorical purposes.

6. As cases like Frey's show, nonfictional narrative always has the
   potential for some conflict between the ethics of referentiality
   and the aesthetics of narrative purpose. Using techniques more
   typically associated with fiction; collapsing several small events
   into a single scene; combining several different people into a
   single character: such choices are typically made to enhance the
   aesthetic quality of the narrative. And they can succeed without
   violating the ethics of referentiality. But they also move the
   author toward the road taken by Frey and others who violate
   that ethics. A full-fledged rhetorical poetics of nonfiction would
   focus a great deal of attention on this potential for conflict not
   in order to fix permanently a dividing line between ethically
   sound and ethically unsound techniques but in order to see
   how and why individual works set that line for themselves and
   what the different ethical and aesthetic consequences of those
   settings are.

Turning to narratives that foreground the synthetic at the expense of the
mimetic, I would like to note why the corpus so far has not included one
(*Atonement,* to be sure, does make its synthetic component prominent, but
its effects also depend on our strong engagement with its mimetic component). The gap follows from my choice between two different principles
of selection, each designed to generate a diverse corpus for the study. The
principle I didn't choose would have generated that diversity by employing
the criterion of selecting narratives with different dominant readerly interests: mimetic, thematic, synthetic, mimetic-thematic, mimetic-synthetic,
thematic-synthetic, and mimetic-thematic-synthetic. Such a group would
have afforded a considerable range of progressions and an extensive range
of interpretive, ethical, and aesthetic judgments. But I opted for a principle
that would generate a sample that would meet three other criteria I deemed
necessary for an adequate study of judgments and progressions. In brief,
the sample would require (1) close attention to different aspects of progression (beginning, middle, ending); (2) it would require the analysis of some
particularly complex and difficult ethical judgments and their affective
consequences; and (3) the sample would require an engagement with the
complications to narrative dynamics presented by hybrid forms. The one
negative consequence of my choice is that it did not lead me to a narrative
with the synthetic component dominant. In choosing such a narrative at
this stage of the study, I can ask not simply, "what judgments does this text
invite us to make and what is the underlying logic of its progression?" but
rather "how do the principles of rhetorical poetics developed in the earlier

chapters help us understand the dynamics of this text, and how might this text complicate those principles?" And in a rhetorical theory equivalent of a harmonic convergence, I choose to ask these questions about Margaret Atwood's "Happy Endings."

Atwood's story is set up as a lesson from a creative-writing-teacher narrator to neophyte students (the implied narratees) about plot in general and endings in particular. It begins this way:

> John and Mary meet.
> What happens next?
> If you want a happy ending, try A.

> A
> John and Mary fall in love and get married. They both have worthwhile and remunerative jobs which they find stimulating and challenging. They buy a charming house. Real estate values go up. Eventually, when they can afford live-in help, they have two children to whom they are devoted. The children turn out well. John and Mary have a stimulating and challenging sex life and worthwhile friends. They go on fun vacations together. They retire. They both have hobbies which they find stimulating and challenging. Eventually they die. This is the end of the story. (213–14)

The middle of "Happy Endings" consists of five variations on A (B through F) that all have the same ending as A. "Happy Endings" itself ends as follows:

> You'll have to face it, the endings are the same however you slice it. Don't be deluded by other endings, they're all fake, either deliberately fake with malicious intent to deceive, or just motivated by excessive optimism if not by downright sentimentality.
> The only authentic ending is the one provided here:
> *John and Mary die. John and Mary die. John and Mary die.*

> So much for endings. Beginnings are always more fun. True connoisseurs, however are known to favor the stretch in between, since it's the hardest to do anything with.
> That's about all that can be said for plots, which anyway are just one thing after another, a what and a what and a what.
> Now try How and Why. (216; emphasis in original)

If we plunge right in and apply the main concepts of rhetorical poetics, our analysis would look something like this: The synthetic clearly trumps the mimetic in the six variations of the plot. John and Mary are counters that the implied Atwood licenses the narrator to move around at will. In each story they—and the other characters who sometimes replace them as the focus of the main action (Madge, James, and Fred)—are all stereotypes (conventional happy couple, exploitative male, woman who allows herself to be exploited, etc.). Their lives also play out according to formulaic patterns. For this reason, although A appears to be that rare thing, a narrative without instabilities, it has much the same function as B through F: it takes its stereotypical characters through one conventional trajectory to the predictable ending. Indeed, by E, the narrator is flaunting the triumph of the synthetic over the mimetic:

> Yes, but Fred has a bad heart. The rest of the story is about how kind and understanding they both are until Fred dies. Then Madge devotes herself to charity work until the end of A. If you like, it can be "Madge," "cancer," "guilty and confused," and "bird watching." (215)

As often happens, the foregrounding of the synthetic brings the thematic component into greater prominence, and at this stage we can hypothesize that Atwood's purpose is to persuade her audience of the limitations of writing for—and reading for—the plot. Indeed, attending to our interpretive and ethical judgments seems to support that hypothesis. Given the stereotyped characters and plots, our interpretive and ethical judgments are very clear and straightforward, but there is not much at stake in them: they have no significant affective consequences. Strikingly, however, that very lack of affective consequence itself points to the positive function of the judgments, the way they contribute to the achievement of Atwood's thematic purpose. Along with the larger thematic point about endings, the story makes many local thematic points through its satirical send-ups of a range of cultural ideas about such matters as relationships, sex, self-image, what constitutes happiness, and the language we use to describe these things, but none of these is especially startling. Consequently, the interpretive and ethical judgments point to a positive if limited aesthetic achievement, since the thematic points are those that many would already agree with. In other words, although the story effectively deploys our interpretive and ethical judgments in the service of its thematic points, the stakes of the story are not particularly high and so the story's aesthetic achievement is less than that of any of the short stories we have examined in Part One or Part Two.

Now while that commentary employs the concepts I have been using in a reasonably intelligent way, the analysis is flawed from the beginning because it misses one of the story's major affective components and thus one of its primary effects: its contagious sense of play with these stereotypes of character and plot, and, indeed, with the whole idea of the lesson. One way to get at this effect is to note that, although the narrator insists on the inevitability of the single ending "John and Mary die," the story's mood is far more upbeat than that insistence would lead us to expect. If we want to apply not just the concepts of rhetorical poetics but also its principles, then we should start with the a posteriori principle and reason back from effects to causes.

How does the foregrounding of the synthetic help create the story's playful spirit? First, because that foregrounding itself involves a lot of play. Notice, for example, the repetition in A (above) of the phrase "stimulating and challenging" to describe John and Mary's jobs, sex life, and hobbies. Such repetition would normally be a sign of an incompetent, even lazy, writer, but given the insistence on the characters as synthetic counters, the repetition has a different and double-layered effect. The first effect is that it adds to our understanding of the narrator's general disdain for plot. She is conducting a demonstration of the way all plots inevitably converge on a single ending (even if some plots pretend to end happily by stopping before they reach their true conclusion), and, wanting to get to that ending, she can't be bothered with the niceties of style. The second effect is to call attention to the implied Atwood's performance as the constructor of this narrator, a performance that conveys a certain wicked delight in that construction because it allows her to use the narrator's formulaic repetition of "stimulating and challenging" to cue the audience to her own play with that formula: this is an odd threesome to apply that same formula to. In particular, what exactly does it mean to have a sex life that is at once "stimulating and challenging"? In this way, Atwood's play points to the ultimate poverty of what appears to be a strong positive description.

In other words, the foregrounding of the synthetic allows us to focus not simply on the thematic point of the narrator's lesson for her fledging writers but even more on the implied Atwood and her performance. That performance suggests that she is playing a deeper game for her audience than the narrator is for her narratees. Perhaps the most obvious and compelling sign of the distance between the narrator and the implied Atwood and of Atwood's deeper game is that, despite the narrator's insistent lesson,

"Happy Endings" does not end with "John and Mary die" but rather with "Now try How and Why."

That ending also appropriately contains the most important clue to Atwood's deeper game. That game is to have "Happy Endings" exemplify what can be done with How and Why without calling attention to what she is doing because doing so would spoil both the fun and her more serious point about reading for How and Why rather than What. In other words, when the narrator says "Now try How and Why," the connoisseur readers—Atwood's authorial audience—can see the line as the conclusion of Atwood's own successful try and, thus, her arrival at her distinctive happy ending. Atwood's trick—and the source of her contagious joyful play—is the old one of hiding something in plain sight, in this case her exemplification of what can be done with How and Why as the narrator carries out her denigration of What. If we focus only or even primarily on the narrator's point about What, as in my initial analysis, we miss the fun—and the achievement. But if we look past the What to the How and Why of "Happy Endings," we recognize how inventive Atwood is with "the stretch in between" "John and Mary meet" and "Now try How and Why" and how deceptively easy she makes that invention seem.

These points can be illuminated by recalling the discussions of the surprise ending of "Roman Fever" and *Atonement* in Part One. My initial analysis of "Happy Endings" not only misses its playful spirit, but by not registering the distance between implied author and narrator, it also misses the way in which "Now Try How and Why" is not simply a straightforward farewell in the form of the narrator's instruction to her students. The story's last line is also the completion of the implied author's performance, appropriately surprising us by violating the narrator's dictum about all endings, and cuing us to find the value added in the story's own handling of How and Why.

The How resides not in the stereotypical characters and events of the John-and-Mary stories but rather in both the attitude of play Atwood conveys in the double-voiced telling (as with "simulating and challenging") and in the unpredictability of the moves between one variation and the next. To put this point another way, the implied Atwood asks her connoisseur audience—her dropping that term into the narrator's concluding remarks is another case of hiding in plain sight—to engage with her performance at every level from the style to the use of stock characters to the sudden shifts in events and the anticlimaxes within each variation. In D, for example, Fred and Madge's "charming house"—all houses in "Happy Endings" are "charming"—is "by the seashore and one day a tidal wave approaches. Real estate values go down" (215).

In other words, we move from section to section not because we are invested in the characters and their fates: John and Mary (or Fred and Madge) die and we don't feel much one way or the other; nor do we hope against hope that in the next section they will avert this fate. Instead, we are invested in discovering what new variation on the underlying pattern of "John and Mary meet, John and Mary live together, John and Mary die" the implied Atwood will come up with and what local satiric points she'll make within that variation. The principle of progression gives Atwood a fair amount of leeway—about the specifics of the variation (in teaching the story, one can help the students grasp the principle of progression by inviting them to invent two other variations), and even, to some extent, the numbers of them (she could do, say, five or seven, rather than the six she gives us, though fewer than five will reduce the story's effect and more than seven will likely yield diminishing returns). The order of the variations follows the principle of increasing emphasis on the symthetic qauality of the material.

I have quoted variation E above, and Variation F begins "If you think this is all too bourgeois, make John a revolutionary and Mary a counter-revolutionary and see how far that gets you" (215). How does one make a high-spirited and sophisticated story out of a focused demonstration by a narrator that attention to plot is limiting? This is How.

And Why would the implied Atwood undertake that How? In her own terms, to show that effective stories can—and by extension often do—depend more on their How than on their What. If the narrator's lesson is about the tyranny of the single ending, "John and Mary die," Atwood's lesson is not just that it is possible to escape that tyranny, but also that the power of stories resides not in their events but in the treatment of these events. Translating Atwood's Why into the terms of this study, we can say that her How is designed to show that effective progressions can depend as much on the dynamics of the relationship between implied author and authorial audience as on the dynamics of instability-complication-resolution. Thus, the lack of the affective consequences for our interpretive and ethical judgments of the characters in the six variations of the John-and-Mary plot is a sign of how those judgments matter so much less than the ones associated with the dynamics of the implied author-authorial audience relationship.

At this point, then, we can see one of the ways in which "Happy Endings" adds to the principles of rhetorical poetics. The story displays a new way of generating narrativity. It contains but subordinates the standard elements—the introduction and complication of instabilities involving the characters and the judgments associated with those instabilities—to a different kind of narrative movement: that of the implied author's dynamic performance, the logic of which only gradually emerges as the other kind of narrativity continues to recede, and our judgments of it.

"Happy Endings" offers us a set of interpretive judgments about the implied author's moves that are—I can't resist—stimulating and challenging. The implied Atwood is asking, "can you keep up with me?" and much of the pleasure of the story comes from our satisfaction in being able to answer yes—but only in the sense of following closely behind. To the extent that we were able to anticipate Atwood's every move, we would find these judgments much less stimulating and challenging. Our ethical judgments are closely connected to our interpretive ones. Atwood's performance is built on the values of trust and reciprocity—I will hide but I will trust you to find me because I am hiding in plain sight; I will require some effort to be found, but that effort will make the finding more rewarding. But just as important, her performance affirms the value of sharing in high-spirited play with and about the dynamics of narrative. For these reasons and for Atwood's mastery of the requisite craft, "Happy Endings" is an impressive aesthetic achievement.

Now the class of works that foreground the synthetic at the expense of the mimetic is itself diverse, so I do not mean to suggest that this analysis of "Happy Endings" provides a clear template for analyzing all such works. Instead, it is to suggest that the concepts of rhetorical poetics, when subordinated to the principles for employing these concepts, especially the a posteriori principle, are well-suited for dealing with such metafictions. More extensive work with more texts of this general kind (or indeed, even with "Happy Endings") might very well lead to some new or revised concepts. But, as I noted in chapter 3, the same can be said about more extensive work with more texts that foreground the mimetic. The more general point, which I have expressed before, also brings me to the happy ending of *Experiencing Fiction:* rhetorical poetics always has the "Construction in Progress" sign out, even as it remains open for business 24/7.

# Alice Munro, "Prue"

Prue used to live with Gordon. This was after Gordon left his wife and before he went back to her—a year and four months in all. Some time later, he and his wife were divorced. After that came a period of indecision, of living together off and on; then the wife went away to New Zealand, most likely for good.

Prue did not go back to Vancouver Island, where Gordon had met her when she was working as a dining-room hostess in a resort hotel. She got a job in Toronto, working in a plant shop. She had many friends in Toronto by that time, most of them Gordon's friends and his wife's friends. They liked Prue and were ready to feel sorry for her, but she laughed them out of it. She is very likable. She has what eastern Canadians call an English accent, though she was born in Canada—in Duncan, on Vancouver Island. This accent helps her to say the most cynical things in a winning and light-hearted way. She presents her life in anecdotes, and though it is the point of most of her anecdotes that hopes are dashed, dreams ridiculed, things never turn out as expected, everything is altered in a bizarre way and there is no explanation ever, people always feel cheered up after listening to her; they say of her that it is a relief to meet somebody who doesn't take herself too seriously, who is so unintense, and civilized, and never makes any real demands or complaints.

The only thing she complains about readily is her name. Prue is a schoolgirl, she says, and Prudence is an old virgin; the parents who gave her that name must have been too shortsighted even to take account of puberty. What if she had grown a great bosom, she says, or developed a sultry look? Or was the name itself a guarantee that she wouldn't? In her late forties now, slight and fair, attending to customers with a dutiful vivacity, giving pleasure to dinner guests, she might not be far from what those parents had in mind: bright and thoughtful, a cheerful spectator. It is hard to grant her maturity, maternity, real troubles.

Her grownup children, the products of an early Vancouver Island marriage she calls a cosmic disaster, come to see her, and instead of wanting money, like other people's children, they bring presents, try to do her accounts, arrange to have her house insulated. She is delighted with their presents, listens to their advice, and, like a flighty daughter, neglects to answer their letters.

Her children hope she is not staying on in Toronto because of Gordon. Everybody hopes that. She would laugh at the idea. She gives parties and goes to parties; she goes out sometimes with other men. Her attitude toward sex is very comforting to those of her friends who get into terrible states of passion and jealousy, and feel cut loose from their moorings. She seems to regard sex as a wholesome, slightly silly indulgence, like dancing and nice dinners—something that shouldn't interfere with people's being kind and cheerful to each other.

Now that his wife is gone for good, Gordon comes to see Prue occasionally, and sometimes asks her out for dinner. They may not go to a restaurant; they may go to his house. Gordon is a good cook. When Prue or his wife lived with him he couldn't cook at all, but as soon as he put his mind to it he became—he says truthfully—better than either of them.

Recently he and Prue were having dinner at his house. He had made chicken Kiev, and crème brûlée for dessert. Like most new, serious cooks, he talked about food.

Gordon is rich, by Prue's—and most people's—standards. He is a neurologist. His house is new, built on a hillside north of the city, where there used to be picturesque, unprofitable farms. Now there are one-of-a-kind, architect-designed, very expensive houses on half-acre lots. Prue, describing Gordon's house, will say, "Do you know there are four bathrooms? So that if four people want to have baths at the same time there's no problem. It seems a bit much, but it's very nice, really, and you'd never have to go through the hall."

Gordon's house has a raised dining area—a sort of platform, surrounded by a conversation pit, a music pit, and a bank of heavy greenery under sloping glass. You can't see the entrance area from the dining area, but there are no intervening walls, so that from one area you can hear something of what is going on in the other.

During dinner the doorbell rang. Gordon excused himself and went down the steps. Prue heard a female voice. The person it belonged to was still outside, so she could not hear the words. She heard Gordon's voice, pitched low, cautioning. The door didn't close—it seemed the person had not been invited in—but the voices went on, muted and angry. Suddenly there was a cry from Gordon, and he appeared halfway up the steps, waving his arms.

"The crème brûlée," he said. "Could you?" He ran back down as Prue got up and went into the kitchen to save the dessert. When she returned he was climbing the stairs more slowly, looking both agitated and tired.

"A friend," he said gloomily. "Was it all right?"

Prue realized he was speaking of the crème brûlée, and she said yes, it was perfect, she had got it just in time. He thanked her but did not cheer up. It seemed it was not the dessert he was troubled over but whatever had happened at the door. To take his mind off it, Prue started asking him professional questions about the plants.

"I don't know a thing about them," he said. "You know that."

"I thought you might have picked it up. Like the cooking."

"She takes care of them."

"Mrs. Carr?" said Prue, naming his housekeeper.

"Who did you think?"

Prue blushed. She hated to be thought suspicious.

"The problem is that I think I would like to marry you," said Gordon, with no noticeable lightening of his spirits. Gordon is a large man, with heavy features. He likes to wear thick clothing, bulky sweaters. His blue eyes are often bloodshot, and their expression indicates that there is a helpless, baffled soul squirming around inside this doughty fortress.

"What a problem," said Prue lightly, though she knew Gordon well enough to know that it was.

The doorbell rang again, rang twice, three times, before Gordon could get to it. This time there was a crash, as of something flung and landing hard. The door slammed and Gordon was immediately back in view. He staggered on the steps and held his hand to his head, meanwhile making a gesture with the other hand to signify that nothing serious had happened, Prue was to sit down.

"Bloody overnight bag," he said. "She threw it at me."

"Did it hit you?"

"Glancing."

"It made a hard sound for an overnight bag. Were there rocks in it?"

"Oh."

Prue watched him pour himself a drink. "I'd like some coffee, if I might," she said. She went to the kitchen to put the water on, and Gordon followed her.

"I think I'm in love with this person," he said.

"Who is she?"

"You don't know her. She's quite young."

"Oh."

"But I do think I want to marry you, in a few years' time."

"After you get over being in love?"

"Yes."

"Well. I guess nobody knows what can happen in a few years' time."

When Prue tells about this, she says, "I think he was afraid I was going to laugh. He doesn't know why people laugh or throw their overnight bags at him, but he's noticed they do. He's such a proper person, really. The lovely dinner. Then she comes and throws her overnight bag. And it's quite reasonable to think of marrying me in a few years' time, when he gets over being in love. I think he first thought of telling me to sort of put my mind at rest."

She doesn't mention that the next morning she picked up one of Gordon's cufflinks from his dresser. The cufflinks are made of amber and he bought them in Russia, on the holiday he and his wife took when they got back together again. They look like squares of candy, golden, translucent, and this one warms quickly in her hand. She drops it into the pocket of her jacket. Taking one is not a real theft. It could be a reminder, an intimate prank, a piece of nonsense.

She is alone in Gordon's house; he has gone off early, as he always does. The housekeeper does not come till nine. Prue doesn't have to be at the shop until ten; she could make herself breakfast, stay and have coffee with the housekeeper, who is her friend from olden times. But once she has the cufflink in her pocket she doesn't linger. The house seems too bleak a place to spend an extra moment in. It was Prue, actually, who helped choose the building lot. But she's not responsible for approving the plans—the wife was back by that time.

When she gets home she puts the cufflink in an old tobacco tin. The children bought this tobacco tin in a junk shop years ago, and gave it to her for a present. She used to smoke, in those days, and the children were worried about her, so they gave her this tin full of toffees, jelly beans, and gumdrops, with a note saying, "Please get fat instead." That was for her birthday. Now the tin has in it several things besides the cufflink—all small things, not of great value but not worthless, either. A little enameled dish, a sterling-silver spoon for salt, a crystal fish. These are not sentimental keepsakes. She never looks at them, and often forgets what she has there. They are not booty, they don't have ritualistic significance. She does not take something every time she goes to Gordon's house, or every time she stays over, or to mark what she might call memorable visits. She doesn't do it in a daze and she doesn't seem to be under a compulsion. She just takes something, every now and then, and puts it away in the dark of the old tobacco tin, and more or less forgets about it.

# Ann Beattie, "Janus"

The bowl was perfect. Perhaps it was not what you'd select if you faced a shelf of bowls, and not the sort of thing that would inevitably attract a lot of attention at a crafts fair, yet it had real presence. It was as predictably admired as a mutt who has no reason to suspect he might be funny. Just such a dog, in fact, was often brought out (and in) along with the bowl.

Andrea was a real estate agent, and when she thought that some prospective buyers might be dog lovers, she would drop off her dog at the same time she placed the bowl in the house that was up for sale. She would put a dish of water in the kitchen for Mondo, take his squeaking plastic frog out of her purse and drop it on the floor. He would pounce delightedly, just as he did every day at home, batting around his favorite toy. The bowl usually sat on a coffee table, though recently she had displayed it on top of a pine blanket chest and on a lacquered table. It was once placed on a cherry table beneath a Bonnard still life, where it held its own.

Everyone who has purchased a house or who has wanted to sell a house must be familiar with some of the tricks used to convince a buyer that the house is quite special: a fire in the fireplace in early evening; jonquils in a pitcher on the kitchen counter, where no one ordinarily has space to put flowers; perhaps the slight aroma of spring, made by a single drop of scent vaporizing from a lamp bulb.

The wonderful thing about the bowl, Andrea thought, was that it was both subtle and noticeable—a paradox of a bowl. Its glaze was the color of cream and seemed to glow no matter what light it was placed in. There were a few bits of color in it—tiny geometric flashes—and some of these were tinged with flecks of silver. They were as mysterious as cells seen under a microscope; it was difficult not to study them, because they shimmered, flashing for a split second, and then resumed their shape. Something about the colors and their random placement suggested motion. People who liked country furniture always commented on the bowl, but then it turned out that people who felt comfortable with Biedermeier loved it just as much. But the bowl was not at all ostentatious, or even so noticeable that anyone would suspect that it had been put in place deliberately. They might notice the height of the ceiling on first entering a room, and only when their eye moved down from that, or away from the refraction of sunlight on a pale wall, would they see the bowl. Then they would go immediately to it and comment. Yet they always faltered when they tried to say something. Perhaps it was because they were in the house for a serious reason, not to notice some object.

Once, Andrea got a call from a woman who had not put in an offer on a house she had shown her. That bowl, she said—would it be possible to find out where the owners had bought that beautiful bowl? Andrea pretended that she did not know what the woman was referring to. A bowl, somewhere in the house? Oh, on a table under the window. Yes, she would ask, of course. She let a couple of days pass, then called back to say that the bowl had been a present and the people did not know where it had been purchased.

When the bowl was not being taken from house to house, it sat on Andrea's coffee table at home. She didn't keep it carefully wrapped (although she transported it that way, in a box); she kept it on the table, because she liked to see it. It was large enough so that it didn't seem fragile, or particularly vulnerable if anyone sideswiped the table or Mondo blundered into it at play. She had asked her husband to please not drop his house key in it. It was meant to be empty.

When her husband first noticed the bowl, he had peered into it and smiled briefly. He always urged her to buy things she liked. In recent years, both of them had acquired many things to make up for all the lean years when they were graduate students, but now that they had been comfortable for quite a while, the pleasure of new possessions dwindled. Her husband had pronounced the bowl "pretty," and he had turned away without picking it up to examine it. He had no more interest in the bowl than she had in his new Leica.

She was sure that the bowl brought her luck. Bids were often put in on houses where she had displayed the bowl. Sometimes the owners, who were always asked to be away or to step outside when the house was being shown, didn't even know that the bowl had been in their house. Once—she could not imagine how—she left it behind, and then she was so afraid that something might have happened to it that she rushed back to the house and sighed with relief when the woman owner opened the door. The bowl, Andrea explained—she had purchased a bowl and set it on the chest for safekeeping while she toured the house with the prospective buyers, and she . . . She felt like rushing past the frowning woman and seizing her bowl. The owner stepped aside, and it was only when Andrea ran to the chest that the lady glanced at her a little strangely. In the few seconds before Andrea picked up the bowl, she realized that the owner must have just seen that it had been perfectly placed, that the sunlight struck the bluer part of it. Her pitcher had been moved to the far side of the chest, and the bowl predominated. All the way home, Andrea wondered how she could have left the bowl behind. It was like leaving a friend at an outing—just walking off. Sometimes there were stories in the paper about families forgetting a child somewhere and driving to the next city. Andrea had only gone a mile down the road before she remembered.

In time, she dreamed of the bowl. Twice, in a waking dream—early in the morning, between sleep and a last nap before rising—she had a clear vision of it. It came into sharp focus and startled her for a moment—the same bowl she looked at every day.

She had a very profitable year selling real estate. Word spread, and she had more clients than she felt comfortable with. She had the foolish thought that if only the bowl were an animate object she could thank it. There were times when she wanted to talk to her husband about the bowl. He was a stockbroker, and sometimes told people that he was fortunate to be married to a woman who had such a fine aesthetic sense and yet could also function in the real world. They were a lot alike, really—they had agreed on that. They were both quiet people—reflective, slow to make value judgments, but almost intractable once they had come to a conclusion. They both liked details, but while ironies attracted her, he was more impatient and dismissive when matters became many sided or unclear. But they both knew this; it was the kind of thing they could talk about when they were alone in the car together, coming home from a party or after a weekend with friends. But she never talked to him about the bowl. When they were at dinner, exchanging their news of the day, or while they lay in bed at night listening to the stereo and murmuring sleepy disconnections, she was often tempted to come right out and say that she thought that the bowl in the living room, the cream-colored bowl, was responsible for her success. But she didn't say it. She couldn't begin to explain it. Sometimes in the morning, she would look at him and feel guilty that she had had such a constant secret.

Could it be that she had some deeper connection with the bowl—a relationship of some kind? She corrected her thinking: how could she imagine such a thing, when she was a human being and it was a bowl? It was ridiculous. Just think of how people lived together and loved each other. . . . But was that always so clear, always a relationship? She was confused by these thoughts, but they remained in her mind. There was something within her now, something real, that she never talked about.

The bowl was a mystery, even to her. It was frustrating, because her involvement with the bowl contained a steady sense of unrequited good fortune; it would have been easier to respond if some sort of demand were made in return. But that only happened in fairy tales. The bowl was just a bowl. She did not believe that for one second. What she believed was that it was something she loved.

In the past, she had sometimes talked to her husband about a new property she was about to buy or sell—confiding some clever strategy she had devised to persuade owners who seemed ready to sell. Now she stopped doing that, for all her strategies involved the bowl. She became more deliberate with the bowl, and more possessive. She put it in houses only when no one was there, and removed it when she left the house. Instead of just moving a pitcher or a dish, she would remove all the other objects from a table. She had to force herself to handle them carefully, because she didn't really care about them. She just wanted them out of sight.

She wondered how the situation would end. As with a lover, there was no exact scenario of how matters would come to a close. Anxiety became the operative force. It would be irrelevant if the lover rushed into someone else's arms, or wrote her a note and departed to another city. The horror was the possibility of the disappearance. That was what mattered.

She would get up at night and look at the bowl. It never occurred to her that she might break it. She washed and dried it without anxiety, and she moved it often, from coffee table to mahogany corner table or wherever, without fearing an accident. It was clear that she would not be the one who would do anything to the bowl. The bowl was only handled by her, set safely on one surface or another; it was not very likely that anyone would break it. A bowl was a poor conductor of electricity: it would not be hit by lightning. Yet the idea of damage persisted. She did not think beyond that—to what her life would be without the bowl. She only continued to fear that some accident would happen. Why not, in a world where people set plants where they did not belong, so that visitors touring a house would be fooled into thinking that dark corners got sunlight—in a world full of tricks?

She had first seen the bowl several years earlier, at a crafts fair she had visited half in secret, with her lover. He had urged her to buy the bowl. She didn't *need* any more things, she told him. But she had been drawn to the bowl, and they had lingered near it. Then she went on to the next booth, and he came up behind her, tapping the rim against her shoulder as she ran her fingers over a wood carving. "You're still insisting that I buy that?" she said. "No," he said. "I bought it for you." He had bought her other things before this—things she liked more, at first—the child's ebony-and-turquoise ring that fitted her little finger; the wooden box, long and thin, beautifully dovetailed, that she used to hold paper clips; the soft gray sweater with a pouch pocket. It was his idea that when he could not be there to hold her hand she could hold her own—clasp her hands inside the lone pocket that stretched across the front. But in time she became more attached to the bowl than to any of his other presents. She tried to talk herself out of it. She owned other things that were more striking or valuable. It wasn't an object whose beauty jumped out at you; a lot of people must have passed it by before the two of them saw it that day.

Her lover had said that she was always too slow to know what she really loved. Why continue with her life the way it was? Why be two-faced, he asked her. He had made the first move toward her. When she would not decide in his favor, would not change her life and come to him, he asked her what made her think she could have it both ways. And then he made the last move and left. It was a decision meant to break her will, to shatter her intransigent ideas about honoring previous commitments.

Time passed. Alone in the living room at night, she often looked at the bowl sitting on the table, still and safe, unilluminated. In its way, it was perfect: the world cut in half, deep and smoothly empty. Near the rim, even in dim light, the eye moved toward one small flash of blue, a vanishing point on the horizon.

Altieri, Charles. *The Particulars of Rapture: An Aesthetics of the Affects.* Ithaca: Cornell University Press, 2003.

Anzaldúa, Gloria. *Borderlands/LaFrontera: The New Mestiza.* New York: Norton, 1998.

Aristotle. *Poetics.* Translated by James Hutton. New York: Norton, 1982.

Armstrong, Nancy. "Why Daughters Die: The Racial Logic of American Sentimentalism." *The Yale Journal of Criticism* 7: 2 (1994): 1–24.

Atwood, Margaret. "Happy Endings." In *McGraw-Hill Book of Fiction,* edited by Robert DiYanni and Kraft Rompf. New York: McGraw-Hill, 1995. 213–16.

Austen, Jane. *Emma.* Edited by R.W. Chapman. Oxford: Oxford University Press, 1963.

_____. *Mansfield Park.* Edited by R.W. Chapman. Oxford: Oxford University Press, 1963.

_____. *Persuasion.* Edited by R. W. Chapman. Oxford: Oxford University Press, 1963.

_____. *Northanger Abbey* and *Persuasion.* Edited by R. W. Chapman. Oxford: Oxford University Press, 1963.

_____. *Pride and Prejudice.* Edited by R. W. Chapman. Oxford: Oxford University Press, 1963.

_____. *Sense and Sensibility.* Edited by R.W. Chapman. Oxford: Oxford University Press, 1963.

Baker, Carlos. *Hemingway: The Writer as Artist.* Princeton: Princeton University Press, 1972.

Barthes, Roland. *S/Z.* Translated by Richard Miller. New York: Hill and Wang, 1974.

Beattie, Ann. "Janus." *Where You'll Find Me and Other Stories.* New York: Simon and Schuster, 1986. 103–12.

Bennett, Warren. "Character, Irony, and Resolution in Hemingway's 'A Clean, Well-Lighted Place.'" *American Literature* 42 (March 1970): 70–79.

Bierce, Ambrose. "The Crimson Candle." In *The Collected Writings of Ambrose Bierce.* New York: The Citadel Press, 1946. 543.

_____. "An Occurrence at Owl Creek Bridge." In *The Collected Writings of Ambrose Bierce.* New York: The Citadel Press, 1946.

Booth, Wayne C. *The Company We Keep: An Ethics of Fiction.* Berkeley: University of California Press, 1988.

_____. *The Essential Wayne Booth.* Edited by Walter Jost. Chicago: University of Chicago Press, 2006.

_____. *The Rhetoric of Fiction.* 2nd ed. Chicago: University of Chicago Press, 1983.

_____. *A Rhetoric of Irony.* Chicago: University of Chicago Press, 1974.

Brodsky, Joseph. "On Grief and Reason." In *Homage to Robert Frost* by Joseph Brodsky, Seamus Heaney, and Derek Walcott. New York: Farrar, Straus, and Giroux, 1996. 5–56.

Brooks, Peter. *Reading for the Plot: Design and Intention in Narrative.* New York: Knopf, 1984.

Brown, Julia Prewitt. *Jane Austen's Novels: Social Change and Literary Form.* Cambridge, MA: Harvard University Press, 1979.

Butte, George. *I Know That You Know That I Know.* Columbus: Ohio State University Press, 2004.

Byatt, A. S. *Passions of the Mind: Selected Writings.* New York: Vintage, 1993.

Carroll, Rebecca. "A Reader–Response Reading of Robert Frost's 'Home Burial.'" *Text and Performance Quarterly* 10 (1990): 143–56.

Christian, Barbara. "Beloved, She's Ours." *Narrative* 5 (1997): 36–49.

Cisneros, Sandra. *Woman Hollering Creek and Other Stories.* New York: Random House, 1991.

Cohn, Dorrit. *The Distinction of Fiction.* Baltimore: Johns Hopkins University Press, 1999.

Crane, R. S. "The Concept of Plot and the Plot of *Tom Jones.*" In *Critics and Criticism,* edited by Crane. Chicago: University of Chicago Press, 1952. 616–47.

_____, ed. *Critics and Criticism: Ancient and Modern.* Chicago: University of Chicago Press, 1952.

_____. *The Languages of Criticism and the Structure of Poetry.* Toronto: University of Toronto Press, 1953.

Dubrow, Heather. "The Interplay of Narrative and Lyric: Competition, Cooperation, and the Case of the Anticipatory Amalgam." *Narrative* 14 (2006): 254–71.

_____. "Lyric Forms." In *Cambridge Companion to English Literature, 1500–1600,* edited by Arthur Kinney. New York: Cambridge University Press, 2000. 78–99.

Finney, Brian. "Briony's Stand against Oblivion: Ian McEwan's *Atonement.*" http://www.csulb.edu/~bhfinney/McEwan.html.

Frey, James. *A Million Little Pieces.* New York: Random House, 2003.

Friedman, Susan. "Lyric Subversion of Narrative in Women's Writing: Elizabeth Barrett Browning and Virginia Woolf." In *Reading Narrative: Form Ethics, Ideology,* edited by James Phelan. Columbus: Ohio State University Press. 162–85.

Frost, Robert. "Home Burial." In *The Poetry of Robert Frost,* edited by Edward Connery Lathem. New York: Holt, Rinehart, and Winston. 1969 [1916].

Genette, Gérard. *Essays on Aesthetics.* Translated by Dorrit Cohn. Lincoln: University of Nebraska Press, 2005.

Gerlach, John. "The Margins of Narrative: The Very Short Story, the Prose Poem, and the Lyric." In *Short Story Theory at a Crossroads,* edited by Susan Lohafer and Jo Ellyn Clarey. Baton Rouge: Louisiana State University, 1989. 74–84.

_____. "Narrative, Lyric, and Plot in Chris Offutt's 'Out in the Woods.'" In *The Art of Brevity: Excursions in Short Fiction Theory and Analysis,* edited by Per Winther, Jakob Lothe, and Hans H. Skei. Columbia, SC: University of South Carolina Press, 2004. 44–56.

Gilbert, Sandra, and Susan Gubar. *The Madwoman in the Attic: The Woman Writer and the Nineteenth-Century Literary Imagination.* New Haven: Yale University Press, 1979.

Goldsmith. Oliver. *The Vicar of Wakefield.* New York: Oxford University Press, 2006.

Hagopian, John V. "Tidying Up Hemingway's 'A Clean, Well-Lighted Place.'" *Studies in Short Fiction* 1 (1964): 140–46.

Handley, William R. "The House a Ghost Built: Nommo, Allegory, and the Ethics of Reading in Toni Morrison's *Beloved.*" *Contemporary Literature* 36 (1995): 676–701.

Hare, David. "Holding Forth." *The Guardian,* July 16, 2005.

Hartman, Geoffrey H. "Public Memory and Its Discontents." In *The Uses of Literary History,* edited by Marshall Brown. Durham: Duke University Press, 1995. 73–91.

Heaney, Seamus. "Above the Brim." In *Homage to Robert Frost* by Joseph Brodsky, Seamus Heaney, and Derek Walcott. New York: Farrar, Straus, and Giroux, 1996. 61–88.

Hemingway, Ernest. "The Art of the Short Story." In *Ernest Hemingway: A Study of the Short Fiction* by Joseph Flora. Boston: Twayne Publishers, 1989. 129–42.

_____. *The Complete Short Stories of Ernest Hemingway: The Finca Vigia Edition.* New York: Charles Scribner's Sons, 1987.

Heyne, Eric. "Toward a Theory of Literary Nonfiction." *Modern Fiction Studies* 33 (Autumn 1987): 479–90.

_____. "Mapping, Mining, Sorting." *Narrative* 9 (2001): 322–33.

_____. "Where Fiction Meets Nonfiction: Mapping a Rough Terrain." *Narrative* 9 (2001): 343–45.

Hirsch, Marianne. "Maternity and Rememory: Toni Morrison's *Beloved.*" In *Representations of Motherhood,* edited by Donna Bassin, Margaret Honey, and Meryle Mahrer Kaplan. New Haven: Yale University Press, 1994. 92–110.

Homans, Margaret. "Feminist Fictions and Feminist Theories of Narrative." *Narrative* 2 (1994): 3–16.

Jarrell, Randall. "Robert Frost's 'Home Burial.'" In *No Other Book: Selected Essays,* edited by Brad Leithauser. New York: Perennial, 1999 [1962]. 42–66.

Johnson, Claudia. *Jane Austen: Women, Politics, and the Novel.* Chicago: University of Chicago Press, 1988.

Jost, Walter. "Ordinary Language Brought to Grief: 'Home Burial.'" In *Ordinary Language Criticism: Literary Thinking after Cavell after Wittgenstein,* edited by Kenneth Dauber and Walter Jost. Evanston: Northwestern University Press, 2003. 77–114.

Kafalenos, Emma. *Narrative Causalities.* Columbus: Ohio State University Press, 2006.

Kann, Hans–Joachim. "Perpetual Confusion in 'A Clean, Well-Lighted Place': The Manuscript Evidence." *Fitzgerald/Hemingway Annual* (1977): 115–18.

Keast, W. R. "The 'New Criticism' and King Lear." In *Critics and Criticism,* edited by R. S. Crane. Chicago: University of Chicago Press, 1952. 108–37.

Kearns, Katherine. *Robert Frost and a Poetics of Appetite.* New York: Cambridge University Press, 1994.

Kerner, David. "The Ambiguity of 'A Clean, Well-Lighted Place.'" *Studies in Short Fiction* 29 (1992): 561–74.

_____. "Counterfeit Hemingway: A Small Scandal in Quotation Marks." *Journal of Modern Literature* 12 (November 1985): 91–108.

_____. "The Foundation of the True Text of 'A Clean, Well-Lighted Place': The Manuscript Evidence." *Fitzgerald/Hemingway Annual* (1979): 279–300.

_____. "Hemingway's Attention to 'A Clean, Well-Lighted Place.'" *The Hemingway Review* 13 (Fall 1993): 48–62.

Lardner, Ring. "Haircut." In *The Best Short Stories of Ring Lardner*. New York: Charles Scribner's Sons, 1957. 23–33.

Lehman, Daniel. *Matters of Fact: Reading Nonfiction over the Edge*. Columbus: The Ohio State University Press, 1998.

_____. "Mining a Rough Terrain: Weighing the Implications of Nonfiction." *Narrative* 9 (2001): 334–42.

Lehtimaki, Markku. *The Poetics of Norman Mailer's Nonfiction: Self-Reflexivity, Literary Form, and the Rhetoric of Narrative*. Tampere, Finland: The University of Tampere, 2005.

Lentricchia, Frank. *Robert Frost: Modern Poetics and the Landscapes of the Self*. Durham: Duke University Press, 1975.

Levin, Richard. *New Readings v. Old Plays*. Chicago: University of Chicago Press, 1979.

Lodge, David. "Hemingway's Clean, Well-Lighted Puzzling Place." In *The Novelist at the Crossroads and Other Essays on Fiction and Criticism*. Ithaca: Cornell University Press, 1971. 184–202.

May, Charles E. "Is Hemingway's 'Well-Lighted Place' Really Clean Now?'" *Studies in Short Fiction* 8 (Spring 1971): 326–30.

_____. "Writing Short Stories: My Double Story, with Reflections on Occasion, Tonality, and Direction." In *The Art of Brevity: Excursions in Short Fiction Theory and Analysis,* edited by Per Winther, Jakob Lothe, and Hans H. Skei. Columbia, SC: University of South Carolina Press, 2004. 14–25.

McEwan, Ian. *Atonement*. New York: Doubleday, 2001.

Moglen, Helene. "Redeeming History: Toni Morrison's *Beloved*." In *Subjects in Black and White: Race, Psychoanalysis, Feminism,* edited by Elizabeth Abel, Barbara Christian, and Moglen. Berkeley: University of California Press, 1997. 201–20.

Moreland, Richard C. "'He Wants to Put His Story Next to Hers': Putting Twain's Story Next to Hers in Morrison's *Beloved*." *Modern Fiction Studies* 39:3–4 (1993): 501–25.

Morrison, Toni. *Beloved*. New York: Knopf, 1987.

Mortimer, Armine Kotin. "Romantic Fever: The Second Story as Illegitimate Daughter in Wharton's 'Roman Fever.'" *Narrative* 6 (1998): 188–98.

Munro, Alice. "Prue." *The Moons of Jupiter*. New York: Knopf, 1983. 129–33.

Novas, Himilce. *Everything You Need to Know about Latino History*. New York: Penguin, 1994.

Nussbaum, Martha. *Love's Knowledge: Essays on Philosophy and Literature*. New York: Oxford University Press, 1990.

_____. *Poetic Justice: The Literary Imagination and Public Life*. Boston: Beacon Press, 1995.

Oelschlager, Fritz H. "Tragic Vision in Frost's 'Home Burial.'" *Ball State University Forum* 22: 3 (1981): 25–29.

Olson, Elder. "An Outline of Poetic Theory." In *Critics and Criticism,* edited by R. S. Crane. Chicago: University of Chicago Press, 1952. 546–66.

_____. "William Empson, Contemporary Criticism, and Poetic Diction." In *Critics and Criticism,* edited by R. S. Crane. Chicago: University of Chicago Press, 1952. 45–82.

Petry, Alice Hall. "A Twist of Crimson Silk: Edith Wharton's 'Roman Fever.'" *Studies in Short Fiction* 24 (1987): 163–66.

Phelan, James. "Beginnings and Endings." *Encyclopedia of the Novel,* edited by Paul Schellinger. Chicago: Fitzroy–Dearborn, 1998.

_____. *Living to Tell about It: A Rhetoric and Ethics of Character Narration.* Ithaca: Cornell University Press, 2005.

_____. *Narrative as Rhetoric: Technique, Audiences, Ethics, Ideology.* Columbus: The Ohio State University Press, 1996.

_____. *Reading People, Reading Plots: Character, Progression, and the Interpretation of Narrative.* Chicago: University of Chicago Press, 1989.

_____. *Worlds from Words: A Theory of Language in Fiction.* Chicago: University of Chicago Press, 1981.

Poirier, Richard. *Robert Frost: The Work of Knowing.* New York: Oxford University Press, 1977.

Poovey, Mary. "*Persuasion* and the Promises of Love." In *The Representation of Women in Fiction: Selected Papers from the English Institue,* edited by Carolyn G. Heilbrun and Margaret R. Higgonet. Baltimore: Johns Hopkins University Press, 1981. 152–79.

Propp, Vladimir. *Morphology of the Folktale.* Translated by Laurence Scott. Austin: University of Texas Press, 1968.

Rabinowitz, Peter J. *Before Reading: Narrative Conventions and the Politics of Interpretation.* Columbus: The Ohio State University Press, 1998. Originally published 1987.

_____. "Lolita: Solipsized or Sodomized?; or Against Abstraction in General." In *A Companion to Rhetoric and Rhetorical Criticism,* edited by Wendy Olmstead and Walter Jost. Oxford: Blackwell Press, 2004. 325–39.

_____. "They Shoot Tigers, Don't They?: Path and Counterpoint in *The Long Goodbye.*" In *A Companion to Narrative Theory,* edited by James Phelan and Peter J. Rabinowitz. Malden, MA: Blackwell Publishing, 2005. 181–91.

_____. "Truth in Fiction: A Reexamination of Audiences." *Critical Inquiry* 4 (1977): 121–41.

Rader, Ralph W. "The Dramatic Monologue and Related Lyric Forms." *Critical Inquiry* 3 (1976): 131–51.

_____. "From Richardson to Austen: 'Johnson's Rule' and the Eighteenth-Century Novel of Moral Action." In *Johnson and His Age,* edited by James Engell. Cambridge, MA: Harvard University Press,1984. 461–83

Reinert, Otto. "Hemingway's Waiters Once More." *College English* 20 (1959): 417–18.

Richter, David H. "The Chicago School." In *Routledge Encyclopedia of Narrative Theory,* edited by David Herman, Manfred Jahn, and Marie-Laure Ryan. New York: Routledge, 2005. 57–59.

_____. *Fable's End: Completeness and Closure in Rhetorical Fiction.* Chicago: University of Chicago Press, 1974.

_____. "The Second Flight of the Phoenix: Neo-Aristotelianism Since Crane." *The Eighteenth Century: Theory and Interpretation,* 23:1 (1982): 27–48.

Rigney, Barbara. *The Voices of Toni Morrison.* Columbus: The Ohio State University Press, 1994.

Rimmon-Kenan, Shlomith. *A Glance beyond Doubt: Narration, Representation, Subjectivity.* Columbus: The Ohio State University Press, 1996.

Ryan, Ken. "The Contentious Emendation of Hemingway's 'A Clean, Well–Lighted Place.'" *The Hemingway Review* 18 (Fall 1998): 78–90.

Sacks, Sheldon. *Fiction and the Shape of Belief.* Berkeley: University of California Press, 1964.

_____."Golden Birds and Dying Generations." *Comparative Literature Studies* 6 (1969): 274–91.

_____. "Novelists as Storytellers." *Modern Philology* 73: 2 (1976): S97–S109.

Scholes, Robert, Robert Kellogg, and James Phelan. *The Nature of Narrative.* 2nd ed. New York: Oxford University Press, 2006.

Smith, Paul. "A Note on a New Manuscript of 'A Clean, Well-Lighted Place.'" *The Hemingway Review* 8 (Spring 1989): 36–39.

_____. *A Reader's Guide to the Short Stories of Ernest Hemingway.* Boston: G. K. Hall, 1989.

Smith, Sidonie, and Julia Watson. *Reading Autobiography: A Guide for Interpreting Life Narratives.* Minneapolis: University of Minnesota Press, 2001.

Sternberg, Meir. *Expositional Modes and Temporal Ordering in Fiction.* Baltimore: Johns Hopkins University Press, 1978.

Sweeney, Susan Elizabeth. "Edith Wharton's Case of Roman Fever." In *Wretched Exotic: Essays on Edith Wharton in Europe,* edited by Katherine Joslin and Alan Price. New York: Peter Lang, 1993. 313–31.

Tave, Stuart. *Some Words of Jane Austen.* Chicago: University of Chicago Press, 1973.

Travis, Molly. "Speaking from the Silence of the Slave Narrative: *Beloved* and African-American Women's History." *The Texas Review* 13:1-2 (1992): 69–81.

Twain, Mark. *Adventures of Huckleberry Finn: A Case Study in Critical Controversy,* edited by Gerald Graff and James Phelan. Boston: Bedford/St. Martin's, 2004.

Warhol, Robyn. *Having a Good Cry: Effeminate Feelings and Pop Culture Forms.* Columbus: The Ohio State University Press, 2003.

_____. "The Look, the Body, and the Heroine: A Feminist-Narratological Reading of *Persuasion.*" *Novel* 26 (1992): 5–19.

Wharton, Edith (1991). "Roman Fever." In *Roman Fever and Other Stories.* New York: Charles Scribner's Sons, 1997. 3–20.

_____. (1991). "Preface," from *Ghosts* (1937). In *Edith Wharton: A Study of the Short Fiction,* edited by Barbara White. New York: Twayne Publishers. 139–44.

Wilt, Judith. *Abortion, Choice, and Contemporary Fiction.* Chicago: University of Chicago Press, 1989.

Wiltshire, John. *Jane Austen and the Body.* Cambridge: Cambridge University Press, 1992.

Wimsatt, William K. *The Verbal Icon: Studies in the Meaning of Poetry.* Lexington: University of Kentucky Press, 1954.

Wolfe, Joanna. "'Ten minutes for Seven Letters': Song as Key to Narrative Revision in Toni Morrison's *Beloved.*" *Narrative* 12 (2004): 263–80.

Wyatt, Jean. "Giving Body to the Word: The Maternal Symbolic in Toni Morrison's *Beloved.*" *PMLA* 108 (1993): 474–88.

THEORY AND INTERPRETATION OF NARRATIVE
James Phelan and Peter J. Rabinowitz, Series Editors

Because the series editors believe that the most significant work in narrative studies today contributes both to our knowledge of specific narratives and to our understanding of narrative in general, studies in the series typically offer interpretations of individual narratives and address significant theoretical issues underlying those interpretations. The series does not privilege one critical perspective but is open to work from any strong theoretical position.